Social History of Africa

BO-TSOTSI

Recent Titles in
Social History of Africa Series
Series Editors: Allen Isaacman and Jean Allman

BO-TSOTSI

THE YOUTH GANGS
OF SOWETO, 1935–1976

Clive Glaser

HEINEMANN
Portsmouth, NH

JAMES CURREY
Oxford

DAVID PHILIP
Cape Town

Heinemann
A division of Reed Elsevier Inc.
361 Hanover Street
Portsmouth, NH 03801-3912
USA
www.heinemann.com

James Currey Ltd.
73 Botley Road
Oxford OX2 0BS
United Kingdom

David Philip Publishers (Pty) Ltd.
208 Werdmuller Centre
Claremont 7708
Cape Town, South Africa

Offices and agents throughout the world

ISBN 0–325–00219–3 (Heinemann cloth)
ISBN 0–325–00218–5 (Heinemann paper)
ISBN 0–85255–690–X (James Currey cloth)
ISBN 0–85255–640–3 (James Currey paper)

British Library Cataloguing in Publication Data

Glaser, Clive
  Bo-Tsotsi : the youth gangs of Soweto, 1935–1976.—(Social history of Africa)
  1. Gangs—South Africa—Soweto   2. Urban youth—South Africa—Soweto—Social conditions   3. Gangs—South Africa—Soweto—Political activity   4. Soweto (South Africa)—Social conditions—20th century
  I. Title
  364.3'6'0968221
  ISBN 0–85255–690–X (James Currey cloth)
  ISBN 0–85255–640–3 (James Currey paper)

Library of Congress Cataloging-in-Publication Data

Glaser, Clive, 1964–
    Bo-tsotsi : the youth gangs of Soweto, 1935–1976; Clive Glaser.
      p. cm.—(Social history of Africa, ISSN 1099–8098)
    Includes bibliographical references and index.
    ISBN 0–325–00219–3 (alk. paper)—ISBN 0–325–00218–5 (pbk. : alk. paper)
    1. Gangs—South Africa—Soweto.   2. Juvenile delinquency—South Africa—Soweto.
  3. Urban youth—South Africa—Soweto.   4. Soweto (South Africa)—Social conditions.
  I. Title.   II. Series.

  HV6439.S62 S684 2000
  364.1'06'60968—dc21   99–049242

Paperback cover photo: A typical "American" gangster in Sophiatown. Posed photograph for *Drum*, September 1954. Photographer: Bob Gosani. © Bailey's African History Archives. Reprinted with permission.

Printed in the United States of America on acid-free paper.

04 03 02 01 00 SB 1 2 3 4 5 6 7 8 9

If you are an anthropologist who is interested in location life, especially where there are so many street fights during the weekends, study "bo Tsotsi" and you'll get enough information to write a thesis that will excite many universities into honouring you with degrees!

—"Mr J.D.N." of Benoni, *Bantu World*,
Readers' Forum, 7 April 1945

We weep for the young people of our society for they are, in reality, people with problems and not problem children.

—"Father," Soweto, *The World*, 15 February 1971

CONTENTS

ILLUSTRATIONS

MAPS

PHOTOGRAPHS

PREFACE

Phil Bonner and Peter Delius have inspired and encouraged my work throughout my career. Without them, I doubt whether I would have become a historian, let alone taken this project through to its conclusion. I am also grateful to John Iliffe for his superb supervision and guidance while I was preparing my Cambridge Ph.D. I am deeply indebted to my research assistant, Meverett Koetz, who conducted and translated dozens of interviews that added a dimension I could not have achieved on my own. I would like to thank all those interviewees who gave of their time to talk to us. Angus Gibson, who directed the History Workshop Soweto Film Project, allowed me free access to numerous videotaped interviews; and Gail Gerhart, Tom Lodge, Steve Lebelo, and Jeremy Seekings generously gave me copies of interviews they had conducted themselves. Luli Callinicos was enormously helpful in the search for photographic material. The participants in the Social Sciences Graduate Seminar at the University of the Witwatersrand provided a supportive and stimulating academic network in Johannesburg, while Bruce Murray, as head of the "Wits" History Department, offered me space and encouragement to complete the process of writing. Special thanks go to my parents, Harold and Shirley Glaser, and to Victoria Bronstein for assistance in editing the final draft of the book. This project would not have been possible without the financial support of the Cambridge Livingstone Trust and the Human Sciences Research Council in South Africa. Cambridge University's Smuts Fund also helped me to cover travel and other research expenses.

ABBREVIATIONS

AB - Advisory Board
ANC - African National Congress
ANCYL (or CYL) - African National Congress Youth League
ASM - African Students' Movement
BAD - Bantu Affairs Department
BC - Black Consciousness
BCM - Black Consciousness Movement
BPA - Black Parents' Association
BPC - Black People's Convention
BW - Bantu World
CATA - Cape African Teachers' Association
CATU - Cape African Teachers' Union
COSAS - Congress of South African Students
CYL - Congress Youth League
DBE - Department of Bantu Education
GCP - Golden City Post
HWSFP - History Workshop Soweto Film Project
IAD - Intermediary Archive Depot
ICS - Institute of Commonwealth Studies
JCC - Johannesburg City Council
JNEAD - Johannesburg Non-European Affairs Department
MIHS - Morris Isaacson High School
NAD - Native Affairs Department (later BAD)
NAYO - National Youth Organisation
NEAD - Non-European Affairs Department
NP - National Party
NUSAS - National Union of South African Students

OHS - Orlando High School
OWHS - Orlando West High School
PAC - Pan Africanist Congress
RDM - Rand Daily Mail
SACP - South African Communist Party
SAP - South African Police
SASM - South African Students Movement
SASO - South African Students Organisation
SCM - Student Christian Movement
SOYCO - Soweto Youth Congress
SRC - Student Representative Council
SSRC - Soweto Students Representative Council
TATA - Transvaal African Teachers' Association
TRAYO - Transvaal Youth Organisation
UBC - Urban Bantu Council
UDF - United Democratic Front
UCM - University Christian Movement
ULPP - Urban Labour Preference Policy
UNISA - University of South Africa
UP - United Party
WLD - Witwatersrand Legal Division
WRAB - West Rand Administration Board

1

"BEING MANLY": THEMES IN THE HISTORY OF URBAN YOUTH GANGS

In the period between the 1976 Soweto uprising and the February 1990 reform initiatives, black urban youth forced the pace of resistance politics throughout South Africa. The so-called "comrades" were the shock troops of resistance: making the townships ungovernable, policing boycotts and stayaways, defying security forces at mass funerals and meetings, rooting out, isolating, and punishing perceived collaborators. Not surprisingly, "the youth" became a central theme in South African sociological and political analysis. The literature on youth in the late 1970s and 1980s concentrated almost exclusively on their political role.[1] Despite reservations about their immaturity and coercive excesses, their contribution was seen as positive, sometimes heroic.[2] The 1976 uprising, with its immediate background, was often taken as a starting point for the history of South African youth politics and, by extension, the point at which youth entered "relevant" South African history.[3] Since the February 1990 reforms, however, observers have become concerned and often bewildered by the extent of anomie and criminality among black urban youth. A large portion of the activist youth felt that they were shunted aside and underappreciated in the negotiation process. Rising expectations were not matched by concrete changes in their way of life. During the 1990s, unemployment amongst black urban youth spiraled out of control. In 1993 it was reported that fewer than 5 percent of South African school-leavers were absorbed into the job market.[4] If anything, the situation has deteriorated since then. A recent survey suggests that over 80 percent of Soweto's population between sixteen and twenty years old, and about 65 percent of those between twenty-one and twenty-five are unemployed.[5] Many questions have been asked about how to accommodate this so-called "lost generation" in the new South Africa.

The perplexing problems of youth prompted a great deal of historical and sociological research in the 1990s.[6] These studies pointed to complexities and divisions among youth that had gone largely unnoticed in the 1980s literature. For all this, surprisingly little attention was given to the youth constituency, or even the important generational dynamics in township culture, *before* 1976. It was scarcely acknowledged that a powerful, largely apolitical, gang culture dominated the world of township youth from the 1930s to the early 1970s. In fact the social tensions, mostly along gender and generational lines, that this gang subculture provoked were an important feature of township life throughout this period.

This book begins to explore the culture of African gangs in Johannesburg from the mid-1930s, when the population of city-born youth became significant, until the 1976 uprising. From the late 1950s, in the wake of the Western Areas removals, the focus narrows to Soweto itself. Although this study is confined to Johannesburg/Soweto, it is intended to stimulate parallel studies for Durban, Cape Town, and other urban centers where the historiographical blindspots remain virtually intact. Johannesburg is an appropriate starting point both because it represents the biggest concentration of urban Africans in South Africa and because it was the cauldron of the 1976 uprising. By focusing on African urban youth gangs and youth politics before 1976, this book attempts to open up uncharted historical terrain and offer some fresh perspectives on the dilemmas of contemporary urban youth.

In chapters 2 and 3 I describe in detail the "juvenile delinquency" phenomenon and the *tsotsi* youth gang subculture that gripped the townships of Johannesburg during the 1940s and 1950s. The proliferation of urban youth gangs during this period was by no means unique to Johannesburg. Youth gangs were likely to emerge in any urban environment that included a substantial population of poor city-bred youth with limited employment possibilities and a lack of adequate housing, schooling, and recreation facilities. The dissipation of strong ethnic or religious socialization, often associated with urbanization, the destabilization of family life, and the exposure to Western media imagery all fueled gang subcultures.[7] Chapter 4 focuses on youth politics during the 1940s and 1950s. It looks at the relationship between the youth gangs and the political organizations intent on mobilizing youth, especially the Congress Youth League and the Pan Africanist Congress (PAC). Chapters 5 and 6 detail the continuities (and discontinuities) in youth gang culture in Johannesburg in the 1960s and early 1970s as the epicenter of African gang culture shifted from the inner-city black free hold areas to Soweto.[8] Chapter 7 returns to the theme of youth politics. It examines the relationship between the youth gangs of Soweto and the emergent Black Consciousness movement from the late 1960s until the 1976 uprising.

The chapter concludes by attempting to assess the participation of the gangs in the Soweto uprising.

AGE AND SEXUALITY

"Youth" is an ambiguous concept. There is no sociological consensus about its limits. The term has been used to describe a specific political or subcultural element. It has also been used as a rather rigid age-defined category, usually spanning the years fourteen to twenty-five. The most useful discussions on the subject, found largely in social anthropological literature, define youth in terms of social and family hierarchies, independence, and responsibility. Preindustrial African societies were clearly age graded, usually into three distinct phases. The youth slotted into a transitional phase between childhood and adulthood/eldership. In traditional Xhosa society, for instance, this stage is known as *intlombe*, while the Maasai use the male-specific term, *moran* (warriors).[9] In both examples, boys and girls go through a process of initiation from around the time of puberty and sexual awakening. Generational definitions are ultimately inseparable from gender socialization. Girls are supervised more tightly. Their skills in domesticity and child-rearing are honed and they exit the period of initiation earlier than males, at the point of marriage and childbearing. For males the initiation period is seen as a time of boisterous rebellion, mobility, fighting, assertion of independence, and sexual experimentation. Within the age set, sexual and social prestige is attached to being a good fighter. Socially, the young men are kept largely separate from the wider community. Spencer calls it "a ritualised form of rebellion directed against their fathers."[10] Although this rebelliousness and self-expression is tolerated and even encouraged in rural Xhosa society, "real power in the family and community . . . is still being withheld."[11] Similarly, the Maasai elders "at times lose a degree of control over the younger men, but it is they who control the system and perpetuate it, domesticating the moran by stages, and ultimately controlling them."[12] Gradually, as the young men marry, set up their own homesteads, and take on responsibilities, they are accepted into adulthood.

Following Eriksen, Philip Abrams regards adolescence as a "psycho-social moratorium." It is a "distinct biographical episode, a period of time out . . . in which the individual is offered time and space to try out roles, relationships, identities, occupations and life-styles."[13] Youth, then, can be understood more usefully as a phase of socialization than as a fixed age category. The boundaries fluctuate according to sociohistorical context. For instance, according to circumstances, prepubescent boys may join gangs or become gun-toting political cadres; girls may be given more space for experimentation or bear children later; or adolescents may be forced to take on family responsibilities. Also, as is common in urban scenarios, this period of rebellion need not be contained or supervised by the older generation to ensure social continuity. For all its vagueness, however, the concept of youth coheres around the notion of transition between childhood and responsible adulthood; for males it is a phase of mobility, rebellion, experimentation, floating identity, and assertive independence.

Urban youth gang formation has to be seen in some sense as an extension of pre-urban sexual socialization. While girls were socialized into domesticity, boys were given the freedom to embark on an exploration of sexuality and identity.[14] It seems clear that there were continuities between African male age grades and urban youth gangs. It is likely in the case of Johannesburg that neither male peer-group traditions nor parental attitudes shifted dramatically during the period of drift from the countryside. In the 1940s and 1950s, township parents probably retained their basic expectations of, and methods of bringing up, boys and girls. What did change, however, was the social context. In the city, parents lost control of their children, particularly their sons. In the city there was an absence of older-generation kinship supervision, and children had access to money and resources beyond the control of their parents. Perhaps most importantly, sons had no incentive to conform because they could see no viable inheritance; there seemed to be little prestige, power, or dignity associated with eldership in the city, where social mobility was blunted by poverty and racial discrimination, and where older residents had little real leverage over the next generation of youths.

The *tsotsi* gangs of the 1940s and 1950s, as well as the Soweto gangs of the 1960s and 1970s, were expressions of young urban masculinity. Although women were sometimes drawn peripherally into gangs as girlfriends, decoys, and lookouts, the gang subculture was essentially male. The distinctive subcultural clothing style was for males only, and women were excluded from the prestige spheres of gang life such as fighting. The masculine identity of the gang hinged around fighting skill, independence, street wisdom, feats of daring, law-breaking, clothing style, proficiency in the *tsotsitaal* argot, and success with women. Adeptness and success in these areas determined a *tsotsi*'s status and prestige as a "man." Young township women, as objects of subcultural prestige, as trophies of masculinity, were subjected to astonishing levels of sexual violence (Photo 1.1). Male power and control in the gang subculture were underpinned by rape and the threat of rape.[15]

In the high school environment, which was largely gang-free, masculine assertion took different forms. In Soweto the school version of masculinity, on the whole, placed less emphasis on physicality. This should not be exaggerated; as in the gang world, there was a great deal of variety and shading

Photo 1.1   The Mark of Zorro: an ex-girlfriend of the notorious Alexandra gangster, Zorro. He was known for carving a "z" on the forehead of his "molls." (From *Drum*, October 1955. © Bailey's African History Archives. Reprinted with permission.)

within the school constituency. Physical achievements were often given high value in school, particularly in organized sport, and male school students often reacted violently to defend their dignity or protect female students. Clearly, though, there was room for masculine assertion within the intellectual sphere. Boys could, for instance, achieve significant status through academic achievement or debating.

Masculine socialization at school followed its own specific patterns. Unlike gang socialization, it was mediated by the presence of authoritative adults as well as girls. Although male school students were given a certain amount of room to explore their sexuality and to assert their independence, as in the case of most Sowetan male teenagers, school represented a partial extension of parental authority beyond the home. School acted, in a sense, as a substitute for traditional forms of adult supervision. This partly explains the eagerness of most Sowetan parents to send their children to school despite the financial sacrifice. Boys were given some space for exploration but they were restrained from insubordinate excesses and they were prepared for future adult responsibilities. School broadened the paradigm of masculine competition to include more intellectual and profession-oriented spheres. Education itself opened up the white-collar path to upward social mobility, a path denied to the non-school youth. It would be incorrect, then, to argue that assertive young masculinity was exclusive to the world of the gang. Rather, school and gang offered two divergent, competing forms of masculine identity.

This book, which explores gang culture, almost by definition concentrates on the world of men. This does not mean that it ignores the gendered nature of society. On the contrary, it attempts to explore the construction of a particular version of masculinity. Though women are peripheral actors, the notions of gender identity and gendered power relations are central.

STYLE, STATUS, AND TERRITORY

Subcultural style, a term I use broadly to incorporate clothing tastes, social values, leisure activities, and street argot, operates on two levels. First, it represents a withdrawal of social consent; an angry refusal to participate in a social consensus. Second, it insulates and defines the boundaries of a world with its own status structure and routes of accumulation.

During the late 1970s and early 1980s, a number of writers from Birmingham's Centre for Contemporary Cultural Studies portrayed subcultural style as a form of class resistance, even if ultimately self-defeating.[16] They argued that subcultures are an essentially working-class phenomenon in which young males, structurally excluded from social privilege, express their scorn for hegemonic norms. Hegemony, as the Birmingham school saw it, is a social and cultural consensus, albeit shifting, contested, and underpinned by coercion, which allows for the dominance of a ruling class. The working class accepts hegemonic values such as nonviolence, adherence to the law, the sanctity of private property, and the work ethic. A more-or-less consensual dress code also emerges. Subcultures refuse to accept class subordination passively. Perceiving even their parent class to be party to the consensus, they express their own denial of consent through style. Subcultural status, according to the Birmingham school, is derived precisely through the inversion of these hegemonic values.[17] In the case of clothing, withdrawal of consent is expressed through the use of familiar imagery with inflected meaning as in the case of, say, a smart suit worn with short trousers or sports shoes. The middle class is deliberately mocked.[18]

The Birmingham school captured an important element of conscious rebellion and defiance inherent in youth subcultures. The *tsotsi* gangs and the later Soweto gangs rejected the work ethic, held the law in contempt, revered violence, and experimented with drugs. The *tsotsis* were expressing rage at a social status quo that marginalized and subordinated them, a rage directed both at the dominant classes and at their apparently acquiescent parents. Clearly their choices of style in some way mocked the establishment and inverted its values.[19]

The Birmingham school must take credit for politicizing the issue of subculture, for placing it squarely in the realm of social power and competition. The school's class essentialism, however, caused it to underplay the extent to which subcultural style is an expression of control, an adaptation to the ghetto environment.[20] For instance, Phil Cohen, who was associated with the Birmingham school, explained subcultural territoriality and alternative status structures as "magical solutions" to social contradictions that ultimately fail to address the "real" source of those contradictions, namely, class subordination.[21] Cohen failed to acknowledge the extent to which street gangs establish a real power base and local prestige. These solutions are less "magical" than they are practical and immediate. Subcultures invent their own status structures; the gangs seize de facto control over their streets. As Albert Cohen observed in the 1950s, "delinquent" subcultures provide alternative opportunities for upward mobility among those who have the least access to the "legitimate channels" of upward mobility.[22] In his 1965 study of Harlem, *Dark Ghetto*, K. B. Clark argued that a male teenager from Harlem was very likely to turn to delinquency or join a gang because he felt that "he cannot hope to win meaningful self-esteem through the avenues ordinarily available to more privileged individuals. These avenues have been blocked for him through inadequate education, through job discrimination and through a system of social and political power which is not responsive to his needs."[23] Style defines subcultural status. It is forged out of a necessary ducking of social norms to achieve material control over, or at least self-esteem within, the immediate environment.

The Birmingham school underestimated the acquisitive and consumerist aspirations of subcultures. Certainly in the case of the *tsotsis*, the pursuit of wealth, expensive clothes, and social prestige was not merely a mocking gesture. The *tsotsis* had a contradictory attitude towards the white middle class. They simultaneously held middle-class values in contempt and aspired to high levels of comfort and accumulation. Ostentatious style items and free spending symbolized success in the ghetto.[24] Crucially, however, *tsotsis* rejected middle-class methods of accumulation. Steady employment, answering to a boss, was undignified. Robbery, gambling, and bootlegging were prestigious methods of accumulation in the subculture.[25]

In order to protect their realm of power and status, youth subcultures insulate themselves from the outside world and create exclusivity through style. Urban sophistication is one crucial element of this exclusivity. Status is derived through familiarity with urban fashion. "Urban-ness" was central to the *tsotsi* self-image. Dress codes immediately separated city youths from country youths. *Tsotsis* looked down upon those who had come in from the countryside; they referred to the newcomers scornfully as *moegoe* or *bari*.[26] Language is another crucial style element that creates exclusivity. In Johannesburg, proficiency in the street language, *tsotsitaal*, indicated a familiarity with the *tsotsi* subculture. Subcultural status was attached to speaking the language with dexterity and inventiveness. It was a language that involved constant innovation and reinvention; only those who were part of the subculture could retain a mastery of speech. *Tsotsitaal* naturally separated the in-group from the out-group.

Territoriality is common to all youth gangs. The association of a cluster of individuals with each other and with a territory is what gives a gang its definition. Gangs attempt to establish territorial rights over a particular area in order to secure access to local facilities, women, and sources of accumulation. A gang develops prestige on its turf. It follows that the size of the turf itself determines prestige within the subculture. Gangs are intensely parochial phenomena; they rely on neighborhood identification and close familiarity with their terrain to stave off "intruders." Despite the absence of official ownership, gangs see themselves as the effective rulers of territories.

J. S. La Fontaine, observing Kinshasa youth gangs, sums up the role of territory in gang activity:

> The concept of the territory includes the sole right to recruit members within it, sexual access to young girls living within it, and the right to use the area to satisfy requirements for money, food and drugs. A large part of the gang's time is spent in fighting other gangs for exclusive control of a territory or in endeavouring to encroach on the territories of other gangs, particularly by kidnapping or seducing the girls "belonging" to other gangs.[27]

Youth gang wars in Johannesburg were fought essentially over territory. When hostilities developed over competition for women, territorial rights underpinned the conflict since local gangs regarded women living on their turf as their exclusive property.

Among street youth, style and territoriality are interwoven in the construction of masculine status. Manuel Sanchez, one of the protagonists in Oscar Lewis's oral history of a slum neighborhood in Mexico City, epitomizes this. As a fifteen-year-old who spent most of his time on the streets with his male peers in the late 1950s, his personal conception of masculine dignity was inseparable not only from physical courage, but from the notion, literally and figuratively, of holding ground.

I have learnt to hide my fear and to show only courage because from what I have observed, a person is treated according to the impression he makes. That's why when I'm really afraid inside, outwardly I'm calm. It has helped me too, because I didn't suffer so much as some of my friends who trembled when they were grabbed by the police. If a guy shows weakness and has tears in his eyes, and begs for mercy, that is when the others pile on him. In my neighbourhood, you are either a *picudo*, a tough guy, or a *pendejo*, a fool.

Mexicans, and I think everyone in the world, admire the person "with balls," as we say. The character who throws punches and kicks, without stopping to think, is the one who comes out on top. The one who has guts enough to stand up against an older, stronger guy, is more respected. If someone shouts, you've got to shout louder. If any so-and-so comes to me and says, "Fuck your mother", I answer, "Fuck your mother a thousand times." And if he gives one step forward and I take one step back, I lose prestige. But if I go forward too, and pile on and make a fool out of him, then the others will treat me with respect. In a fight I would never give up or say "Enough," even though the other was killing me. I would try to go to my death smiling. That is what we mean by being *"macho,"* by being manly.[28]

GANGS, CRIME, AND RELOCATION

I attempt to show in this book that distinctive gangs emerge once neighborhood peers develop a sense of identity based on an overlapping personal and territorial familiarity. Here I disagree with Don Pinnock, who insists that youth gangs on the Cape Flats were a response to an *absence* of community cohesion. Following the forced relocation of colored communities in Cape Town during the 1960s and 1970s, the kinship and neighborhood networks of the old colored townships, such as District Six, were dispersed. In District Six, Pinnock argues, neighbors, friends, and extended family members kept an eye on local youths and prevented them from getting up to serious mischief. By contrast, the new Cape Flats townships were impersonal; "the isolated family could no longer call on the resources of the extended family or neighbourhood." Unsupervised children searching for support and companionship, Pinnock concludes, drifted into youth gangs and crime.[29] Although Pinnock's picture of District Six in the 1950s and 1960s is somewhat romanticized, he is correct to assert that social networks were severely disrupted by the removals. Nevertheless, he fails to explain why "defensive" youth gangs emerged in the Cape Flats only around 1980, a considerable time lag given that the bulk of relocations took place between the mid-1960s and the mid-1970s. If gang formation was indeed a response to dislocation, gangs, according to Pinnock's model, would have formed in the earliest stages of relocation. Aside from this, Pinnock himself notes that so-called "skollie" gangs proliferated in pre-removal District Six. There is evidence to suggest that social dislocation, leading to an impersonal environment, encourages crime and juvenile delinquency, but this does not necessarily imply simultaneous gang formation. Gangs are a particular kind of youth association that may be more or less criminal according to circumstances. Gangs tend to be relatively protective toward familiar neighborhoods and channel a large part of their violent energy into internal subcultural feuding. Crime and gang formation, while often coinciding, follow separate trajectories. Gangs develop in more settled neighborhoods, when male youths establish a bond with their environment and their peers.

During the latter half of the 1950s and the early 1960s many African communities in Johannesburg were relocated and resettled. Inhabitants of squatter settlements generally moved voluntarily into western Soweto but a number of old-established urban communities, most notably Sophiatown, were forcibly removed to the Sowetan suburbs of Meadowlands and Diepkloof. In chapter 5 I show that the relocated communities of Meadowlands, Diepkloof, and western Soweto complained bitterly about severe crime and juvenile delinquency problems during the 1960s, yet, simultaneously, there was a distinct *lull* in gang formation. The relocation process in Johannesburg, while possibly encouraging juvenile crime, shattered gang organization. It was only towards the end of the 1960s, once neighborhood networks began to cohere, that distinctive territorial gangs emerged on a large scale in the newer parts of Soweto.

GANGS AND POLITICAL MOBILIZATION

Much of the historical literature on South African youth has treated the urban youth constituency as monolithic.[30] There is a tendency in South African scholarship to link the terms "youth" and "student." In fact the erroneous double-barreled concept "youth/student" is used frequently, thus conflating potentially diverse social elements. Whereas "youth" is a generic term, "students" is a very specific, often relatively privileged, subset. The political mobilization of specifically non-student youth has received little attention historiographically.[31]

Youth gang culture remained, in the formal sense, apolitical from the 1930s through to the 1970s. There were moments of ambivalent flirtation between political organizations and gangs, particularly around the 1960 and 1976 upheavals in Johannesburg's townships. But formal political mobilization of the youth was confined almost entirely to the schools, specifically the high schools. It has been little recognized by historians just how marginal the high school population was in relation to the wider township youth population from the 1930s to the early 1970s. Even during the expansion of African schooling under the Bantu Education system from around the second half of the 1950s, urban high school development was frozen, leaving Soweto with a mere eight secondary schools by 1968.[32] In the early 1970s Soweto experienced rapid growth in secondary schooling. It was only then that secondary school students emerged out of relative social obscurity in Soweto to even out the balance between school and street youth.

By the mid-1970s, high school students were uniquely placed to assume political leadership in Soweto. Secondary schools, which cut across narrow, street-level identities, had a unifying influence. They drew together literate youths, with similar experiences and grievances, on a large scale. High schools, with their core of intellectually inquisitive students and their ready-made network of extramural associations, were receptive to the Black Consciousness ideology that filtered down from the black rural universities and Christian groups. University students, as a result of the government's systematic balkanization of black tertiary education during the 1960s, were themselves virtually absent from the city. The parents of Soweto, in the shadow of state repression and under intensified threat of "repatriation," had been drained of political confidence and enthusiasm. School students, with energy and independence, united by a common set of experiences and brimming with a self-belief inspired by Black Consciousness, occupied the political vacuum left by the outlawed Congress movements. By contrast, the masses of non-school youth were apolitical, certainly in any organized sense. Boys, particularly those out of school and unemployed, were drawn in large numbers into gangs, which developed their own forms of expression and, arguably, resistance. Political organizations, even those explicitly recruiting among the young, from the ANC Youth League (CYL) in the 1940s and 1950s to the Black Consciousness movement of the 1970s, failed to organize the street youth effectively.

Students and youth gangs were in many ways antithetical constituencies. Non-schoolgoing male youth incorporated into street subcultures tended to be anti-intellectual, politically cynical, and ill-disciplined. Street youth did not necessarily lack political consciousness, but their anger was expressed through style and channeled into a narrowly focused defense of turf. Despite an often spontaneous sympathy for oppositional campaigns, street youth rarely identified with broadly based political movements. Youths involved in gangs hardly ever signed up for membership in organizations or attended their meetings. The nonviolent, intellectual methods of the African National Congress (ANC) or the Black Consciousness movement made little sense to them.[33]

The objectives of street gangs did, on occasion, overlap with those of political organizations. In the South African townships, gangs shared with oppositional organizations an antipathy for police and other symbols of state authority. In the case of the Sophiatown removals, for example, they were prepared to engage police in physical combat to defend their territories from intrusion. The *tsotsis* and the later Soweto gangs felt tremendous rage toward pass laws, which regulated their legal access to the streets in which they grew up. Here too their interests intersected with those of the ANC and other opposition groups.

One of the central concerns of this book is to examine the relationship between oppositional organizations and street youth in Johannesburg from the 1940s to the 1970s. The Congress Youth League's neglect of the urban gangs and the PAC's subsequent attempt to mobilize them during 1959–1960 are dealt with in chapter 4. The relationship between the Black Consciousness movement and Soweto gangs in the lead-up to the Soweto uprising is explored in chapter 7.

A NOTE ON METHODOLOGY

This book is distilled from my 1990 M.A. dissertation and my 1994 Ph.D. thesis. The M.A. concentrated on the *tsotsi* gangs of the 1940s and 1950s, while the Ph.D. focused on the youth culture of Soweto from the late 1950s until the 1976 student uprising. The bulk of the research, comprising a variety of written and oral sources, was carried out between 1988 and 1992. It hardly needs saying that every source has its own strengths and weaknesses, its own specific problems of subjectivity and accuracy. But it is the job of the historian to contextualize, assess, and balance them and, ultimately, to construct a coherent analytical narrative.

The written source material on gangs is surprisingly substantial. The archive of the Johannesburg Non-European Affairs Department (JNEAD) proved invaluable. It forms part of the West Rand Administration Board archive, which, at the time of the research, was housed at the Intermediary Archive Depot in Johannesburg. The collection includes the records of the Welfare Department and Native Youth Board from the 1930s to the late 1960s. These sections of the JNEAD, which employed a number of black fieldworkers, monitored youth unemployment, "juvenile delinquency," and gang formation in the townships and attempted to create jobs and improve recreational facilities. The JNEAD collection also includes correspondence, memoranda, and minutes of meetings that circulated between local black representatives, township superintendents, police, and central government officials. The JNEAD material not only provides valuable data but offers insights into administrative strategy, as well as the tensions between local and central government over the handling of urban youth.

The local township newspapers, *Bantu World* (1934–1955), *The World* (1958–1977), *Golden City Post* (1955–1965), and the *Post* (1966–1971), ran regular articles and features on gang activity. These newspapers targeted a township audience, and it was essential for them to carry intimate stories of local concern. Since newspapers appear regularly and sequentially, they are a particularly valuable source for developing a sense of historical process. Newspapers are also sensitive to waves of public concern over specific issues. These four papers were largely untapped sources until the late 1980s because the apartheid government restricted access even to back copies under 1970s and 1980s censorship measures. The mainstream white English-language newspapers, *The Star* and the *Rand Daily Mail*, also occasionally ran interesting features on township conditions. They provide a useful gauge of white public perception of township issues. *Drum* magazine is a particularly complicated source because it simultaneously documented township style of the 1950s and 1960s and was itself an important trend setter. Used with sensitivity, however, the magazine can be helpful in establishing a picture of contemporary subcultural style.

The records of several big gang trials are available in the archive of the Witwatersrand Legal Division. Trial records offer some useful details, especially names, age profiles, locations, and clues about gang size. But they can be frustratingly limited sources because the proceedings are narrowly forensic; witnesses focus on describing very specific incidents. Not surprisingly, accused individuals suppress detail and adjust their self-expression in order to protect themselves. Since trials are listed under the name of the first accused, I was able to trace only cases that received newspaper coverage. There is almost certainly a great deal of untapped material in legal records, but the limited index does not indicate which trials involve gangs.

Urban juvenile delinquency and youth unemployment featured prominently in several government commissions, including those of J. de Villiers Louw (1950), S. P. Viljoen (1951), A. van der Sandt Centlivres (1958), M. C. Botha (1962), G. Viljoen (1976), and P. M. Cillie (1980). The reports of these commissions provide valuable data as well as insights into central government thinking on black urban youth issues.

The University of South Africa Library houses a collection of Black Consciousness movement material, which includes minutes of meetings, organizational publications, and police memoranda. This collection was important in assessing the relationship between urban youth and the Black Consciousness movement and in gaining access to the movement's strategic debates on *tsotsi* mobilization.

Bloke Modisane, Can Themba, Don Mattera, Godfrey Moloi, Anthony Sampson, Trevor Huddleston, and Mbulelo Mzamane, to name but a few, wrote extensively about their experiences in the Johannesburg townships. It becomes clear from their assortment of autobiographical and fictional writing that youth gangs were a common feature of township life from the 1950s to the mid-1970s. This kind of writing, especially the explicitly fictional, obviously cannot be trawled for "hard" data but, as the reader follows individuals playing out their lives in a specific historical context, this writing offers an emotional and social texture absent from other written sources.

Oral sources were crucial to this project. Through interviews I was able to unearth intimate details unrecorded in written sources. I was able to include the personal perspectives of former gang members and also township residents who experienced gang activity indirectly. I made use of over a hundred interviews, which can be broken down into three categories: I conducted about forty interviews myself, a research assistant interviewed a further fifty, and I was kindly allowed access to a number of transcribed or videotaped interviews conducted by various colleagues for other purposes.

For my personal interviews I initially approached individuals such as Don Mattera and Godfrey Moloi, who were known to have been involved in gangs in their youth. They, in turn, suggested other potential contacts. I also approached former schoolteachers, social workers, journalists, musicians, and businessmen whose lives, at one point or another, were affected by township youth gangs; people who lived among the gangs but were never directly involved in them. Most of my interviewees were articulate professionals, comfortably conversant in English. In some cases I was able to conduct very detailed interviews and organize follow-up visits.

In 1992 I employed Meverett Koetz, a University of the Witwatersrand postgraduate student, as a research assistant. Meverett was superbly qualified for the job: he had research experience, he was familiar with Soweto, and he spoke Zulu, English, Afrikaans, and *tsotsitaal* fluently. We had long discussions about the themes of my research and we established an informal list of questions. While I worked through individual networks, Meverett targeted areas of Soweto. I developed profiles of specific gangs based on available documentary evidence and then asked Meverett to follow up the most important ones. For instance, he would "ask around" in Mzimhlophe until he found suitable people to talk to about the Hazels gang; similarly with the ZX5 in Phiri or the Dirty Dozen in Moroka/Pimville. These gangs operated twenty years or more prior to the interviews, but they had clearly left an impression on older residents. Meverett worked alone: he felt that my presence would inhibit people from talking. He taped interviews (unless he was asked not to) and then translated and transcribed them in English. It was not always easy for Meverett to win the confidence of people, and many of those who did respond gave fairly cursory answers to his questions. Several of the interviews, however, were richly detailed. His interviewees were generally ordinary residents, many of them women, who had experienced gang culture from the outside. But he did also manage to track down several former gang members who were willing to talk about their experiences. This book, especially the second half, would have lost much of its richness without Meverett's contribution.

In the early 1990s the "Wits" University–based History Workshop, in collaboration with a local film cooperative, Free Film-makers, created a six-part documentary television series entitled *Soweto: A History*. During 1991 and 1992 dozens of Sowetan residents were interviewed on videotape for the project. I was one of the many local historians to be consulted in the early process of framing questions and identifying potential interviewees. The series director, Angus Gibson, later allowed me free access to the unedited interview footage. Even though I had no control over the questioning, issues central to my own research were discussed repeatedly, often without prompting. This is not surprising, since a general history of Soweto would be incomplete without addressing gang culture.

As a postgraduate student in the late 1980s, I saw historical research on urban gangs as politically and socially important. If anything, it became even more relevant during the 1990s and I was increasingly drawn towards this glaring historiographical gap. I make no pretence at having produced the definitive work on the subject. But it is a beginning, and I could not wish for more than that it stimulates debate and further research.

NOTES

1. One major exception is Don Pinnock, *The Brotherhoods: Street Gangs and State Controls in Cape Town*, Cape Town, 1987.

2. On the 1976 uprising, see in particular J. Kane-Berman, *Soweto: Black Revolt, White Reaction*, Johannesburg 1978; B. Hirson, *Year of Fire, Year of Ash: The Soweto Revolt: Roots of a Revolution?* London, 1979; A. Brooks and J. Brickhill, *Whirlwind before the Storm*, London, 1980. On 1980s youth politics, see T. Lodge and M. Swilling, "The Year of the Amabuthu," in *Africa Report*, 31, 2, 1986; Colin Bundy, "Street Sociology and Pavement Politics: Aspects of Youth and Student Resistance in Cape Town, 1985," in *Journal of Southern African Studies*, 13, 3, April 1987, pp. 303–330; D. Niddrie, "New National Youth Congress Launched: Emergency Forces New Forms of Organisation," *Work in Progress*, 47, April 1987; Shaun Johnson, "The Soldiers of Luthuli: Youth in the Politics of Resistance in South Africa," in S. Johnson (ed.), *South Africa: No Turning Back*, London, 1988; J. Hyslop, "School Student Movements and State Education Policy: 1972–1987," in W. Cobbett and R. Cohen (eds.), *Popular Struggles in South Africa,* London 1988.

3. For a striking counterexample, see Philip Bonner, "Family, Crime and Political Consciousness on the East Rand 1939–1955," in *Journal of Southern African Studies,* 14, 3, 1988. This piece was an important inspiration for my own work. Tom Lodge, *Black Politics in South Africa since 1945,* Johannesburg, 1983, addresses gang involvement in the resistance to the Sophiatown removals. See also Paul La Hausse,

"'Mayihlome': Towards an Understanding of Amalaita Gangs in Durban, c 1900–1930," in S. Clingman (ed.), *Regions and Repertoires: Topics in South African Politics and Culture*, Johannesburg, 1991; La Hausse, "The Message of the Warriors: The ICU, the Labouring Poor and the Making of a Popular Political Cultural in Durban, 1925–1930," in P. Bonner, I. Hofmeyr, D. James, and T. Lodge (eds.), *Holding Their Ground: Class, Locality and Culture in 19th and 20th Century South Africa,* Johannesburg, 1989; and A. Mager and G. Minkley, "Reaping the 2 Whirlwind: The East London Riots of 1952," in P. Bonner, P. Delius, and D. Posel (eds.), *Apartheid's Genesis 1935–1962*, Johannesburg, 1993.

4. For an early 1990s survey of youth unemployment and the social conditions of youth generally, see David Everatt and Mark Orkin, *"Growing Up Tough": A National Survey of South African Youth,* Community Action for Social Enquiry (CASE) survey commissioned by the Joint Enrichment Project, Johannesburg, 1993.

5. "Soweto in Transition Project: Second Preliminary Report," Department of Sociology, University of the Witwatersrand, August 1997, pp. 23–24.

6. See, for example, Wilfried Scharf, "The Resurgence of Urban Street Gangs and Community Responses in Cape Town during the Late Eighties," in D. Hansson and D. Van Zyl Smit (eds.), *Towards Justice: Crime and State Control in South Africa*, Cape Town, 1990; Charles Carter, "'We are the Progressives': Alexandra Youth Congress Activists and the Freedom Charter, 1983–1986," in *Journal of Souther African Studies*, 17, 2, June 1991, pp. 197–220; Ari Sitas, "The Making of the 'Comrades' Movement in Natal," and Catherine Campbell, "Learning to Kill? Masculinity, the Family and Violence in Natal," both in *Journal of Southern African Studies*, 18, 3, September 1992; Gill Straker, *Faces in the Revolution: The Psychological Effects of Violence on Township Youth in South Africa,* Cape Town, 1992; Jeremy Seekings, *Heroes or Villains? Youth Politics in the 1980s,* Johannesburg, 1993; Monique Marks, "Organisation, Identity and Violence amongst Activist Diepkloof Youth, 1984–1993," M.A. thesis, University of the Witwatersrand, 1993. The issue is also raised, though rarely directly, in various contributions by N. Chabani Manganyi and Andre du Toit (eds.), *Political Violence and the Struggle in South Africa,* Basingstoke, England, 1990.

7. There is some evidence to suggest that urban youth gangs emerged in Durban, Cape Town, and East London at around the same time, though research on these centers is too patchy to develop a clear periodization or textured picture. In Durban, where the rural hinterland was closer than that of Johannesburg, the *amalaita* and *indlavini* gangs, which were essentially migrant youth associations, tended to predominate. (See La Hausse, "Mayihlome," and "The Message of the Warriors"; William Beinart, "The Origins of the Indlavini: Male Associations and Migrant Labour in the Transkei," *African Studies*, 50, 1991. See also Absolom Vilakazi, *Zulu Transformations*, Pietermaritzburg, 1962, pp. 76–78, on the abaqafi style in Durban in the 1920s.) There did, however, appear to be gangs with some similarity in style to the t*sotsis* among urbanized Indians in Durban. Though Pinnock, *Brotherhoods*, has made an impressive and pioneering study of colored gangs in District Six and the Cape Flats, little is known about African gangs in the townships of Langa or Guguletu prior to the mid-1980s. See also Scharf, "Resurgence of Urban Street Gangs," p. 237, who argues that youth gangs were largely absent from Cape Town's African townships until the mid-1980s. Mager and Minkley, "Reaping the Whirlwind," have also pointed to a substantial *tsotsi* element in East London in the 1940s and 1950s. In other colonial African cities, juvenile "gangsterism" became a no-

ticeable social problem by the 1930s. There were, according to John Iliffe, youth gangs in Lagos and Freetown as early as the 1920s and in Dar es Salaam in the 1930s.

The problem, as in Johannesburg, escalated during and immediately after the Second World War to such an extent that juvenile delinquency became "an obsession of the late colonial period." In the 1950s there were reportedly youth gangs in Ouagadougou and in the Zambian copperbelt, where they called themselves "sugar boys." See J. Iliffe, *The African Poor: A History*, Cambridge, 1987, pp. 187–189. In the late 1950s a juvenile delinquency conference was held in Kampala. Despite all the administrative attention, however, it appears that very few historical or sociological studies have been carried out on urban youth gangs in Africa. One noteworthy exception is J. S. La Fontaine's study of youth associations in Kinshasa during the very early 1960s. As in Johannesburg, youth gangs with a distinctive urban style proliferated in a context of poverty, over-crowding, school shortages, and strained nuclear families. See J. S. La Fontaine, "Two Types of Youth Group in Kinshasa (Leopoldville)," in P. Mayer (ed.), *Socialization: The Approach from Social Anthropology*, London, 1970, pp. 195–197.

8. There is ongoing ambiguity in South Africa over the use of the terms "black" and "African." To avoid confusion, I use the term "black" to refer to all those who do not identify as white. "African," as a subdivision of "black," excludes Indian and colored (mixed race in the local sense) South Africans. There has been a powerful gang tradition in the colored townships of Johannesburg since the 1950s, but this is a story I do not attempt to tell in this book.

9. See I. Mayer and P. Mayer, "Socialization by Peers: The Youth Organisation of the Red Xhosa," in P. Mayer (ed.), *Socialization: The Approach from Social Anthropology*; and Paul Spencer, *The Maasai of Matapato: A Study of Rituals of Rebellion*, Manchester, England, 1988.

10. Spencer, *The Maasai of Matapato*, p. 5.

11. Mayer and Mayer, "Socialization by Peers," p. 162.

12. Spencer, *The Maasai of Matapato*, p. 5.

13. Philip Abrams, *Historical Sociology*, Shepton Mallet, England, 1982, p. 253.

14. See Mike Brake, *The Sociology of Youth Culture and Youth Subculture*, London, 1980, p. vii; he argues that "on the whole, youth cultures and subcultures tend to be some form of exploration of masculinity." See also Albert Cohen, *Delinquent Boys: The Culture of the Gang*, London, 1956, pp. 138–140, in which the assertion of masculinity in the delinquent subculture is emphasized.

15. For an in-depth analysis of sexuality and gender relations in the *tsotsi* sub-culture, see Clive Glaser, "The Mark of Zorro: Sexuality and Gender Relations in the Tsotsi Youth Gang Subculture on the Witwatersrand," *African Studies*, 51, 1, 1992. For the construction of masculinity, see particularly pp. 48–52 and for sexual violence, see pp. 56–60.

16. J. Clarke, S. Hall, T. Jefferson, and B. Roberts, "Subcultures, Cultures and Class," in S. Hall and T. Jefferson (eds.), *Resistance through Rituals: Youth Subcultures in Post-War Britain*, London, 1976; Phil Cohen, "Subcultural Conflict and Working Class Community," in S. Hall, D. Hobson, A. Lowe, and P. Willis (eds.), *Culture, Media, Language*, London, 1980; D. Hebdige, *Subculture: The Meaning of Style*, London, 1984; Brake, *The Sociology of Youth Culture and Youth Subcultures*.

17. Albert Cohen arrived at a similar conclusion without the explicit class analysis. See especially *Delinquent Boys*, pp. 26–28.

18. See Clarke et al., "Subcultures, Cultures and Class," p. 55 and Hebdige, *Subculture: The Meaning of Style*, p. 85.

19. In explaining *tsotsi* style, I develop this line of argument in great detail, perhaps rather uncritically, in chapter 3 of "Anti-Social Bandits." See also Albert Cohen, *Delinquent Boys*, pp. 26–28, who talks of "a delight in the defiance of taboos itself" and "an element of active spite and malice, contempt and ridicule, challenge and defiance" in delinquent subcultures.

20. Although the members of the Birmingham school are sensitive to generation and gender dynamics intersecting with class, they tend to undervalue these social forces in a hierarchy of causality.

21. Phil Cohen, "Subcultural Conflict and Working Class Community," particularly pp. 82–85.

22. Albert Cohen, *Delinquent Boys*, p. 35. See also Irving Spergel, "Youth Gangs: Continuity and Change," *Crime and Justice*, 12, 1990, pp. 171–273. Spergel, pp. 226–227, emphasizes the search for status, reputation, and recognition.

23. K. B. Clark, *Dark Ghetto: Dilemmas of Social Power*, London, 1965, p. 13. Ellis and Newman make a similar observation on Greaser and Gowster gangs in Chicago. See Herbert Ellis and Stanley Newman, "The Greaser Is a 'Bad Ass'; the Gowster Is a 'Muthah': An Analysis of Two Urban Youth Roles," in T. Kochman (ed.), *Rappin' and Stylin' Out*, Urbana, Ill., 1972,

24. For an excellent example of this, see Godfrey Moloi, *My Life*, Johannesburg, 1991, vol. 1 in particular. Moloi, as a youth, was a classic case in point.

25. See "Anti-Social Bandits," pp. 138–141. See also interview with "Ndoza" (HWSFP); he emphasizes the elements of "fun" and prestige in the criminal activity of the Damarras gang in Diepkloof in the 1970s. In this respect, as in others, there were remarkable parallels between *tsotsi* values and the American ghetto "hustling ethic." Hustlers, although generally lone operators, had tremendous street prestige and were perhaps the most important role models for ghetto gangs. They believed in making money but not by working. Their income came from gambling, pool, narcotics, petty theft, and pimping. They were showy, flashy conspicuous consumers, successful city-slickers. Upwardly mobile blacks in professional jobs, semiskilled blue collar workers, and white collar workers were heaped with disdain and referred to as "eight-hour chumps." See Julius Hudson, "The Hustling Ethic," in T. Kochman (ed.), *Rappin' and Stylin' Out*, Urbana, Ill., 1972, pp. 410–424. Ellis and Newman, in their chapter on Greasers and Gowsters in the same volume, p. 376, emphasize the respect of Chicago street youth for hustlers whose attitude is reflected in the comment: "Shit! I can make more in a day hustling in the streets than washing Mr. Charley's car for a week." See also E. G. Wolfenstein, *The Victims of Democracy: Malcolm X and the Black Revolution*, Berkeley, 1981, pp. 172–173, and Albert Cohen, *Delinquent Boys*, p. 135. In the delinquent culture, Cohen observes, "the stolen dollar has an odour of sanctity that does not attach to the dollar saved or the dollar earned." Journalist Stanley Motjuwadi, in an interview, observed that the *tsotsis* regarded any young man who worked from nine to five as a "sissie."

26. La Fontaine makes a similar observation about Kinshasa youth gangs in the early 1960s: "Fashions in dress serve . . . as diacritical signs to mark off the young urbanite both from the parental generation and from those of his contemporaries who are only newly arrived from the provinces." See La Fontaine, "Two Types of Youth Group in Kinshasa," p. 200.

27. La Fontaine, "Two Types of Youth Group in Kinshasa," p. 204.

28. Oscar Lewis, *The Children of Sanchez*, London, 1964, p. 38. There does not appear to have been a substantial gang in Manuel's neighborhood. There seems to have been a far more individualized form of young male assertion. It is difficult to guess whether this was specific to Manuel himself or to his neighborhood. I have uncovered no literature on Mexican or other Latin American youth gang subcultures. Interestingly, Manuel had a tremendously powerful father who held his family together with a mixture of hard work and brute force. It is unlikely that Manuel himself would have joined a gang for fear of his father. Nevertheless, Manuel's attitudes, forged in the streets of Mexico City, seem appropriate and applicable to gang subcultures. His final words resonate, for instance, with the famous *tsotsi* dictum, "live fast, die young, and make a beautiful corpse."

29. Pinnock, *Brotherhoods*, pp. 51–59.

30. See, for example, Bundy, "Street Sociology and Pavement Politics"; and Lodge, *Black Politics in South Africa since 1945*. Hirson, *Year of Fire, Year of Ash*, pp. 192–194, however, does begin to hint at the divergence, as do Brooks and Brickhill, *Whirlwind before the Storm*, p. 151 and p. 208. Scharf shows perhaps the most sensitivity to this issue but in a far more contemporary study, "The Resurgence of Urban Street Gangs." See also Seekings, *Heroes or Villains?* particularly chapter 1, in which the definition and diversity of youth identity are discussed.

31. In South Africa there are very few documented precedents of urban youth gang politicization prior to 1959–1960. Paul La Hausse has suggested that the ICU mobilized the Durban *amalaita* gangs during the 1929 beer boycott. See La Hausse, "The Message of the Warriors," pp. 38–39. Phil Bonner shows how a rehabilitated gangster who joined the Benoni branch of the CYL became a central figure in the 1955 Bantu Education boycott in Benoni. Using his contacts and familiarity with the gangs, "AB," as Bonner calls him, was able to draw the gangs effectively into the boycott campaign. They played a role in policing the boycott, intimidating potential schoolgoers. See Bonner, "Family, Crime and Political Consciousness." On *tsotsi* opposition to the Sophiatown removals, see Lodge, *Black Politics in South Africa since 1945*, pp. 91–113. In "Reaping the Whirlwind," Mager and Minkley examine the involvement of *tsotsis* in political unrest in East London during the 1950s.

32. This figure is taken from a table entitled "Schools in the Bantu Locations/Villages: 30th June 1968," Urban Bantu Councils Collection (Johannesburg 1968–1970), University of South Africa Archive, Pretoria, Acc 244. The table in fact lists only seven secondary schools; it excludes one in Diepkloof, which fell under an autonomous administration called the Bantu Resettlement Board. Secondary schools, as opposed to high schools, went up to Standard Eight. Only five of the seven listed were high schools: Morris Isaacson, Musi, Orlando West, Orlando, and Sekano Ntoana.

33. Similarly, the street youth of the United States kept out of *formal* politics certainly throughout the 1940s, 1950s, and, with some qualification, the 1960s. Clark, *Dark Ghetto*, pp. 13–14 and U. Hannerz, *Soulside: Inquiries into Ghetto Culture and Community*, New York, 1969, chapter 8, point respectively to political apathy on the streets of Harlem in the 1940s and 1950s and in Washington in the early 1960s.

2

"THEIR PLAYGROUNDS ARE THE STREETS": THE JUVENILE DELINQUENCY CRISIS ON THE RAND, 1935–1960

From around the mid-1930s, before the term *tsotsi* was in vogue, public concern mounted over a youth gang and "juvenile delinquency problem" in the townships of the Witwatersrand. In 1938 a conference on juvenile delinquency was organized by the South African Institute of Race Relations (SAIRR), an influential liberal welfarist organization, and enthusiastically supported by the Johannesburg municipal authorities. The observations and analyses that emerged from the conference were taken extremely seriously by the local administrators, but they nevertheless failed to implement effectively any of the wide-ranging recommendations. During the war years, youth gangs, some of them extremely violent, proliferated and the term *tsotsi* took on common township usage. The term initially referred to a specific youth subcultural style but gradually widened to incorporate urban "juvenile delinquents" more generally. By the late 1940s and throughout the 1950s local administrators and many township residents perceived "tsotsiism" to be out of control. Youth gangsterism had become so pervasive that the terms "juvenile delinquency," "tsotsiism," and "youth" became almost synonymous in administrative jargon.

This chapter attempts to establish the socioeconomic context of gang formation in the townships. It draws primarily on the evidence of contemporary outsiders—members of the African township elite, social welfarists, local and central government administrators—who were trying to describe and understand the youth gang phenomenon. The views of the African elite are expressed most clearly in the local *Bantu World* newspaper and township advisory board documentation. The *Bantu World*, though financed by white mining houses and politically conservative, was run by African journalists who focused on social issues of real importance. The newspaper also ran a lively "Readers' Forum." The advisory boards were officially recognized elected structures designed to advise local governments on the administration of urban Africans. Though they lacked executive powers, advisory board representatives often expressed local grievances forcefully and many of them retained popular credibility well into the 1950s. A number of boardmen, especially in the 1930s and 1940s, had links to the ANC. Generally they were small businessmen or professionals. Aside from organizing the juvenile delinquency conference in 1938, the SAIRR, the most important of the independent welfare organizations operating on the Rand, continued to conduct research on the issue of gangs and juvenile crime throughout the 1940s and 1950s. Liberal sociologist Ellen Hellmann, probably the most informed and sensitive commentator on urban social issues during this period, wrote extensively on urban African youth. Church-linked groups and individuals also became involved in the issue. Prominent among them was the philanthropist Ray Phillips.

The Johannesburg Non-European Affairs Department (JNEAD), responsible for the hands-on administration of the townships, had close ties to the welfarist lobby and took the advisory boards seriously. Numerous letters and memoranda on youth gangs and crime circulated between the office of JNEAD's manager, its Welfare Division, welfare organizations, and the advisory boards. The central government was no less interested—several commissions dealt directly or indirectly with the issue between 1940 and 1960—but it was concerned more with social control than with the plight of individuals. The African elite, welfarists, JNEAD, and the central government all saw "juvenile delinquency" as a social and moral crisis that had to be headed off, and there was a surprising conformity in the discourse on the subject. But the central government's position differed starkly from that of the other groups over the strategy of influx control. Whereas the welfarist lobby and local administrators emphasized the need to upgrade and invest in the townships, the central government repeatedly fell back on influx control as the solution to all urban ills. For the central government—and this applies to the United Party as well as the Nationalists—the flow of Africans into the city was the primary problem rather than inadequate urban conditions.

Few of the subcultural insiders were able to give anything but impressionistic insights into the broader socioeconomic issues that fed into youth gang formation and crime. The available sources are therefore inevitably limited and subjective. Nevertheless, through a careful and critical reading it is possible to piece together a detailed picture of the social and economic context of the so-called juvenile delinquency problem. This analysis of the crisis is grouped into five broad themes, each of which will be explored in turn: urban family instability and the breakdown of generational hierarchy; inadequate schooling; youth unemployment; poverty, overcrowding, and the shortage of social facilities; pass laws and urban illegality.

THE URBAN FAMILY

"Ere long, we shall be ruled by our children in our own homes."
—S. B. Sibiya, *Bantu World*, Readers' Forum, 7 September 1946

From as early as the mid-1930s, one of the most common explanations for urban African juvenile delinquency was urban/rural discontinuity and social dislocation. This kind of explanation was expounded regularly by literate older-generation Africans, welfarists, and government officials. The explanation tended to romanticize and simplify rural African society and set up "the city" as its evil opposite. In rural society, it was argued, youths were socialized effectively. They were taught respect for elders; they had a wide support network in the extended family; they accepted social laws and moral values and thus became constructive and integrated members of society. In the city, youths were exposed to all sorts of "immoral" influences such as crime, prostitution, and irresponsible cinema; in the city, youths of eighteen were registered as independent adults who could marry and seek employment without parental consent; in the city, youths lost access to wider kinship support and socialization networks as the nuclear family replaced the extended family. In short, generational hierarchy was breaking down; the parents were losing respect and control. Without parental control and effective socialization of youth into society, it was argued, juvenile delinquency was inevitable.

Many older *Bantu World* readers looked back nostalgically at the ordered precolonial rural society. Take, for example, Douglas Mbopa who wrote to the newspaper in 1935:

Sir—In the olden days before the advent of Western Civilisation, the Bantu had a thorough control over their children. One never heard of Bantu youth misbehaving.

They had chiefs who ruled, there were laws and customs which were not to be broken. Boys were trained to be straight and truthful and be worthy subjects to their chiefs to obey seniors and to fear touching anything that would degrade them. Boys grew up to their manhood trying to abide by their customs and laws.[1]

Although recognizing the terrible inadequacy of education, housing, health, and recreation facilities, a writer in 1938 emphasized the "moral breakdown" that accompanied the transition from rural to urban society.[2] Yet another writer, in 1939, reminisced about the "old customs" under which youths were content and controlled. The "present generation of youth," he lamented, had lost its respect for the older generation; their values and morals were degenerating.[3] *Bantu World* itself emphasized this theme. The following extracts from *Bantu World* editorial pages between 1937 and 1940 illustrate this:

> Juvenile delinquency is primarily, although not altogether, a product of town life and its main incidence is urban . . . the temptations of youth are so much more varied than those of the rural areas.[4]
> On account of the lack of education facilities, thousands of boys and girls are growing wild in the midst of the dazzling splendour of Western Civilisation, with its picture and dance halls, its lipsticks and cigarette smoking, its drinking parties and gangsters. Can such ignorant boys and girls, living in the midst of such complicated life, be expected to cultivate the good qualities of the human heart and mind?[5]

This older-generation African elite was proud of its urbanity and literacy yet rejected the permissiveness of the city. Its members equated the rejection of the traditional age hierarchy with criminality, disobedience with deviancy and delinquency.

The white liberal social welfare organizations tended to place the rural/urban adaptation argument alongside a number of other socioeconomic factors. Ellen Hellmann's work epitomized this approach. Her 1939 study, *Problems of Urban Bantu Youth*, gave equal weight to the issues of youth unemployment, early school-leaving, and family problems arising from urban dislocation. In rural tradition, she argued, relationships in the immediate family emphasized respect and obedience and did not encourage familiarity and confidence. But, although there was this stress on authority within the immediate family,

> the child is subject not only to his parents but to the wider body of relatives. Moreover, the parents do not bear the sole responsibility of rearing the child, but are assisted by their kindred. The maternal relatives temper the severity of the behaviour pattern between parents and paternal relatives and the child. These behaviour patterns complement each other. The child pays respect to those in authority over him; he has an outlet for his demands for familiarity; and he receives respect from those junior to him. The whole tribal system appears to be balanced and to meet the full range of the child's needs.[6]

She went on to argue that extended kinship networks had all but ceased to function in the urban context:

> If relatives live nearby, this is usually fortuitous, not designed. Urban conditions, in which a family has little choice but to take a vacant house in a location or a vacant room in a slum-yard, make it almost impossible for relations to settle close together.[7]
>
> The interdependence of the kinship group living and working together in a homestead no longer exists. . . . [D]espite the numerous exceptions which are found, the individual family is the stock unit in urban areas. It is an economic unit and very largely independent of its kin for other purposes as well.[8]

Hellmann observed that urban parent–child relationships remained fairly constant. The emphasis on deference and obedience continued despite the huge shift in environment. The child's upbringing, however, lacked the balance and the crucial outlets of "tribal" family life. Children consequently became unruly and rebellious. The parents' difficulty in disciplining their children was exacerbated by parental absence from the home due to wage labor and by the very real possibility of escape for children who felt they had been too severely dealt with.[9]

The findings of the 1938 Juvenile Delinquency Conference, which was supported by both the Union Social Welfare Department and the local Johannesburg Native Affairs Department, outlined four main causes of urban African delinquency: poverty, inadequate housing, lack of education, and unstable families. The last-mentioned issue incorporated urban/rural adjustment. The Native Affairs Commission of 1940, sponsored by the central Union Native Affairs Department (NAD), picked up on the urban/rural adjustment issue to strengthen its advocacy of tightened influx control regulations. The uncontrolled drift of Africans to the cities, the commission insisted, was at the root of urban depravity:

> It cannot be denied that the bare human facts as disclosed in the papers at the Conference need to be more widely known and their full implications realised. The increase in the number of cases of juvenile delinquency appearing before the Courts in Johannesburg—an increase of 63.8% during the single year 1937/1938—is distinctly alarming; the continual migration of the rural population to the towns—in Johannesburg an increase of 100.65% between 1921 and 1936—must, if continued, defeat every effort at amelioration; and the growth and extension of the promiscuous society which Johannesburg is breeding up is a dreadful reflection on our civilization: for it is a society in which, in the abandonment of all tribal sanctions and coupled with a corresponding failure to adopt Christian stan-

dards of morality, the old Bantu obligations and affections and sanctity of family life are completely disappearing. An undisciplined, unmoral, lawless community is fast being created, which will become increasingly difficult to control with the years.[10]

The commission's strategy, then, for dealing with the growing juvenile delinquency problem was to screen out from the cities all juveniles who did not have jobs or stable, legal guardians. The SAIRR was heavily critical of the commission's approach. In a memorandum replying to the commission's draft report it pointed out that the majority of cases of juvenile delinquency came from among the more permanently urbanized rather than the recently urbanized section of the African population. In other words, for the commission's strategy to be effective, the government would have to send settled, legal urban residents *back* to the rural areas. For the SAIRR, the solution to the problem lay rather in upgrading urban facilities and improving standards of living. Juvenile delinquency was not inevitable if the urban standard of living was adequate; "delinquency is lowest in those families where good wages, a stabilised family life, decent housing and regular school attendance are to be found."[11] In other words, Africans could adjust to urban life more effectively if their urban status was acknowledged and their needs taken seriously. Whereas the NAD argued that Africans were inevitably rural people whose lifestyle was inappropriate to the city, liberal social welfarists tended to argue that social problems such as juvenile delinquency emerged out of sudden, harsh processes of adjustment to the city and that solutions lay in speeding up rather than retarding that adjustment.

Under the "natural protection" of the war years, South African industry continued to boom, and Africans, responding to labor needs, continued to pour into the cities. Urban facilities, inadequate as they were by the late 1930s, did not keep pace with the urban influx. State policy hovered in an indecisive no-man's-land between encouraging and discouraging a settled urban African population. The urban African population was allowed to expand but little was done to cater to its needs. There were chronic shortages, particularly in housing and education. Statistically, juvenile crime and gang formation continued to escalate but, as a social issue, it seemed to fade into the background as the war effort took precedence over most internal social issues. But by the late 1940s, juvenile delinquency flooded back into the public consciousness. Advisory board members once again decried delinquent youth; the *Inter-Departmental Inquiry into Native Juvenile Unemployment* was set up under S. P. Viljoen; and social welfarists organized another conference. Although more concrete factors such as youth unemployment and inadequate education started to take center stage in explaining the growing crisis, the urban/rural adjustment argument continued to be

popular. For instance, in a Joint Advisory Board memorandum drawn up in
November 1950 by, amongst others, R. V. Selope Thema, P. Q. Vundla, and
Paul Mosaka, the "disruption of modern industrial society" was seen as the
crucial context of township crime. "It has substituted a money economy for
the cattle economy of the African; it has broken down tribal solidarity with
its social sanctions; it has undermined the authority of the chief and of the
parents; it has accorded a freedom to women and children which is expressing itself by a challenge to authority." The writers then went on to say that
the government had not allowed any viable urban social alternative to emerge.
Despite massive urbanization, "especially following the 1913 Land Act,"
the government had refused to recognize Africans as urban citizens and hence
had taken no care over the African urban environment.[12] The Viljoen Report, which came out in 1951, also pointed to an absence of tribal youth
control mechanisms both to keep youth "in their place" and to imbue them
with a sense of social responsibility.[13] Ellen Hellmann, in a speech to the
SAIRR in 1951, reiterated many of the points she had made in her 1939
thesis. Again she emphasised the "difficulties of adjustment" during a period of "intensive culture contact" as Africans shifted from a rural to an
urban environment.[14]

Closely related to the issue of urban/rural dislocation was urban family instability. Welfarists drew a clear correlation between family instability and juvenile delinquency; children of unstable families, they argued, received little supervision or guidance. These children, particularly the male children, had an enormous amount of free time to roam
the streets. Teenage girls tended to be drawn more effectively into housework, especially the many who were already mothers with responsibilities.[15] An SAIRR-sponsored study of the family lives of eighty-seven
Diepkloof Reformatory inmates during the mid-1930s pointed out that
only about one-third came from a home with both mother and father
present. Fifty-four of the eighty-seven belonged to gangs.[16] In a study of
juvenile court statistics in 1939 it was found that, of the 900 cases handled
by the Probation Office, about 40 percent had one or both parents de-
ceased, and fully one-third of the total lived completely independently
of parents or guardians.[17]

The high rate of illegitimacy in the Rand townships tended to be linked
uncritically to family instability. Ellen Hellmann, in a study of 216 sample
township families in 1939, found that roughly 34 percent of the families
numbered illegitimate children among the family group or were "irregular"
in that the parents were not married.[18] At a social welfare conference in
September 1944, a welfare worker, a Mr. Radebe from Orlando, stressed the
need to stabilize the home environment of the urban African family if juvenile delinquency was to be effectively combated. He estimated that 60 to 70

percent of Orlando residents had not entered into a form of marriage.[19] The Viljoen Report of 1951 expressed concern about the effects of illegitimacy on children: "It would seem that the majority of Native children born in the urban areas are illegitimate, a potent force undermining parental control and weakening disciplinary forces which are so necessary to the maintenance of a stable society." [20] It was rarely recognized that illegitimacy itself had little bearing on family instability. Officially consecrated marriages were often as unstable as casual unions. Conversely, informal unions occasionally led to fairly stable families.[21]

The absence from the home of working mothers was regularly raised as a major contributing factor to the poor supervision of children. Wages for unskilled African male workers were invariably inadequate to support a family in Johannesburg. The result was that wives had to seek a supplementary income, through formal or informal means. The SAIRR emphasized that wage levels were related to family stability. If the father earned enough, the institute researchers argued, mothers would stay at home and keep a much tighter rein on their children. "The absence of the mother from any home is a menace to the well-being of the children of that home."[22] Even in stable families, then, children remained virtually unsupervised throughout the day and they were susceptible to the counterinfluence of gangs.[23]

One of the key targets of blame for juvenile delinquency, particularly in the prewar period, was independent African women.[24] Local administrators, welfarists, and older-generation African men saw the issue of family instability as inevitably associated with the interrelated issues of beer brewing, prostitution, and "loose" and independent women. Beer-brewing encouraged delinquency, it was argued, because it exposed children to "immoral" and illegal activities from an early age and because it gave women an independence that, by extension, destabilized families. On the subject of beer-brewing "and other illicit occupations of mothers to supplement family income," a Joint Council memorandum in the mid-1930s commented: "This, of course, means not only neglect, but the children's early familiarity with society as an enemy and the law as something to be broken rather than to be maintained in the common interest."[25]

Their opinions were, of course, informed by a network of gendered, "Western civilized" prejudices. There was no established connection between beer-brewing and delinquency. On the contrary, a beer-brewing mother was probably more able to give her children attention than other working mothers because she tended to work at home. But these linkages remained strong in the minds of many male observers. An excellent example can be found in a 1938 *Bantu World* editorial that bemoans the undermining of "old customs" with the advent of Western civilization:

But nothing was done by those who urged for their abandonment to replace them by such methods as would have ensured the security of our
family life and the safety of our youth. Instead women were given to
understand that in the eyes of God they were the equal of men and could
do as they liked; children were made to understand that as soon as they
became of age they were no longer under parental control. . . . [Poverty]
has driven many women—some of them "respectable" members of our
well known churches—to the selling of illicit liquor in order to supplement the meagre earnings of their husbands. But in the course of time this
awful business brings family quarrels which eventually lead to separation, because women have discovered that by selling liquor they can become economically independent of men's controls.[26]

The issue of African urban family instability was clouded not only by a
whole range of cultural prejudices but also by administrative control objectives. Many white policy-makers, for instance, used it as a pretext to
restrict urban African settlement, while members of the African male
elite evoked the issue to assert, or reassert, as they saw it, traditional
patriarchal values. Nevertheless, it would be a mistake to discount family instability as a factor in the high levels of gang formation and juvenile crime in the Rand townships. The specific patterns of urbanization
and employment did lead to extraordinary instability among urban African families. To start with, African workers were generally unskilled;
this ensured a high job turnover and meant that workers were constantly
on the move looking for new or better-paid jobs. In addition, the migrant
labor system and the associated pass laws often broke up family units.
In the process of urbanization, many men left families behind in the
rural areas. Most recently urbanized single men still hoped to reestablish
themselves in the countryside in the long run. This discouraged them
from making firm commitments to urban women and their children. Many
urban marriages were merely relationships of convenience to ensure access to housing, which was assigned only to recognized married couples.[27]
Although it should perhaps not be exaggerated, urban African children
were lacking in parental supervision, and kinship support was usually
thin in the city. Moreover, single-headed households almost certainly
experienced material deprivation as one income was stretched to breaking point. For young males, juvenile gangs provided an obvious alternative locus for emotional and sometimes material support.

SCHOOLING

In the crowded streets of Sophiatown, Newclare and the native townships
and locations, over 10,000 native children are running wild. There are no

schools to accommodate them, for the schools—such as they are—are filled
to overflowing. They are the adults of the future, but their chance of becoming reasonably decent, law-abiding citizens is slender. Their playgrounds
are the streets—among cars, carts and the mixed traffic of the native quarters.

—*The Star*, editorial, 16 November 1938

From the 1930s to 1960, roughly one-third of African children of
schoolgoing age on the Witwatersrand attended school. In 1937 the *Bantu
World* claimed that of the 90,000 African children of schoolgoing age on the
Reef only 18,000 were in school.[28] A study by Ellen Hellmann in 1939
emphasized that school attendance was clustered in the lower grades. Fifty-
four percent of those in school were in the subgrades, while roughly 10
percent reached Standard Five, the first official year of secondary schooling, and a meagre 3.8 percent were in Standard Six and above.[29] It is particularly important to focus on secondary as opposed to primary school attendance since secondary schools had a strikingly similar age profile to that
of the bulk of the gangs (roughly fifteen to twenty-one). Although some
Standard Five students could be as old as sixteen or even seventeen, the
average age was fourteen-and-a-half.[30] By 1949, fewer than 7,000 Africans
were enrolled in secondary school in Pretoria and on the Witwatersrand
combined. Of these, over half were in Standard Five. There were 820 Standard Sevens and only 63 matriculants.[31] Although primary schooling did
expand almost immediately after the introduction of Bantu Education in the
mid-1950s, a significant expansion in secondary schooling was only noticeable in the 1960s (and, even then, it was concentrated in the rural areas).
National secondary school figures remained virtually stagnant until 1960.[32]
Unless school enrollment patterns on the Rand and in Pretoria differed drastically from national patterns, it is safe to assume that secondary school
enrollment on the Rand and in Pretoria remained below 7,000 throughout
the 1950s. Truancy rates were also extremely high. An annual average of
4,000 children "disappeared" from African schools on the Rand during the
1950s.[33] Given that there were at least 37,000 Africans aged fifteen to eighteen resident in Johannesburg alone by 1961, it is clear that schoolgoers
represented a startlingly small proportion of the adolescent urban African
population on the Rand throughout the 1940s and 1950s[34] (Photo 2.1).

There were three basic reasons for low school enrollment, early school-
leaving, and truancy. First, schooling was not compulsory and there were
far too few schools and teachers to accommodate even those children who
did want to attend school.[35] Second, the quality of education was extremely
low. Children rejected inferior, unstimulating teaching made worse by the
overcrowded conditions. Moreover, schooling was impractical. A school
education did not necessarily enhance a school-leaver's employment oppor-

Photo 2.1   "Much has been done—more needs to be done. For hundreds of thousands of youngsters such as these their primary education is that of the street arab, qualifying them, with little check, for the university of crime." This picture and caption appeared in R.H.W. Shepherd and B. G. Paver, *African Contrasts: The Story of a South African People*, Cape Town: Oxford University Press, 1947, p. 233. Shepherd and Paver express the anxiety of white philanthropists about "urban Bantu youth" in the 1940s. Note how these youths, though extremely poor, aspire to the *tsotsi* style, especially in their choice of hats. (Photo attributed to "Messrs Garthorne and Keartland.")

tunities. In a study of over 500 African school-leavers on the Rand in 1939, Hellmann found that 25 percent of these children refused to go to school against the wishes of their parents.[36] To begin with, the worst teachers and the worst conditions tended to be concentrated in the substandards. Hellmann observed:

> To anyone who has watched the dreary classes of sub-standard children, heard their monotonous rote spelling of words and repetition of phrases, it is not surprising that after languishing in the sub-standards for three or four years the child emerges bored, listless and unwilling to continue his schooling.[37]

In addition, pupils had no incentive to stay on at school because there appeared to be no attractive job opportunities for them on completion of their schooling. The pupils saw African teachers and clerks receiving similar wages to those of unskilled laborers. There also appeared to be no possibilities for upward mobility, despite education, because of the color bar.[38] The de Villiers Louw Commission of 1950 recognized these problems. The standard of African schooling was so bad, the commission complained, that children preferred to join youth gangs. The commission also recommended that schooling should provide skills more immediately necessary to the economy. Children, the commission argued, would then be employable once they left school, and they would recognize some value in attending school.[39]

Finally, most urban African families could not afford to send their children to school. Children were under pressure from a very early age to become economically active. Parents often preferred to have their children contributing to the household income rather than wasting their time at school. In Hellmann's study of school-leavers, she found that 37 percent left school out of economic necessity, either to seek employment or because their parents were unable to afford fees, books, and school clothes.[40]

The ANC, with its deep commitment to education, was naturally alarmed by the low levels of school attendance and emphasized the link between dropping out of school and juvenile delinquency. The ANC president, A. B. Xuma, set the tone in 1945 when he blamed the high incidence of juvenile crime on the country's failure to invest adequately in black education:

> No country can expect to be free from crime when it spends proportionately such a small amount on the education of one section of its children as South Africa does. When 60 to 65 per cent. of African children of school-going age in the towns are unable to go to school through lack of accommodation, it must be clear that they are merely being qualified to become juvenile delinquents and later gaolbirds—simply because society has neglected them and does not try to discipline them or create a social environment conducive to happy, useful citizenship.[41]

UNEMPLOYMENT

> There is a gap—a hiatus—between school-leaving and employment. What fills this gap? Gambling and drinking—idle congregation on the streets, joining a gang, harmless pursuits gradually becoming less harmless.
> —Ellen Hellmann, memorandum, April 1951[42]

African urban juvenile unemployment, like inadequate schooling, started to attract major public and administrative attention from around the mid-1930s. The two issues often went hand in hand, as administrators and social welfarists tried to explain the massive rate of "idleness" amongst urban African youths. Unemployment was a major focus of the 1938 Juvenile Delinquency Conference, and in 1948 the Native Youth Board was established under the chairmanship of Ray Phillips with the intention of placing African youths in jobs. Nevertheless, the youth unemployment problem continued to escalate during the 1950s. In July 1950 the Youth Board conducted an extensive survey, which arrived at a figure of 20,800 unemployed youths in Johannesburg's African townships.[43] It is impossible to reach any certainty with the figures available, but they do suggest that, at the time of the investigation, at least half of the urban African males of Johannesburg between the ages of fourteen and twenty were neither in school nor employed.[44] In November 1961 the Johannesburg NEAD provided the following figures for youth unemployment. Of the 23,400 males in the fourteen to eighteen age group, 6,500 were at school, 5,500 were registered as employed, and 11,400 were "unemployed or unable to work." The corresponding figures for the 14,400 females in this age category were 4,200, 285, and 9,950.[45] In other words, roughly 47 percent of the males were neither in school nor employed. Although the equivalent figure for females was higher at 68 percent, this caused less official alarm as girls were expected to be drawn heavily into domestic duties. It is also probable that unemployment was generally underestimated because of the high incidence of illegal urban residence.

Youth unemployment levels contrasted sharply with adult unemployment. The official male adult (nineteen years old and above) unemployment rate of around 8 percent was not unusually high by world standards. W.J.P. Carr, the manager of the Johannesburg NEAD, made this observation in a 1960 memorandum: "The incidence of male adult unemployment is very low at the moment . . . unemployment hits those in the 16 to 19 age group hardest."[46]

The factors involved in youth unemployment remained fairly constant from the mid-1930s to the early 1960s.[47] Probably the most important reason for urban youth unemployment was the competition urban youths faced from migrants on the job market. Employers on the Rand, despite influx control legislation, preferred to employ migrants rather than local youths. Migrants tended to be more acquiescent, "respectful," and reliable than their urban counterparts. Furthermore, they were prepared to accept lower wages. Employers of both industrial and domestic labor tended to feel this way.[48] In an official letter to the Johannesburg Regional Employment Commissioner, W.J.P. Carr wrote in 1955: "Native juveniles who are urbanised are often unreliable, work-shy and selective in their choice of a job—many prefer to exist by gambling and other nefarious means, and make little or no contribution to the maintenance of their families. . . . Employers because of these facts, are unwilling to employ native juveniles."[49]

In another letter in 1956, Carr reiterated the point that urban African youths "tend to be unreliable, work-shy, aggressive and unco-operative when offered employment."[50] These allegations were not entirely unfounded, but the unemployment problem was exacerbated by these very impressions held by the employers. The latter were usually prejudiced toward urban youths and unwilling to give them a chance.[51] They often bypassed local labor bureaus in the 1950s and employed people directly through contacts in the countryside. Throughout the 1940s and 1950s, municipal authorities throughout the Pretoria–Witwatersrand–Vereeniging area generally turned a blind eye to these breaches of influx control in order to avoid discouraging local industry. Domestic employers, like industrialists, preferred to employ rural workseekers, thus restricting the chief avenue of employment open to female urban youths.[52] Urban youths found it virtually impossible to penetrate the industrial and domestic labor market in any significant way.

There were two other practical considerations for employers. First, urban youths tended to have less strength and stamina than adults, and they had very little experience of hard physical work.[53] Second, the Wage Board fixed wage levels for juveniles. Industrialists might have been more amenable to employing urban youths at wages below Wage Board levels but once wages were fixed, employers were determined to find the most productive possible workers.[54] Unionized adult workers, fearing that they would be undercut by juvenile workers should wage fixing be removed, rejected interference with Wage Board controls.[55]

The attitude of urban youths toward employment was influenced by youth gang culture. *Tsotsi* culture rejected discipline, hard work, and "respectable" employment. Any form of informal, quasi-legal employment was preferable to consistent, badly paid legal employment. In a July 1950 memorandum the Native Youth Board commented:

> The Employment Officers of the Board have . . . discovered that numbers of Native lads are not in school, nor are they interested in obtaining employment. The lads, most of whom are city born, lounge about the Townships, live on their parents, act as "runners" for the Chinese "Fah Fee" game, sell articles on the Orlando/Pimville trains, gamble with dice or cards, engage in smuggling dagga or liquor, pick pockets and drift into crime.[56]

Crime, often organized in gangs, provided an alternative means of subsistence for urban youths. The need to find regular employment was therefore less urgent. In a front-page article in June 1950 the *Bantu World* commented: "It is common knowledge amongst Africans in the townships that many of these [unemployed] youths think it is a waste of time working for small wages while, by means of robbery, they are able to collect large sums of money."[57]

The Viljoen Report of 1951 adopted a similar line of argument: "Juveniles out of employment develop spontaneously into tsotsis in order to find an outlet for their energies as well as a means of earning a livelihood by illegal means."[58] Unemployment and youth gang culture, therefore, reinforced one another. Unemployment was a far more conceivable option for urban youths with the alternative of gang life. Simultaneously, unemployment helped to swell the ranks of the *tsotsi* gangs.

The pass laws made the prospect of finding jobs additionally unattractive. To get a job, a youth had to register officially, and this could often expose dubious urban status. Moreover, passes were necessary for youths to travel even from their townships to the city. Without the correct documentation this could lead to their arrest. In 1948 Ray Phillips commented: "The pass laws militate against their finding jobs. They fear that if they enter the towns they will be detained by the police for their lack of passes. They fear they may be returned to the smaller centres, where the type of employment they seek is unavailable."[59]

In 1951, Boys' Club officials reiterated the point: "It is not always easy for a boy to come up to the City owing to the Pass Law Regulations under which he might be arrested."[60] Noting the low rate of registration for unemployment among African youths in 1960, W.J.P. Carr observed that "some of these boys are reluctant to come forward for employment because, for one reason or another, their papers are not in order and they fear arrest and persecution if they bring themselves to the notice of the authorities."[61]

During the 1930s and 1940s the juvenile delinquency problem was left in the hands of various social welfare organizations, but by the late 1940s it became clear that the efforts of the philanthropists had been in vain; they were unable to stem the growing tide of juvenile unemployment. By the early 1950s the state, both local and central, became increasingly anxious about the youth problem on the Rand. It recognized that welfare organizations were inadequate to cope with the problem. Large-scale state intervention was needed. Youth unemployment was targeted as the key issue.

In 1951 the Inter-Departmental Committee on Native Juvenile Unemployment was established. This committee was aimed at investigating the extent of and reasons for juvenile unemployment on the Rand and in Pretoria. The committee report argued that there were direct links between juvenile unemployment and "tsotsiism."[62] The central state apparently started to identify juvenile unemployment, which led to "tsotsiism," as politically threatening.[63] Following the Viljoen Report, the central state showed tremendous interest in finding employment for African youths on the Rand. It attempted to provide the Johannesburg municipal government with active assistance in this regard. In February 1953 the Director of Native Labour and representatives from the Central Labour Bureau met with local state officials to discuss the issue. Central government officials, eager to handle the problem in a forceful way, called for greater coordination between local authorities and the central state.[64] They offered assistance to local labor bureaus wherever possible.[65] The Secretary of Native Affairs H.S.J. Van Wyk was convinced that the *tsotsi* problem could best be combated by overcoming African juvenile unemployment.[66]

At the 1953 meeting between local and central government labor officials, the state decided to embark on a three-pronged strategy, based largely on the recommendations of the Viljoen Report, to combat juvenile unemployment on the Rand. First, "[it] was the intention of the Minister of Labour to grant to those industries employing juveniles exemption from the various wage instruments to allow of [sic] the payment of a lower wage than that applicable to adults." It was hoped that more local juveniles would be employed if Wage Board instruments were removed. Second, the Department of Labour committed itself to exploring avenues for juvenile employment in commerce and industry "and to endeavour to persuade commerce and industry to give preference in filling such vacancies to location youths in preference to youths from rural areas or Native Territories." Finally, the central government intended to place the allocation of jobs on the Rand more firmly under Central Labour Bureau control. All workseekers had to be officially registered at the local bureaus, which, in turn, had to supply the Central Labour Bureau with regular reports on job registration and job placement. This fitted into the Central Labour Bureau strategy to screen out illegal migrant workseekers and encourage the employment of urban juveniles.[67]

In mid 1953 the Johannesburg Department of Native Affairs launched a juvenile employment drive. Initially, the department appeared to have some success. Between September 1953 and April 1954, 17,987 juveniles (sixteen to twenty-one years of age) were registered as employed and 15,197 found employment.[68] The official surplus was only 2,790 but thousands of youths had managed to avoid registration.[69] The figures for 1955 showed a marked increase in the official surplus. Between February and October 1955, 38,695 juveniles officially registered as workseekers. Of these, 23,396 were placed in employment. A balance of 15,299 failed to find employment.[70] These figures probably indicate a tightening up of the registration procedure between April 1954 and February 1955 rather than a deterioration in juvenile employment over this period. In fact, the number of job placements was significantly higher during 1955. Nevertheless, in line with the central government's newly acquired concern over this issue, the new Secretary of Native Affairs, Van Rensburg, was angry and perplexed by the 1955 juvenile unemployment figures. He demanded more details and an explanation from the Johannesburg Registration Officer.[71] The pace of placing juveniles in employment flagged until, by the early 1960s, between 2,000 and 4,000 registered juvenile workseekers were being placed annually.[72] But even this very limited success of the Johannesburg Juvenile Employment Section has to be qualified on two accounts. First, it is unclear to what extent state intervention made a difference to the overall employment situation. In other words, the majority of those placed in employment might well have found employment anyway. Second, and more importantly, almost as many juvenile workers lost jobs as those who were placed. It was not uncommon to find that overall employment figures had gone down over a three-month period despite the fact that over a thousand were placed in employment.[73] Ultimately, the juvenile unemployment problem was as serious in the early 1960s as it had been in the early 1950s.

SOCIAL FACILITIES

Our children are left loitering in the streets absolutely with nobody to guide them along proper channels of life; and of course the devil finds work for them.
—C. P. Molefe, *Bantu World*, Readers Forum, 20 July 1935

By the mid-1930s, urban Africans were already experiencing severe overcrowding problems and, to avoid claustrophobic households, thousands of male children made a natural home of the streets.[74] During the war years the housing shortages became much worse. While squatter settlements sprouted throughout the Rand, more and more children poured into the streets, and efforts at providing them with alternative stimulus and recreation were hopelessly inadequate. Gang life became increasingly popular.

According to Hellmann, by the early 1950s Johannesburg had a housing backlog of between 25,000 and 50,000. She observed: "The consequence of this extreme congestion on family life is obvious: lack of privacy, inability of children to work or play in the crowded home and the necessity for them to make the street their home."[75] After fighting in the war, W.J.P. Carr returned to the Johannesburg municipal administration in 1945 to find that both the overcrowding and the juvenile delinquency problems had become much more serious than they had been in the prewar years. Carr observed that there was nothing to attract the youths to their homes. Youths, desperate "to get out from under the feet of the adults," went out onto the streets to find their own amusement.[76]

Throughout the 1940s and 1950s, social welfare and church bodies struggled to provide "suitable" recreation for township youths. If the home environment was disastrous and employment and schooling were scarce, they reasoned, youths could at least be guided and controlled to an extent through leisure activities. In West Native Township, which, unlike Sophiatown and Alexandra, fell directly under JNEAD control, there was some infrastructure for youth recreation. The Anglican Board Mission was very active in "West Native." Ray Phillips organized soccer teams that became a "tremendous drawcard" for the youth; his wife, Dora, ran the Wayfarers for girls, which organized sewing classes, picnics, and netball. But, even in West Native Township, their work was a "drop in the ocean."[77] There were also numerous independently organized soccer and boxing clubs that were extremely popular, but these clubs, with their emphasis on physical prowess and competitiveness, did not necessarily discourage gang association.[78]

Throughout the 1940s and 1950s there were persistent calls from welfarists, local administrators, and government commissions for improved recreation facilities "to counteract the lure of the streets."[79] The state, both local and central, encouraged organizations such as the Boy Scouts, Wayfarers, and Pathfinders but allocated no material resources to them. What resources were made available to alleviate the "youth problem" tended to be allocated to the creation of employment. Despite the lack of resources, these organizations often attracted fairly substantial memberships. Nevertheless, their success in counteracting the lure of gang life was minimal, largely because they recruited most effectively from the schoolgoing population. They appeared to make no substantial inroads among youths who were already involved with gangs.[80]

The one leisure time activity that was unambiguously popular among township youth was the cinema. Local administrators often encouraged the township movie industry and even provided municipal mobile film units, in the hope of drawing children away from street life. Carr, for instance, felt that if the movies were adequately monitored to allow only "healthy and wholesome" entertainment, they could counteract youth gangsterism.[81] Ultimately this approach was swamped in a wave of outrage against movie influences. By the mid-1940s the centrality of cinema to *tsotsi* style and imagery was abundantly clear. In a 1946 editorial, *Bantu World* complained bitterly that "hundreds of African children . . . are running wild in the streets of our big cities" and that it was "in the cinemas where they receive an education which prepares them for a life of thieving and killing."[82] Movies were easily available and reasonably cheap. They offered a respite from the crowded home and squalid street environments; they provided a glimpse of romantic and inaccessible worlds. As I show in chapter 3, it was not surprising that movie imagery became fundamental to *tsotsi* subcultural style.

PASS LAWS

P. Q. Vundla: I am satisfied that the cause of the majority of crimes in the townships is the passes.

Col. Grobler: What?

P. Q. Vundla: The pass laws. The young men go to the pass office, they are given a definite time within which they have to find employment, if not, they have to leave. Only this morning I took a young boy to the Superintendent—he was born at Masinga, his parents stay in Western Native Township—he was told to leave Johannesburg, he will never leave Johannesburg, the next time you meet him he will be in gaol. He is going to resort to crime.

—Extract from minutes of NEAD Conference, December 1955[83]

Although the pass laws only became a major social issue for township youth after the National Party takeover in 1948, the issue was by no means unique to the post-1948 era. From as early as the mid-1930s, numerous city-born African youths were forced into an underground existence in the absence of official urban status. To survive in the urban underground, youths had to avoid tax and unemployment registration. The easiest survival route was to join a street gang. In the early 1930s Africans became liable to pay tax at the age of eighteen, which, in itself, became a motivation to avoid official urban status and seek security in gang life.[84] In 1937 *Bantu World* noticed this connection between the pass laws and juvenile delinquency.

The conception of our Native location as reservoirs of labour rather than homes for our town Native population and the operation of the trek pass system which obliges a man to "move on" in the event of his losing his job and failing to find another within a certain period of time, results often in women and children being left without any claim to remain in the town in which the children may have been born. Usually the only alternative in such circumstances are [*sic*] to live precariously, dodging the police, or to wander homeless about the country.[85]

In the late 1940s and early 1950s, the National Party tightened influx control particularly in dealing with "excess" unemployed urban youths. The connections between delinquency, gang association, and the pass laws became more apparent. Hundreds of youths were rounded up and jailed or sent to the rural areas. But the hardened ones stayed in the cities, often after serving jail sentences, and lived a twilight gang existence. Periods in jail tended to harden their criminality and registering as unemployed was impossible because it would expose their lack of urban status.[86]

In the mid-1950s advisory board member P. Q. Vundla became vocal in pointing out the connection between the pass laws and the prevalence of criminal gangs. He railed against the government, which tried to justify its clampdown on urban youth by claiming that it was encouraging the employment of permanently urban youths. This was invalid, he argued, both because city-born youths were often included in the clampdowns and also because there was no significant improvement in youth employment. "What about this influx control? That was brought into being they told us so that only Johannesburg youngsters will get employment in Johannesburg. If we don't get employment for these youngsters then we are waging a futile campaign." He also argued that children who were sent to jail for pass offenses made contacts with and learnt things from gang members. "Many of these boys don't fear to go to jail, if they have been to jail, they are deemed to be heroes." The pass laws were forcing township youths into a criminal existence.[87] In 1956, during a Non-European Housing Committee meeting at which advisory board members were present, Vundla was again vocal on the issue:

> Mr. Vundla wanted to know why it was that a boy, born in Johannesburg and whose parents were in Johannesburg, should be refused entry into the urban area. Many months elapsed sometimes before the boy was given permission to remain and work in Johannesburg. It often happened that when a man lost his job in Johannesburg and wished to seek other employment, he was told to leave Johannesburg and return to the place where he was born. As his family was in Johannesburg he remained in the area. He would go into hiding from the police and would become a menace to society as he had no legitimate means of earning a living.[88]

Early in 1957 an article in *The Star* dealing with crime in Alexandra identified the pass laws as an important factor in gang activity. The pass laws were seen as particularly destructive in that they interfered with job opportunities. "One resident said that the reason for the existence of these gangs is the number of unemployed young Natives who have not been given passes to work in Johannesburg. 'They have nothing to do all day and they also have no money. They expect to live on us workers.'"[89]

The issue remained alive in the early 1960s. In 1961 three advisory board members from South West Bantu Townships asserted that youngsters became delinquents and gang members *in response* to being endorsed out of the city and not vice versa as government sources claimed.[90]

I have shown earlier how, in the contexts of urban adaptation and juvenile unemployment, there was a divergence in strategy between local and central state authorities. Influx control lay at the center of this disagreement. Whereas the local Johannesburg administration argued that urban juvenile delinquency could best be combated by improving urban conditions and expanding juvenile job opportunities, the central government tended to place its faith in influx control.[91] By limiting the number of Africans permanently settled in the city, the central administrators asserted, jobs could be found more easily for local youths, and resources would be less thinly spread. Although this strategic divergence became much more pronounced in the era of Nationalist rule, it was apparent during the 1930s and 1940s as well.[92] In the early 1950s there was a great deal of continuity in the administrative staff of the Johannesburg NEAD, while the central administrators were more ardent adherents to influx control strategy than their predecessors. There was enormous tension at local government level as the central administration placed permanent inspectors in W.J.P. Carr's offices to ensure that ministerial instructions were carried out.[93]

Influx control backfired tragically as a strategy for combating juvenile delinquency. Instead of allowing the administration to concentrate its energy and resources on a limited number of strictly legal urban youths, the pass laws created a massive population of influx-control refugees who lived a shadowy illegal existence in the townships. Hounded by police and without any chance of finding legal employment, their best chance for urban survival lay in joining criminal street gangs.

Juvenile criminality and youth gangs emerged almost organically out of the social and economic dead ends that township youths faced throughout the 1930s, 1940s, and 1950s. The typical male township teenager lived in an unstable family unit from which one or both of his parents were absent. Perhaps his mother worked at home, selling beer or washing clothes, but she was likely to be overloaded with responsibilities, and her ability to offer him emotional support or guidance was severely restricted. His household was drastically overcrowded; any real privacy was impossible. He had left school because his household could not afford to keep him there, especially since schooling was in any case unlikely to secure him a better job in the future. He was unemployed. Although he tried looking for a job on a number of occasions, he soon became disillusioned. He was also worried that he would lose his urban status if his passbook was found not to be in order. Besides, many of his friends were earning a substantial living through robbery. There were no decent recreation facilities in his vicinity. While his sisters tended to do a great deal of housework, looking after young children, cleaning, or preparing meals, very few of the boys he knew were expected to do the same. He spent the major part of his day without supervision or any structured activity. Gang life seemed attractive; it offered companionship, a sense of belonging, and a possible means of income.

NOTES

1. *Bantu World (BW)*, 13 July 1935.

2. *BW*, 18 June 1938, letter from Golden J. Sithole, Adam's College.

3. *BW*, 2 December 1939, letter from Walter B. Nhlapho. Nhlapho was a respected member of the Johannesburg African elite and a regular contributor to the *BW* letters pages.

4. *BW*, 25 September 1937, article on editorial page, "Poverty and Delinquency."

5. *BW*, 21 October 1939, editorial. See also *BW*, 2 March 1940, "Alarming Increase in Juvenile Lawlessness among Africans."

6. Ellen Hellmann, *Problems of Urban Bantu Youth*, South African Institute of Race Relations, Johannesburg, 1940, p. 5. For another good example of this approach, see Joint Council Collection, Historical Papers Library, University of the Witwatersrand, Johannesburg (JC), AD 1433, "Juvenile Vagrancy and Delinquency," undated memorandum (ca. 1936).

7. Hellmann, *Problems*, p. 5.

8. Hellmann, *Problems*, p. 6.

9. Hellmann, *Problems*, pp. 7–10.

10. South African Institute of Race Relations Collection, Historical Papers Library, University of the Witwatersrand, Johannesburg (SAIRR), B25, Native Affairs Commission Draft Report, Cape Town, 1940, par. 6.

11. SAIRR B23, memorandum submitted to the Continuation Committee of the Delinquency Conference, undated (ca. 1940). Interestingly, W. Eiselen, the Chief Inspector of Native Education in the Transvaal, also supported government intervention to improve African schooling in the urban areas. He saw the expansion of education as crucial for the social control of youth. See NTS 8/331 (7642), letter from Eiselen to the Secretary for Native Affairs with a TED memorandum enclosed, and NTS 8/331, Eiselen's speech to Bantu Juvenile Delinquency Conference, 1938.

12. West Rand Administration Board Archive, Intermediary Archive Depot, Johannesburg, IAD WRAB 351/1, "Memorandum on the Growing Incidence of Crimes of Violence in the African Townships," 19 November 1950. The memo was drawn up by an elected committee of the Joint Advisory Board.

13. S. P. Viljoen, *Report on the Inter-Departmental Committee on Native Juvenile Unemployment on the Witwatersrand and in Pretoria* (Viljoen Report), Pretoria, 1951, pp. 5–6.

14. Ellen Hellmann Papers (EHP), memorandum, "Bantu Youth in Our Cities," presented as a speech to the SAIRR, 26 April 1951.

15. See Hellmann, *Problems*, p. 43.

16. SAIRR B14, J. L. Reyneke, "A Preliminary Investigation of African Juvenile Delinquency," undated memorandum (ca. 1935).

17. IAD WRAB 351/2, NEAD and NAD, Research and Welfare Branch, "Non-European Juvenile Delinquents," June 1938–June 1939, Probation Office and Juvenile Court

Statistics. The juvenile court generally dealt with children of eighteen or younger, but they occasionally stretched their age limit to twenty-year-olds.

18. See, for example, *BW*, 8 July 1937, Francis Le Mas, "The Neglect of Bantu Youth." See also Hellmann, *Problems*, p. 16; in a study of 216 sample township families in 1939, Hellmann found that roughly 34 percent of the families numbered illegitimate children amongst the family group or were "irregular" in that the parents were not married.

19. IAD WRAB 351/2, South African National Congress on Post-War Planning of Social Welfare Work, 27 September 1944.

20. Viljoen Report, p. 6.

21. See P. Bonner, "Family, Crime and Political Consciousness on the East Rand 1938–1955," *Journal of Southern African Studies*, 15, 1, 1988, pp. 398–401.

22. SAIRR B23, Memorandum submitted to the Continuation Committee of the Delinquency Conference, undated (ca. 1940).

23. There are numerous references to the issue of parental absence from the mid-1930s to the late 1950s in newspapers, social welfare organization reports, and local Johannesburg administrative documents. See, for example: *BW*, 18 September 1937, editorial; *BW*, 3 September 1940; IAD WRAB 351/3, L. Nkosi, "The Nsibanyoni Gang," April 1940; IAD WRAB 351/2, letter from P. Mashego to the Welfare Officer, undated (ca. August 1944); *The Star*, 11 January 1957, comments by W.J.P. Carr on the delinquency problem; IAD WRAB 285/7, A. S. Marais, Director of NEAD Boksburg, "Urban Bantu Youth Problem and Its Possible Solution," 24 June 1959; *The Star*, 20 October 1959, letter from Boyle S. Ndukwana of Dube.

24. For an interesting argument about independent African women and "moral panic," see Kathy Eales, "Rehabilitating the Body Politic: Black Women, Sexuality and the Social Order in Johannesburg 1924–1937," seminar paper presented at the African Studies Institute, University of the Witwatersrand, 2 April 1990.

25. SAIRR B25.3, Johannesburg Joint Council of Europeans and Africans, "Native Juvenile Destitution and Delinquency," undated (ca. 1935). See, for another example, IAD WRAB 351/2, letter from the Manager JNEAD (Graham Ballenden) to Senior Probation Officer, 15 December 1941.

26. *BW*, 29 October 1938.

27. See Phil Bonner, "African Urbanisation on the Rand between the 1930s and the 1960s: Its Social Character and Political Consequences," *Journal of Southern African Studies,* 21, 1, March 1995.

28. *BW*, 10 April 1937, p. 20; *BW*, 13 November 1937, p. 16. For other early estimates, see *BW*, 12 Jan 1935; and Joint Council Collection, Historical Papers Library, University of the Witwatersrand, Johannesburg (HPL), Cj2, minutes of meeting of the Committee on Juvenile Delinquency of the Johannesburg Joint Council of Europeans and Non-Europeans held at the Bantu Men's Social Centre, 24 August 1937 (figures include Alexandra).

29. Hellmann, *Problems*, pp. 34–35.

30. M. C. Botha, *Verslag van die interdepartementele Komitee insake ledige en niewerkende Bantu in die Stedelike Gebiede* (Report of the Interdepartmental Committee into Idle and Unemployed Bantu in the Urban Areas), Pretoria, 1962 (henceforth Botha Report), par. 276.

31. Viljoen Report, p. 8.

32. For the 1949 figure, see Viljoen Report, p. 8. For the 1960 figure, see Colin Bundy, "Street Sociology and Pavement Politics: Some Aspects of Student/Youth Consciousness during the 1985 Schools Crisis in Greater Cape Town," *Journal of Southern African Studies*, 13, 3, April 1987; this figure is taken from Bundy's table, "The Expansion of African Education since 1960," p. 311.

33. See the Botha Report, par. 14 and corresponding footnote. The figure refers to children who registered at the beginning of the year and stopped attending classes during the year. Truancy had become a major problem as early as the mid-1930s. In Hellmann's twelve sample Rand schools in 1936, there were truancy rates, i.e.: percentage of nonattendance to enrollment, of between 5 and 21 percent. See *Problems*, p. 28.

34. See my calculations in "Anti-Social Bandits: Juvenile Delinquency and the Tsotsi Youth Gang Subculture on the Wittwatersrand, 1935–1960," M.A. thesis, University of the Wittwatersrand, 1990, p. 37–38; for the 37, 000 total see IAD WRAB 401/44/20, memorandum from NEAD Johannesburg to Interdepartmental Committee on Native Juvenile Delinquency, 16 November 1961. Note also that the truancy rate was extremely high.

35. JC AD4133, "Juvenile Vagrancy and Delinquency," undated memorandum (ca. 1936). See also the newspaper *Umteteli wa Bantu*, 11 March 1944, which deals with the opening of a new Anglican mission school in Orlando with a capacity of 495. Hundreds of children apparently had to be turned away and the newspaper complained that African schooling was hopelessly inadequate on the Rand.

36. Hellmann, *Problems*, p. 54.

37. Hellmann, *Problems*, p. 41.

38. Hellmann, *Problems*, p. 70.

39. J. de Villiers Louw, *Report of the Commission Appointed to Inquire into Acts of Violence Committed by Natives at Krugersdorp, Newlands, Randfontein and Newclare*, Pretoria, 1950, UG47/1950, par. 189–190. See also IAD WRAB 351/1, Report of the Manager, W.J.P. Carr, to the Technical Subcommittee, 19 March 1957.

40. Hellmann, *Problems*, pp. 54–55.

41. Xuma's address to the ANC conference in Bloemfontein, reported in *BW*, 22 December 1945.

42. EHP, File 51, "Bantu Youth in our Cities," 26 April 1951, p. 13.

43. IAD WRAB 285/7 Native Youth Board, "Report on the Investigation into African Juvenile Unemployment in Four Johannesburg Townships," July 1950.

44. See my calculations in "Anti-Social Bandits," p. 44.

45. IAD WRAB 285/7, memorandum from NEAD Johannesburg to Interdepartmental Committee on Native Juvenile Delinquency, 16 November 1961.

46. IAD WRAB 285/7, memorandum: "Juvenile Unemployment, Johannesburg," by W.J.P. Carr, submitted to the Town Clerk and Bantu Affairs Commissioner, 20 September 1960. See also 351/2, record of discussion between the manager, NEAD Johannesburg and Joint Native Advisory Board, 1 March 1961. For a more detailed analysis of available juvenile unemployment statistics from the late 1930s to the early 1960s, see "Anti-Social Bandits," pp. 41–44.

47. For an excellent summary of the factors in 1939, see Hellmann, *Problems*, pp. 131–133.

48. This point is made in the Viljoen Report. See also Bonner, "Family, Crime and Political Consciousness," and Deborah Posel, *The Making of Apartheid 1948–1961: Conflict and Compromise,* Oxford, 1991, pp. 158–164.

49. IAD WRAB 401/25/1, letter from Carr to the Regional Employment Commissioner, 22 December 1955.

50. IAD WRAB 401/25/1, letter from Carr to the Native Affairs Commissioner of Johannesburg, 17 October 1956.

51. See Bonner, "Family, Crime and Political Consciousness," pp. 404–405.

52. According to the Viljoen Report, unemployment among urban African female youths was "probably worse" than among male youths.

53. IAD WRAB 351/2, "Appeal to His Worship the Mayor from the Association of Non-European Boys' Clubs," letter from NAD, Johannesburg, to the Mayor, enclosed in a letter from Carr to Councillor Hurd, 23 May 1951.

54. Bonner, "Family, Crime and Political Consciousness," pp. 404–405.

55. Trade Union Council of South Africa Collection, Historical Papers Library, University of the Witwatersrand, Johannesburg (TUCSA), memorandum from African Textile Workers Industrial Union (Witwatersrand Branch) to Native Juvenile Employment Commission, 6 June 1951; TUCSA Collection, "Findings: Native Juvenile Delinquency," reply of the Western Province Local Committee of the South African Trade and Labour Council to Native Juvenile Employment Commission questionnaire, undated (ca. 1950).

56. IAD WRAB 285/7, Native Youth Board, "Report on the Investigation into Native Juvenile Unemployment in Four Johannesburg Townships," July 1950.

57. *BW*, 24 June 1950. See also IAD WRAB 285/7, extract from minutes of meeting between NEAD and Native Youth Board deputation, 28 September 1950; IAD WRAB 210/5, minutes of meeting between NEAD and the Executive Committee of the Joint Native Advisory Board, 18 September 1957.

58. Viljoen Report, p. 7.

59. *The Star*, 20 July 1948.

60. IAD WRAB 351/2, "Appeal to His Worship the Mayor," enclosed in a letter from Carr to Councillor Hurd, 23 May 1951.

61. IAD WRAB 285/7, W.J.P. Carr, "Juvenile Unemployment, Johannesburg," memorandum submitted to the Town Clerk and Bantu Affairs Commissioner, 20 September 1960.

62. Viljoen Report, pp. 7–10.

63. The de Villiers Louw Commission of 1950, UG 47/1950, which was appointed to investigate acts of violence in Krugersdorp, Randfontein, Newclare, and Newlands, identified youth gangs as major catalysts of violence in all four locations. Youth gang involvement is mentioned on virtually every page of the report. Chapter 4 of this book contains a more detailed exploration of state fears of youth gang politicization.

64. IAD WRAB 401/25/1, letter from the Acting Deputy Manager to the Manager, Johannesburg NAD, 19 February 1953.

65. For instance, see IAD WRAB 401/25/1, letter from the Director of Native Labour to the Johannesburg Native Commissioner, 4 May 1953, offering central state assistance in tackling youth unemployment.

66. IAD WRAB 401/25/1, letter from H.J.S. van Wyk, Secretary of Native Affairs, to the Director of Native Labour, Johannesburg, 1 February 1954. See also the comments of Dr. P. Van Rensburg of the Native Affairs Department in an article in *The Star*, 10 February 1954.

67. The strategy is summarized in IAD WRAB 401/25/1, letter from the Acting Deputy Manager to the Acting Manager, Johannesburg NAD, 19 February 1953.

68. IAD WRAB 401/25/1, Monthly Reports from the Registering Officer, City of Johannesburg, on juvenile unemployment. These figures are computed from monthly statistics.

69. Carr admits to this himself in IAD WRAB 401/25/1, letter from the Manager to the Native Commissioner of Johannesburg, 17 October 1957.

70. IAD WRAB 401/25/1, letter from Carr to the Employment Commissioner, Johannesburg, 22 December 1955.

71. IAD WRAB 401/25/1, letter from Van Rensburg, Secretary of Native Affairs, to the Registration Officer, Johannesburg, 24 November 1955.

72. IAD WRAB 285/7, Quarterly Reports, Registration Officer to the Manager, July 1960–March 1962.

73. IAD WRAB 285/7, Quarterly Reports. See, for example, the figures for October–December 1960.

74. See *BW*, 18 September 1937, editorial, "Poverty and Delinquency"; and *BW*, 18 June 1938, letter from Golden J. Sithole, calling for better education, health, housing, and wholesome recreation to combat the juvenile delinquency problem.

75. EHP, File 51, "The Sociological Background to Urban African Juvenile Delinquency," 16 August 1953, p. 3.

76. Interview, Carr (a).

77. Interview, Carr (a).

78. Interview, Mattera (b).

79. The quotation comes from a Johannesburg Joint Council memorandum cited in *BW*, 8 August 1942. See also the following: SAIRR B23, memorandum on Native Juvenile Delinquency, 1938; *The Star*, 14 November 1938, editorial; *BW*, 17 August 1946, editorial; IAD WRAB 351/2, C. Norman Crothall, "A Practical Suggestion Towards the Prevention of Delinquency amongst Native Juvenile-Adults in Large Urban Areas," 11 April 1947; *Sunday Times*, 7 September 1958; UG 47/1950; Viljoen Report, 1951; A. van der Sandt Centlivres, *Report of the Riots Commission/Dube Hostel, 14/15 September 1957*, Johannesburg, March/April 1958, par. 91; Botha Report, 1962, par. 69.

80. See Clive Glaser, "The Mark of Zorro: Sexuality and Gender Relations in the Tsotsi Youth Gang Subculture on the Witwatersrand," *African Studies*, 51, 1, 1992, pp. 48–50, for a discussion of the competing attraction of youth gangs and the Boy Scout movement.

81. See Carr's letter to *The Star*, 15 January 1954.

82. *BW*, 17 August 1946, editorial.

83. IAD WRAB 351/1, Extract from minutes of conference attended by the Deputy Commissioner of Police, Witwatersrand Branch, Area Officers, members of the Non-European Affairs Committee, and members of the Advisory Board, Johannesburg, 14 December 1955.

84. SAIRR B25.3, Johannesburg Joint Council of Europeans and Africans, "Native Juvenile Destitution and Delinquency," undated (ca. 1934).

85. *BW*, 25 September 1937, editorial.

86. See John Lazar, "Conformity and Conflict: Afrikaner Nationalist Politics in South Africa 1948–1961," D. Phil. thesis, Oxford University, 1987, p. 97. In chapter 4 I discuss how the intensified application of pass laws politicized *tsotsis*.

87. Interview, Moloi; *The Star* 20 July 1948; *BW*, 30 September 1950, letter from Charles Riksha Finquana; *Drum*, November 1951, feature article, "The Birth

of a Tsotsi"; IAD WRAB 351/2, letter from the Johannesburg NAD to the Mayor, 23 May 1951.

88. IAD WRAB 351/1, extract from minutes of conference attended by the Deputy Commissioner of the SAP, Witwatersrand Branch, Area Officers, members of the Non-European Affairs Committee and members of the Advisory Board, Johannesburg, 14 December 1945.

89. IAD WRAB 210/6, minutes of meeting between NEAD Housing Committee and members of the Advisory Boards, 28 March 1956. Mr. Malize, a member of the Jabavu AB, raised the issue earlier that year: see IAD WRAB 351/1, extract from minutes of Jabavu AB meeting, 23 February 1956.

90. IAD WRAB 351/2, minutes of meeting of South West Bantu Township No. 3 AB, 15 June 1951. The three members in question were Messrs. Ramokgadi, Ngqase, and Ncwana.

91. Interview, Carr (a).

92. It is interesting to contrast the arguments in the Native Affairs Commission draft report with those in an SAIRR memorandum compiled in response. See SAIRR B25, Native Affairs Commission Draft Report, Cape Town, 1940, par. 6; and SAIRR B23, memorandum submitted to the Continuation Committee of the Juvenile Delinquency Conference, undated (ca. 1940). Johannesburg local government strategy on this issue tended to be in line with that of the SAIRR.

93. Interview, Carr (a).

3

THE *TSOTSI* ERA: YOUTH GANGS ON THE WITWATERSRAND DURING THE 1940s AND 1950s

In contemporary usage, a *tsotsi* refers very broadly to an urban African criminal. During the second half of the 1940s and throughout the 1950s, however, the meaning of *tsotsi* was far more specific. A *tsotsi* was a young man who dressed, spoke, and behaved in a clearly identifiable way. He imitated American "city slicker" clothing styles, spoke *tsotsitaal*, indulged in some kind of criminal or quasi-legal activity, and generally moved around in gangs. As I suggested in chapter 1, it is useful to conceptualize the *tsotsis* of the 1940s and 1950s as a subculture. *Tsotsis* constituted what the contemporary sociologist, C. V. Bothma, described in 1951 as "a society of the adolescent" with a clear sense of identity forged in the furnace of a hostile urban environment.[1] They formed an insular masculine culture that shared much in common with, but was nevertheless distinct from, their "parent" township culture. In the first section of this chapter I examine some of the early social forerunners to *tsotsi* youth gangs and then explore the emergence and meaning of the word *tsotsi*. In the second section I examine the boundaries and internal structures of the subculture which emerged in the early 1940s and assess its prevalence on the Witwatersrand during the 1940s and 1950s. In the next three sections I discuss *tsotsi* values and style.

THE RISE OF THE BO-TSOTSI

By 1943 the term *tsotsi* had not entered common usage. There had been no reference to the word in either newspapers or administrative documents.

Nevertheless, throughout the 1930s and early 1940s, township youth gangs with many similarities to the later *tsotsi* gangs started to emerge. Probably the earliest African youth gang formations in the South African cities were the *amalaita*. These distinctive gangs emerged, particularly in Durban and Johannesburg, as early as the 1920s. They continued to exist in the urban areas until well into the 1940s and even 1950s. But, although state officials often failed to differentiate between the various urban youth gangs, *amalaitas* represented a tradition of urban youth gangs separate from those that were precursors of the *tsotsis*.[2] *Amalaita* gangs were made up of young male migrant domestic workers who lived in white suburban domestic quarters. *Amalaita* gang members tended to have a strong rural consciousness that was particularly evident in the fact that they continued to participate in the circumcision ritual. Gang association could be seen as a way of coping with an alien urban environment. Although *amalaitas*, generically, did not all have the same ethnic background, the specific *amalaita* gangs did tend to associate along ethnic lines. On weekdays, gang members were employed as domestic servants; their *amalaita* identity only became apparent on their "day off," Sunday.[3] Another early form of youth gang formation, extremely common among young Pondo migrants from as early as the 1930s, was that of the *indlavini*. The *indlavini* were renegade youth bands that had broken away from traditional Pondo age structures. The *indlavini* consisted of youths who had shaken off traditional courtship and initiation rituals. Although the *indlavini* were heavily influenced by urban life through migrancy and displayed a number of characteristics associated with the *tsotsis*, such as territorial violence and sexual aggression, they were essentially a rural phenomenon.[4] By contrast, the gangs that can be identified as *tsotsi* forerunners were township based and, even if some of their members were technically migrants, asserted a strong urban identity.

In a book published in 1962, Absolom Vilakazi argued that the most important cultural forerunner to the *tsotsis* in Natal was a social stratum called the *abaqhafi*. The *abaqhafi* apparently emerged in the urban areas during the early 1920s. Like the *tsotsis*, they were adolescents heavily influenced by American movie images, particularly those of the Wild West. Their style was modeled on cowboys. But most young urban Africans could not afford real cowboy outfits, so cheap imitations emerged: ordinary handkerchiefs were used instead of mufflers, and trousers were tied under the knees to imitate breeches. Vilakazi said nothing about *abaqhafi* gang formation. It would appear that the *abaqhafi* were an amorphous stratum of Natal youth, whose chief expression existed at the level of clothing style. Vilakazi argued that, through migrancy, the style became popular amongst rural youths. But, whereas the *abaqhafi* style remained popular in the countryside, it gave way to the *tsotsi* style in the urban areas. "In the urban areas, what would have been the *abaqhafi* in the past are now called the *tsotsis*." By the 1950s, *abaqhafi* style in Natal actually became symbolic of rural lack of sophistication.[5]

In the Pretoria townships youth gangs, generically called *funanis*, emerged during the 1930s. Like the *tsotsis*, these gangs asserted their urban identity and were influenced by American gangster imagery. They spoke an embryonic form of *tsotsitaal*, called *flaaitaal*. The *funanis* self-consciously differentiated themselves from the *amalaita* gangs. The term *tsotsi* eventually came to incorporate what had been the *funanis*.[6]

In Johannesburg, there were a number of precursors to the *tsotsis*. By the early 1940s the Blue Nines and *malalapipes* had become a common feature of township life, particularly in Sophiatown and Alexandra. The Blue Nines and *malalapipes* were amorphous strata of ragged, homeless children and young adolescents who engaged in begging and petty theft. The *malalapipes* got their name from the discarded junkyard pipes in which they slept and sought shelter.[7]

In 1940, on the request of Graham Ballenden, the manager of the NAD in Johannesburg, an Orlando Boys' Unit employee, Lucas Nkosi, was asked to gather information and write a report on local youth gangs. According to Nkosi, a number of juvenile gangs had sprung up in Orlando in the late 1930s, the best known of which were the Nsibanyoni Gang, the Board Gang, and the Station Gang. Each gang tended to have between fifteen and twenty members aged between thirteen and twenty-one. The gang members were generally unemployed and engaged in informal employment or petty theft; they smoked dagga and gambled on the streetcorners; they were influenced by American movies and those who could afford it attempted to imitate American clothing fashions. Nkosi added that similar gangs operated in Alexandra, Pimville, and Sophiatown but the Orlando gangs were generally "better behaved" than those of the other townships.[8] In January 1942 the Orlando Residents' Association requested a meeting with Ballenden to discuss the deteriorating juvenile delinquency problem in Orlando.[9] The meeting took place and in September 1942 Ballenden commented: "It would appear that delinquency amongst children . . . is on the increase. Cases have recently been reported where children have operated in 'crime gangs.'"[10] Similar problems were being experienced in West Native Township. One resident wrote to Ballenden complaining that "people are simply stunned, they do not know what to do. The location is controlled by wicked boys."[11]

In early 1942, administrative attention was drawn to the activities of the Tuta Rangers, a massive criminal juvenile gang operating in Alexandra.[12] According to the Norwood and Wynberg police, the gang was tightly organized, making it extremely difficult to pin any incriminating evidence on the members. The Tuta Rangers apparently operated on a smaller scale in

Sophiatown. The Superintendent of West Native Township commented that "a common threat in Sophiatown is 'I will call the Tuta Rangers from Alexandra to fix you up.'"[13] The Alexandra gang consisted of between 150 and 180 members ranging from fifteen to thirty years of age. The gang was known to have robbed "respectable Natives and unprotected women" and to have broken up dances and concerts. Several shooting incidents in Alexandra were believed to have been associated with the gang. With the money they raised from criminal activities, the Tuta Rangers hired expensive lawyers to defend members under prosecution. According to Lieutenant-Colonel Horak, Deputy Commissioner of Police for the Witwatersrand Division, it had been established "that members of these gangs are children of respectable stand-owners in Alexandra township, and their parents have no control whatso-ever over them."[14]

In Johannesburg, a more generic term for young township "city slickers" was "clevers." Rather than referring to a specific youth gang, "clevers" rep-resented a stratum of urban African youth: unemployed, stylish, influenced by American movie images.[15] The term "clevers" survived into the *tsotsi* era and, in some contexts, could be used synonymously with *tsotsis* but gener-ally without the criminal and gang connotations.

Tsotsitaal was an important element of *tsotsi* subcultural identity during the late 1940s and 1950s. Like the *tsotsi* gangs themselves, *tsotsitaal* had its precursors. The first distinctive language used by township youth gangs, particularly the *funanis* of Pretoria, was known as *shalambombo*. It was a language intelligible exclusively to the "in-group" based on Zulu and Xhosa. *Shalambombo* was self-consciously a "secret language" that delineated a group identity. The word *shalambombo* comes from two Zulu words: *shala* meaning "shunning" and *mbo-mbo* meaning "covering over" or "turning upside-down."[16] Around 1935, *flaaitaal*, a "secret" language with an Afri-kaans basilect, took over as the most popular language among the urban youth gangs, first, it seems, in Pretoria and then on the Rand. *Shalambombo* gradually faded out.[17] *Flaaitaal* evolved into *tsotsitaal* during the 1940s. *Tsotsitaal* had a greatly expanded vocabulary and was also more widely spoken; it became an almost universal language among the African urban youth.[18]

The term *tsotsi* entered township vocabulary around 1943–1944. The word referred to a style of narrow-bottomed trousers that became popular among urban African youth in the early 1940s.[19] In American gangland slang, the narrow-bottomed pants were called "zoot-suits." It is possible that the word *tsotsi* comes directly from the word "zoot-suit," with a pronunciation shift. C. V. Bothma provided a more plausible suggestion: that the word came from the South Sotho *ho tsotsa*, which means "to sharpen," referring to the shape of the trousers.[20] There is some evidence to suggest that the fashion became popular after the movie *Stormy Weather* was screened in the town-ships in the early 1940s.[21] The style was reinforced by another influential movie, *Cabin in the Sky*, screened in Johannesburg between 1945 and 1950.[22] To be "in fashion," township boys had to wear *tsotsis*; these became a cru-cial symbol of urban sophistication. "All the youngsters used to wear these pants," recalls Norris Nkosi, who belonged to the notorious Spoilers gang during the late 1940s and early 1950s.[23] The "sharper" the trouser bottoms, the more fashionable the youth was deemed to be.[24] Initially, then, *tsotsi* referred to a style fashionable among township youth. The late Stanley Motjuwadi, who was a "man-about-town" and a regular writer for *Drum* magazine during the 1950s, remembered that the term was associated with a style of dress "which was worn by any self-respecting city slicker. To be 'with-it' you had to dress like that. Dressing like that meant you were an urban kid. As opposed to a well-mannered, well-brought up, God-fearing country kid."[25] All youths who wore those pants were called *tsotsis*. Gradu-ally, however, the meaning shifted. *Tsotsi* became synonymous with *skelm* or "villain" or "trickster."[26] A *tsotsi* became "someone who is rude towards everything"; disrespectful towards elders, laws, and employment. For teen-agers, the mere act of wearing long trousers was deemed to be precocious; parents still expected their teenage sons to wear shorts in the 1940s.[27] Al-though older people tended to view all those who wore *tsotsi* trousers as gangsters, this was not necessarily the case. The trousers were almost man-datory among teenage boys by the late 1940s.[28] The subculture, therefore, acquired a name and a dominant style around 1943–1944. However, much of what later became associated with the concept *tsotsi* had already started to take shape by the mid- to late 1930s.

The first written reference to *tsotsis* can be found in the *Bantu World* Readers' Forum in April 1945. Between April and June 1945 a vigorous debate raged in the Readers' Forum over the nature of what most readers called the "Bo-tsotsi." Whereas some readers argued that the *tsotsis* were a dangerous scourge, others argued that *tsotsis* were essentially harmless youths very concerned with their clothing style. Clearly, by April 1945 the *tsotsis* had made a major impact on township life. The first letter in this series was written by a Mr. J.D.N. of Benoni. This letter is an important historical document: while providing a useful clue to periodizing the emergence of the *tsotsi* subculture, it also offers some rich descriptive passages and helps to establish subcultural parameters:

As a result of the introduction of fashions in dressing, of broad-brimmed hats and narrow trousers—which have been christened "tsotsi"—not ex-cluding the different kinds of bright-coloured shirts, ties and sports jack-ets, of all designs, there has emerged into popularity (I wonder if I should

[handwritten marginal note: emergence of tsotsi sub-culture.]

say Notoriety) a class of young men in Johannesburg who answer to the fancy name of "bo tsotsi."

This class of budding "men of tomorrow" forms the bulk of the cinema goers, "cultured" audiences of shows and concerts and the "Jive Kings" of Johannesburg and the Reef locations. They are common in the streets, where they are sometimes in the company of young damsels whose very fine broad-brimmed and decorated straw hats make them very attractive to the "bo tsotsi"; although I would rather wear such a hat on the beach, they haunt the dance halls, they sleep latest, and most of them are more artful than the "artful Dodger" in Charles Dickens' "Oliver Twist" when it comes to "borrowing" your wallet or playing "hide and seek" with the Police.

You would think there was never such a thing as work when you saw how some of them "burn the candle at both ends" in idling and moving about from pillar to post. Those who work, among them, represent a very small percentage of the "tsotsi" population. They are a defect in the "tsotsi" body.

Talk of drinking and I'll tell you to consult Mr. "tsotsi" who knows more about the manufacture and price control of every kind of location beer (or "Boil," as it is sometimes called) than he knows his own name. Consult him on how you can be happy and he will philosophise to you with the words: "Eat, drink, steal and be happy for tomorrow you go to gaol!"

If you are an anthropologist who is interested in location life, especially where there are so many street fights during weekends, study "bo tsotsi" and you'll get enough information to write a thesis that will excite many universities into honouring you with degrees!

Step into a train and you'll find that our friends form the majority of the passengers; peep into a prison cell and you'll find a regal choice of them, go anywhere, in any place, as long as there's room for mischief there, you'll find your "tsotsi" gentlemen.

"Bo tsotsi!" The Reef is exhausted by the terror that they wrought [*sic*], parents bewail every day the sad fate of the existence of these "guys," they are a thorn in the flesh these poor victims of ruthless delinquency. Yet they seek to be helped out of this dungeon of the giant Mischief.

Only by patient reform and moral training, on the side of parents, can we be rid of this trivial nuisance: but how can it be done? Has it been tried? And to what extent? I pause for a reply.[29]

It is clear from this letter that a distinctive *tsotsi* subculture had emerged by the mid-1940s on the Rand. Many of the elements of subcultural identification observed by the writer—clothing style, street fights, attitudes to work—will be explored in more detail later in this chapter.

SUBCULTURAL BOUNDARIES

Both contemporary observers, such as Mr. J.D.N., and historians have tended to use the term *tsotsi* very loosely. Little effort has been made to get to grips with the definitional ambiguities of the concept. What was the relationship between youth gangs and the wider subculture? Were all *tsotsis* necessarily gang members? What did a "gang" entail? Were *tsotsis* necessarily criminals? In this section I explore some of these ambiguities and attempt, ultimately, to infuse the subcultural definition with some precision.

During the mid- to late 1940s *tsotsi* seemed to have a broad subcultural, fashion-centered connotation. Gradually, though, throughout the 1950s, the criminal and gang connotations strengthened but remained somewhat ambiguous. In the *Bantu World* Readers' Forum *tsotsi* debate, between May and July 1945, several of the readers defended *tsotsis* as being harmless adherents to fashion. Fashion, rather than criminality or gang formation, was seen by these readers as the essence of the *tsotsi* phenomenon. Thus, a Mr. Nzima wrote, "Let them be! a fashion never harmed anyone, and the present fashion is the best for the time."[30] Another contributor, Walter Nhlapo, took a similar position: "Why should these children apologise for their clothes? It is a fallacy that certain clothes signify corruption or degradation of the spirit."[31] Even when the criminal gang connotation had become widespread, the term *tsotsi* continued to embrace young "city-slickers" who were neither in gangs nor involved in criminal activity. A *tsotsi* was a "slick guy" who dressed and behaved in a particular way.[32] For Peggy Bel Air, who grew up in Sophiatown and became a prominent member of the Americans gang, the word represented "a style, a way of life."[33] The stovepipe trousers remained the key identifying symbol.[34]

During the early 1950s, most township residents perceived the subculture to be undifferentiated: zoot trousers implied *tsotsi*, which, in turn, implied membership of a criminal gang.[35] According to Norris Nkosi, *tsotsi* trousers were so pervasive that elderly people described almost any youth wandering around the streets as a *tsotsi*.[36] Stan Motjuwadi made a similar observation: "The ordinary elderly citizens mistook all those youths who wore the style for a bad element."[37] It would be safe to say that the subculture extended to include urban youths who were neither gang members nor criminals. Subcultural identity cut across gang membership and criminality. A young male could be a member of the "in-group" if he wore *tsotsis*, drank alcohol and smoked dagga freely, spoke *tsotsitaal* well, and demonstrated a familiarity with the township environment. Nevertheless, the criminal gangs constituted the *core* of the subculture; they epitomized subcultural style and behavior (Photos 3.1 and 3.2).

Photo 3.1 Sophiatown gangsters in their flashy convertible, early 1950s. (Photographer: Bob Gosani. © Bailey's African History Archives. Reprinted with permission.)

Members of the subculture tended to cluster in groups, but these subcultural clusters took a number of forms, varying in degree of cohesion and size. There was also a great deal of shading in the extent to which these groups participated in violent or criminal activity. Three different gang formations were discernible within the *tsotsi* subculture: "big shot" gangs, "small-time" criminal gangs, and noncriminal street-corner networks. The divisions were rarely clear-cut; these three categories often merged into one another.

The "big shot" gangs were gangs with name and fame in the townships. Individuals were known, and they dressed distinctively. Their criminal activity tended to be slick and well organized. They often ran protection rack-

Big-Shots: older experienced, often ran dens

Photo 3.2   The Spoilers gang of Alexandra posing at a shebeen, late 1950s. (Photographer: Peter Magubane. © Bailey's African History Archives. Reprinted with permission.)

ets and gambling dens. Leadership figures would often be older—in their late twenties or early thirties. These gangs liked to distinguish themselves from the common *tsotsis*. Motjuwadi explained:

> To be a gang member in especially the old townships had a certain exclusivity attached. It was like a closed club with a clear identity. Sure, they broke the law occasionally, but they weren't involved in heavy crime. Apart from gang warfare. If you became a member of a gang it's prestigious. You aren't a nobody. The muggers were despised. . . . The old gangs were looked up to in a way. . . they commanded some respect and they were envied by youngsters.

The famous gangsters enjoyed dressing well and "liked to associate with socially acceptable people" such as musicians and politicians. They had a known, coherent membership. "So-and-so is a member of the Americans, so-and-so is a member of the Berlins." They almost had a register of membership.[38] The Spoilers of Alexandra did not like to be called *tsotsis*, claims ex-Spoiler Norris Nkosi: "The small-time gangs were not of our class."[39]

Where does one draw the line between "big-time" gangs and smaller *tsotsi* gangs? According to Henry Miles, who was a teenager in Alexandra in the latter half of the 1950s, there were only three "real" gangs during the 1950s, the "Big Three": the Americans, Spoilers, and Msomis.[40] Whereas these three were clearly the best-known youth gangs in the Witwatersrand townships, a number of other gangs could realistically be placed in the "big-time" category, including the Black Caps (best known during the 1940s), the Jakes Gang and the Berliners of Sophiatown, the Cooperatives of West Native Township, the XYs of Newclare, the Otto Town Gang of Orlando, the Apaches and Berlins from Orlando East, the Black Swines of White City. All these gangs controlled large areas, had large memberships with known leaders, and ran extensive crime operations. They aspired to high style. The Torch Gang of Orlando was an ambiguous case. It was as familiar and as large as the other big-time gangs but its membership was incoherent and its style (apart from its notorious custom of shining torches in mugging victims' faces) was not distinctive. The gang was more interested in theft than in exclusivity and style.

Motjuwadi claimed that the bigger, slicker gangs had "a kind of a code" not to mug and steal from township residents. "They were township kids themselves. The township residents [were] their parents. They [were] known."[41] Nkosi supports this view. "The Spoilers," he insists, "were decent guys."[42] There is some evidence to suggest that the Americans had social scruples. Their criminal operations, whether robbing railway trucks or pickpocketing, tended to be carried out in the Johannesburg central business district rather than the townships.[43] The Spoilers and Msomis did not need to mug township residents because these gangs ran extensive protection rackets. Although protection rackets can hardly be construed as socially scrupulous, the Spoilers operations did have a professionalism that set them apart from petty muggers. Residents of Alexandra, it seems, would feel safer running into a group of Spoilers in a dark alley rather than some nameless *tsotsi* gang (provided, of course, they had paid their protection fees). Spoilers took pride in their operations; they did not like to be associated with petty criminals. It is impossible to determine whether this attitude of professional pride extended beyond the "Big Three." Clearly, however, the well-known, bigger gangs operated more professionally and less arbitrarily than anonymous *tsotsi* gangs. Their very familiarity with the residents seemed to place some restriction on their activities. One notable area of exception, however, was in their treatment of women. Their sexual violence and arrogance were in line with the wider subculture.[44] Sexual violence aside, serious and overt violence was, for the most part, confined to inter-gang warfare. In dealing with residents, coercion was unstated; the violence was latent. So a well-known gangster would walk into a restaurant and, in a very

courteous manner, order a meal that, it was understood, he would not pay
for. An anonymous *tsotsi* would have to hold the proprietor up with a knife
or gun to get his meal.

Small-time *tsotsi* gangs ranged in membership from as little as three or
four to as much as twenty.[45] In some cases their membership could be as
large as those of some big-time gangs, but the small-time gangs had shifting
memberships without clear organizational structures or hierarchies. The gangs
would often remain nameless; if they had names, the names were only known
very locally. These small, often anonymous, criminal *tsotsi* gangs were extremely common; they preyed off the community shamelessly, mugging and
pickpocketing residents in trains and on the streets. They lacked the polish
and exclusivity of the big-time gangs and they tended to be more overtly
violent toward township residents.[46] Occasionally, individuals from these
gangs would "graduate"; "some would become refined from the money they
made and they would go and join the bigger gangs after that."[47] The *tsotsi*
term for a gang was *rasj* or *rensj*, from the common cowboy word "ranch,"
which referred to a group of cowboys based at a cattle post.[48] The term *rasj*
was used to describe the smaller, less formal groups rather than the big-time
gangs.

The street-corner networks, also referred to as *rasjs*, were essentially
noncriminal, unarmed, and defensive. It was, however, extremely difficult
to draw a distinction between the criminal and noncriminal *rasj*. Many of
the *rasjs* arose to protect themselves against violent, bullying local gangs,
but their own response was often violent and shaded into criminality. Bloke
Modisane, in his autobiography, *Blame Me on History*, recalls how his own
little *rasj* emerged in Sophiatown.

> I did not learn . . . the daredevil hero complex of the American male; I
> wanted to be with the good boys against the bad boys, so we formed a
> street-corner gang: Philip Spampu, Mannass, Ncali, Valance, Dwarf, Niff
> and I; we were the Target Kids, with targets drawn on the sides of the
> shop on Gold and Victoria Road. Target was for girls and we wrote the
> names of the girls we wanted; but we were also a kind of vigilante group
> concerned with keeping our corner safe from the marauding gangs of
> Sophiatown; we were neither thieves nor thugs, and never carried knives
> but we never hesitated to use violence against the *tsotsis*, the bull-catch-
> ers who attacked, robbed and stripped people. We answered the *tsotsis*
> with violence, which was a kind of lingua franca, and, in effect, we too
> were *tsotsis*; legally we should have handed them over to the police, but
> we were black, the *tsotsis* were black and the law was white. We had no
> intention of being produced by whites as witnesses against blacks, this
> would have exposed us to the vengeance of the *tsotsis*, arranged us in the
> line of knives and guns, and to the scorn of other Africans. The *tsotsis*

were violent men; the force of violence was the only voice they respected; it was a comforting morality adequately masking the violence within us, we were little giants with power complexes, filled with acts of cruelty, injustice and oppression. We cleansed ourselves with rationalisations, armed in point with pious indulgences, like a Christian straight out of a confession box.

We grouped round our corner singing pop songs, making instrument sounds with the mouth, whistling wolf calls at the passing parade of girls, daring each other on.[49]

This is an interesting quotation in a number of respects. First, it reflects the spontaneity and essentially defensive nature of the street-corner *rasj*. Second, it reveals an ambiguous identification with *tsotsis*; Modisane and his friends simultaneously set themselves up in opposition to the *tsotsis* and absorbed the logic of the subculture. They hated the violence of the *tsotsis* and yet were violent themselves; they actually did take on "the daredevil hero complex of the American male." Their identification with the *tsotsis* was ultimately stronger than it was with "the law."

rasjs:
some times
were friends
as young
boys who
emerged
into "gang"

There were also street-corner *rasjs* that were less ambiguously nonviolent and noncriminal. According to Henry Miles, there were not many substantial gangs in Orlando: "there were many street-corner *rasjs* that were of no significance; harmless and useless." They would club together, wear the same clothes and call themselves a *rasj*.[50] Many of these networks emerged quite spontaneously out of play groups consisting of boys between six and ten years old. As they got older, minor skirmishes broke out between the emerging *rasjs*. For some street-corner networks, the fights became increasingly violent as the networks defended their respective territories from rivals. The *rasjs* clustered around street-corner shops, which, because of their potential for both odd jobs and petty theft, became a central territorial element.[51] "McCoy" Mdlalose, who grew up in Sophiatown, recalls that there were numerous little street-corner protection networks in his neighborhood during the 1940s and 1950s. His own group did not dress up particularly stylishly and they did not have a name. They would stand about at the Chinese and Indian shops trying to pick up treats. They played dice and "heads and tails" with coins, often for small sums of money. They spoke *tsotsitaal* together. Some of them, like Mdlalose himself, went to school.[52] These street-corner *rasjs* were on the periphery of the wider *tsotsi* subculture. They were not classic *tsotsis* but they spoke *tsotsitaal*, wore *tsotsi* trousers, were involved in petty gambling, and were heavily influenced by American movies.

In Pretoria, C. V. Bothma identified what can perhaps be considered a fourth *tsotsi* gang category: the *hepkets*. The *hepkets* aspired to high *tsotsi* style and yet were clearly nonviolent and noncriminal. In terms of style, they could be mistaken for "big-league" gangsters. But they were generally employed, educated, and law-abiding.[53] They resembled those who in the 1960s and 1970s were known throughout the Rand as "ivies."[54]

The *tsotsi* subculture, then, was far from monolithic; it contained a great deal of variety and stratification within it. Despite the shading, however, there were enough points of commonality and identification for a case to be made that it did in fact represent a fairly coherent subculture. The "big-league" gangs, although often consciously separating themselves from *tsotsis*, were the subcultural role models. The streetcorner gangs, in all their shades of style, violence, and criminality, constituted the bulk of the subculture.

Quantifying the subculture is a treacherous task. There is quite literally no hard data on gang membership or subcultural participation. Nevertheless, it is possible to create a powerful picture, albeit impressionistic, of the prevalence of the subculture, both in the wider sense and in terms of gang membership.

Perhaps the best starting point is the material presented in chapter 2 on the delinquency crisis and unemployment because these phenomena are highly quantifiable. In the eyes of both township residents and administrators there was a very strong connection between the juvenile delinquency phenomenon and *tsotsi* gangs; the problems were seen as largely indistinguishable. I showed that from the war years to the early 1960s probably the majority of urbanized African youths on the Rand were out of school or unemployed. For the unemployed male youths there were few available outlets other than township youth gangs.

Elsewhere I have compiled a list of roughly one hundred township gangs that operated on the Witwatersrand between 1940 and 1960. This list contains only the gangs that can be referenced concretely. The list only touches the surface of gang membership since the overwhelming majority of gangs were nameless or too little known to be mentioned in newspapers, autobiographies, and NEAD reports or to remain imprinted in the memory of interviewees.[55]

One possible way in which to assess the prevalence of *tsotsi* gangs is to observe the reactions of township residents to them. The spate of letters in *Bantu World* in May to July 1945 clearly demonstrates the massive impact that the *tsotsi* subculture had made on the consciousness of township residents. One Brakpan resident summed up the spirit of these letters when he commented: "The talk of the day and the question of the time is 'Bo-tsotsi' and their effect upon human peace and morality."[56] The style, as opposed to the criminality and gang formation associated with it, penetrated well beyond the unemployed youth constituency. One *Bantu World* reader estimated that "about 90 per cent of the students from the reef and Pretoria wear 'bottoms.'"[57] During the late 1940s and 1950s most teenage boys, it seems, wore *tsotsis*, though not all those who wore the trousers could be presumed to be gangsters.[58] *Tsotsitaal*, petty gambling, and the imitation of American style were also common to the majority of young males.[59]

The best documented evidence suggesting the massive impact of *tsotsi* criminal gangs on the Rand can be found in township advisory board minutes between 1955 and 1958. Board members complained constantly about *tsotsi* terror, about youths out of control, and about police neglect. The streets of the townships and the trains were unsafe during the day, let alone at night, because of the *tsotsi* "menace." Residents avoided making official reports to the police because they feared *tsotsi* reprisals. Township residents made regular requests to the authorities to allow civil guards to operate, which, the board members seemed to agree, was the only way to combat marauding *tsotsi* gangs.[60] Alexandra, Sophiatown, and Newclare, being freehold townships and "nobody's baby," were not represented by advisory boards. Thus there is no advisory board information about gangs in these areas. Nevertheless, there is some evidence to suggest that the *tsotsi* gang presence was probably even more powerful in these townships than elsewhere. A *Bantu World* editorial in 1955, for instance, commented: "At Alex Township, *tsotsis* have gone out of hand. Europeans and Africans walk the streets of that township after sunset, at their peril. . . . The people see no remedy other than to appoint civic guards, to clean the *tsotsi*-infested streets of their township."[61] In 1957 Captain Rocco de Villiers, an "expert" on township gangsterism, was interviewed in *The Star*. According to him, the *tsotsi* gang problem was particularly serious in Sophiatown and Newclare. He observed wryly, "I have had more shots fired at me in Newclare in one year than in all the time I was fighting in North Africa—fortunately they are bad shots."[62]

There was a clear perception among ANC politicians that gangsterism was rife among their potential urban youth constituency. In his autobiography, ANC stalwart Moses Dlamini recalls the violent death in 1956 of his seventeen-year-old cousin, Abel, who led a gang called the Terrors in White City. At Abel's funeral, Dlamini's father, who was a member of the Congress Youth League, asked in anguish, "How many of them have died like this . . . butchering one another mercilessly for trifles? How shall our people get their freedom with the majority of our youths turned to gangsters?"[63]

Godfrey Moloi grew up in Orlando and had links with the local Otto Town Gang during the 1950s. He later made his fortune in the alcohol trade. "It was unusual to find a male teenager who wasn't in a gang," he recalls. Those who "escaped" came from a "small fringe of decent families" who tended to be churchgoing and who often sent their children to distant places for their schooling.[64] "One way or another," observed Stan Motjuwadi, "just about every young boy was sucked into the gangs, though most of them were fairly harmless."[65] Henry Miles, commenting on his experiences as a teenager in Alexandra, confirms this: "Most of the teenagers belonged to harmless smaller gangs. . . . Every street corner had a *rasj*. Every street corner had a leader and there were sort of hangers on."[66] Nkosi and Mdlalose attest that there were numerous street-corner networks of youths coming together for mutual support throughout the townships.[67]

Clearly, there was enormous social pressure on male teenagers to join gangs. "Even if you didn't like the gang," observed Motjuwadi, "you were forced to join for your own protection."[68] There was a general understanding that a teenage male who lived in a particular area was a member of the gang that controlled that area. Thus, in Orlando East, "if you lived in Pirate territory you were thought to be a member of the Pirates."[69] Peggy Bel Air's recollections of Sophiatown are similar. "If you grew up in a particular street and there was a gang which operated there, you would automatically become a member because all your friends were part of it. You've got to join them. It was the obvious thing. There were some young guys who kept out of it and we called them sissies. 'Ag man, just leave him alone. He's a sissie.'"[70] Peter Magubane was never a member of the Berlins gang but he lived in the Berlin area. "If you lived in Berlin territory you were effectively a member of the gang whether you liked it or not." Young males who resisted membership were victimized. Very few youths in Berlin territory were not Berlins. According to Magubane, this pattern was common throughout the townships. "If you can't defend yourself, you become a victim."[71]

Judging from the number of cataloged gangs between 1940 and 1960, the scale of the reaction to "tsotsiism" and the extent of social pressure on township adolescents to join gangs, it seems reasonable to assert that, during the late 1940s and 1950s, the majority of African male youths on the Rand belonged to gangs, whether "big-league" or street-corner *rasj*.

THE *TSOTSI* VALUE SYSTEM

As I argued in chapter 1, the *tsotsi* value code simultaneously scorned the middle-class social consensus and helped to create an alternative, insulated, subcultural structure. This is clearly demonstrated in the *tsotsi* attitude toward law, violence, and the work ethic.

Open defiance of the law was "natural" to the *tsotsi* subculture. Crime was more than simply a material issue; it became a central subcultural theme during the 1940s and 1950s. "The resorting to crime is a way of attempting to get one's own back against a hostile society in whose functioning one plays no part," commented William Carr about *tsotsis* in a 1957 memorandum.[72] In 1953 Ellen Hellmann noted with alarm that the increasing lawlessness of urban youth involved "a rejection of moral norms, which amounts

to a repudiation of the rule of law." In the same memorandum she continued: "The growing prevalence of an attitude which condones theft from a
European and describes it by the vernacular 'work' points to the emergence
of a tradition of this nature. Certainly the various types of gangs, usually
referred to as 'tsotsi' gangs, which are becoming conspicuous in the urban
African scene, are developing a tradition of criminality and of idealization
of gangsters."[73]

Tsotsi crime involved a brazen openness that was not necessarily concerned with maximizing criminal efficiency. In one of its many comments
on *tsotsi* crime, *Drum* magazine observed: "The *tsotsi* and his fellow-thugs
are more familiar to the Johannesburger than the policeman, they parade
themselves openly and arrogantly on the streets, dress in their conspicuous
'uniform' and with little fear of the law."[74]

Throughout the 1950s, *tsotsi* gangs were responsible for numerous *public*
sexual assaults and brazen armed robberies in township residents' houses.[75]

In some ways, *tsotis*' defiance of the law was an area of cultural commonality with their parents' culture, particularly in the defiance of beer-
brewing and pass laws. When their parents defied the law, the *tsotsis* would
happily cooperate. *Tsotsis* often assisted in the illegal domestic beer-brewing industry, particularly as lookouts. Numerous *tsotsis* were passless and
constantly evading the law. "'Getting by' without a pass is an indication of
skill," observed Ellen Hellmann. "Going to gaol for beer-brewing is bad
luck. Hence going to gaol altogether tends to lose its moral stigma."[76] There
also tended to be very little moral censure for *tsotsis* who robbed from whites
(but only criminal subcultures and gangs were prepared to put such activity
into practice). Parents also tended not to question their *tsotsi* sons on the
source of goods and income they brought into the household.[77] The attitude
of the *tsotsi* subculture to the law, however, differed from that of its parent
culture in two distinct ways. First, of course, most victims of *tsotsi* criminal
activity were ordinary African township residents. In other words, *tsotsis*
defied the law where, technically, it gave protection to the average township
resident. Consequently, *tsotsis* were generally hated and feared. Second,
tsotsis displayed an arrogant, open defiance of the law that went well beyond anything in the parent culture. In some areas, breaking the law was
"common sense" to the parent culture, but lawbreakers generally weighed
up the risks carefully and drew no attention to themselves.

Crime and gangsterism were glorified by *tsotsis*. Their styles of dress,
speech, and behavior were heavily influenced by gangster images in movies, books, and comics. This will be dealt with in more detail later. What is
significant to note at this point is their admiration for, and idolization of,
gangsterism. Anthony Sampson, for instance, describes an outing during the
early 1950s to a "non-European" cinema showing the popular *Street with*

No Name. The *tsotsis*, who represented the major part of the audience, jeered at the FBI and cheered for the arch villain, Stiles. "The scene shifted to the gangsters' hideout. A hush from the audience. Richard Widmark appeared in one corner. A shriek from the house. 'Stiles! Attaboy! Go it, Stiles!'" In one scene, a short gangster killed a night watchman with a knife, and a *tsotsi* in the audience shouted "Kort Boy!" (Kort Boy was a Roof gangster, famous for his skills with a knife, who ended up serving eighteen years in jail for murder.) Finally, "Stiles was shot dead by the FBI. The audience groaned, as the FBI took over."[78] As early as 1940, Lucas Nkosi, a member of the Orlando Boys' Unit, pointed to the idolization of screen gangsters by young local gang members. He also noted that they idolized real gangsters such as the notorious William Goosen who had escaped from prison. The *tsotsis* followed Goosen's progress eagerly in the newspapers and pretended to be him in their games.[79] Younger boys hero-worshiped the older and more experienced *tsotsis* as well as the adult criminals with whom they came into contact.[80]

Tsotsis regarded a jail sentence as a status symbol. Not only was it proof of substantial criminal activity, but it also meant coming into contact with other high-status criminals. P. Q. Vundla, a prominent advisory board member, explained this to members of the South African Police Force in 1955. "Many of these boys don't fear to go to gaol, if they have been to gaol, they are deemed to be heroes."[81] Boston Snyman, a veteran gangster who eventually became a member of the Msomis in the late 1950s recalls, in his earlier days, being impressed by the words of a big-time gangster: "A thug gets his confirmation behind bars, you must go to jail for a genuine offence or a frame up. When you come out from the can you can pronounce yourself a gangster."[82] Major gangs, most notably the Americans, Spoilers, and Msomis, had "branches" in local jails. Because *tsotsi* gangs were so territorially based, little actual recruitment took place in the prisons, but anyone with neighborhood links was more or less forced to join the prison gang for protection. Jail gang competition could be ferocious.[83]

The *tsotsis* had no respect for private property. They considered themselves entitled to anything they could lay their hands on. Can Themba's description of *tsotsis* on the trains captures this sense of entitlement:

> There is little method in the operations of these criminals. Many pickpockets just put their hands into your pocket and take what they want. More likely than not you will not feel anything as you struggle for breath in the crowd. If you do, what matter? They out-brave you and threaten you with violence. The younger pickpockets go down on their knees, cut a hole into your trousers with a razor blade, and then let slide into their hands whatever comes forth.

But the true terror for train users comes from the rough-house thugs who hold people up at the point of a knife or gun, or simply rob and beat up passengers. The fear among passengers is so deep that some people don't even want to admit that they have been robbed. And pay days— Fridays, month-ends, from half-past four in the afternoon—are the devil's birthdays.[84]

There is some evidence that one or two of the better organized gangs, particularly in Sophiatown, were fairly scrupulous in selecting their victims. They tended, it would seem, to concentrate on white and state targets rather than on residents in their own community.[85] Even for the more scrupulous gangs, however, this became increasingly difficult as security was systematically stepped up in the white areas throughout the 1950s.[86]

Tsotsi gangs were fiercely territorial. Gangs fought each other frequently to retain control of streets or neighborhoods.[87] African urban youths, who were denied conventional legal ownership, carved out their exclusive territories. This was a central concern for *tsotsi* gangs, from the big-time Americans who sought to be "Kings of Sophiatown" down to the insignificant street-corner gangs who fought for "ownership" of their streets as though their lives depended on it. Ownership was important to them, but it was an ownership based on physical strength and cunning rather than on legal codes. These were rarely fights to establish local criminal monopolies. On the contrary, gangsters generally robbed people from outside of their own territories. Rather, territorial competition was driven by the need for prestige and dignity.

Violence was very much a way of life for the *tsotsis*. Most of the smaller, poorer street-corner gangs would confine themselves to inter-gang fistfights or knife fights and the occasional mugging.[88]

But violence could become much more serious than this, particularly among the bigger, better-equipped gangs. Murders, assaults, and rapes carried out by youths were daily occurrences. The Johannesburg Juvenile Court reported a substantial escalation in youth violence during the late 1940s and 1950s.[89]

During the 1950s the bigger gangs were extremely well armed. The Americans, Berlins, and Vultures of Sophiatown were involved in regular gun battles.[90] The Torch Gang, which operated generally in Orlando, roved around "armed with revolvers, crowbars, knives and clubs."[91] The Spoilers of Alexandra, according to the *Golden City Post*, owned an entire warehouse in which they kept their ammunition.[92] In the early 1950s, revolvers could be bought on the black market for £5 and quality knives for 3s. 6d.[93]

Gang warfare was probably the most common form of violent activity for the *tsotsis*. Wars regularly broke out over territorial competition, sexual rivalry, personal insults, and gambling debts. In order to assert their authority or take revenge, bigger gangs would often carry out horrific ritual violence. In one case an eighteen-year-old Orlando youth was kidnapped by a band of about thirty youths and hacked to death at his home in front of his grandmother.[94] The most startling example of all occurred in the Johannesburg Fort in 1958. After a history of bitter, brutal rivalry for the control of Alexandra, dozens of members of the Spoilers and Msomis were arrested in a huge police swoop. The Spoilers had been all but destroyed by the Msomis prior to the crackdown and were eager for revenge. Four awaiting-trial Msomis were placed in a cell full of Spoilers. The four were subjected to a ritualized trial and then kicked to death. The next morning their mutilated and dismembered corpses were found scattered over the floor of the cell.[95]

Violent achievements and physical strength were symbols of status within the *tsotsi* subculture. Male children in the townships grew up with tremendous respect for the knifemen. Special prestige was accorded to killers. A *tsotsi* interviewed in *Drum* talks about his attitudes as a ten-year-old during the late 1940s. "Our heroes were the boys who could steal and stab. The more stabbings they did, the bigger they were. The 'biggest shot' of all was the one who had killed somebody—either with a knife or a gun."[96] Moses Dlamini, in his autobiography, recalls how his sixteen-year-old cousin, Abel, became a hero of "the underworld" after he had personally killed eleven people in gang warfare in Jabavu in 1955.[97] Gang leaders were chosen for their physical prowess and strength, and gangs often only admitted a member if he could point to some impressive personal act of strength or violence.[98]

THE NON-WORK ETHIC

A Kliptown *tsotsi* commented in 1951: "I am a *tsotsi*, it is true. I don't care to work. Working at a regular job does not pay. I can make more money by stealing—at least most of my friends do. That is why they won't work."[99] *Tsotsis* rejected the idea of steady employment. In fact they were regularly referred to as "won't-works" by exasperated government personnel concerned about high youth unemployment.

Both the Viljoen Commission of 1951 and the M. C. Botha Commission of 1962 argued that the *tsotsi* culture actually *exacerbated* urban youth unemployment. In analyzing the youth unemployment problem of the early 1960s M. C. Botha distinguished between the *bona fide* unemployed and the *ledige* ("idle" or "lazy") youths who deliberately avoided finding employment. Not only did the gangs encourage a negative attitude towards work, the Botha Commission argued, but they actually provided an alternative support network and attracted youths away from "normal" employment. Youth unemployment and *tsotsi* culture were seen as mutually reinforcing one another.[100]

Tsotsis saw regular wage labor as undignified, unprofitable, and a denial of freedom. As one *tsotsi* explained to Ray Phillips: "Why should I accept a job from the Native Youth Board at 25–30 shillings a week when I made 100 Pounds last month by gambling?"[101] In sheer material terms, crime offered *tsotsis* a higher standard of living and a more exciting lifestyle than wage employment. As *Drum* observed: "A *tsotsi* may earn as much as 5 Pounds a day; how else could he earn such big money? With that he can look after his girlfriends, keep his parents and gamble away the rest." When asked why he became a *tsotsi*, Jeremiah Majola of Alexandra explained, "I wanted to have a lot of money to have a good time and give my girls a good time. Sometimes I made 50 Pounds in one day with the gun."[102]

Education was seen in a similar light to steady employment. Only a trickle of African children stayed in school beyond primary school. As I pointed out in chapter 2, throughout the 1950s an annual average of only about 7,000 African children attended high school on the Witwatersrand. There was also an extremely high truancy rate among those who did register at township schools. Education was seen as boring and restrictive. It also very rarely improved the chances of employment. Although the majority of *tsotsis* were semiliterate through subgrade school attendance or extensive comic book reading, educational achievement held no status at all within the *tsotsi* subculture.[103] In fact, speaking English could often hamper social acceptance as it was seen as a sign of showing off education. *Tsotsis* felt that "teachers have the knowledge, but they [the *tsotsis*] have the sense."[104] They emphasized being streetwise rather than educated; a youth became a "clever" through knowledge and experience of the street rather than through schooling. *Tsotsis* were scornful of those who took schooling seriously and relished waylaying and harassing schoolgoers.[105]

Linked to their rejection of employment and education was a pervasive hedonism. The archetypical *tsotsi* did not believe in living for the future; he searched for immediate excitement and danger, immediate gratification. He rejected all "responsible" and "respectable" notions of saving for and investing in the future. He aspired to extravagant lifestyles: if he got hold of money, he would spend it—on gambling, alcohol, clothing, and girlfriends. Spending his days working at jobs or at school seemed senseless when there was an exciting, dangerous life out in the streets.

Being unemployed and out of school was an important symbol of subcultural identification. It was possible to hold down a job or go to school and, after hours, adhere to *tsotsi* style, but it was unusual to find an employed or schoolgoing youth who was also a fully-fledged gang member.[106] Apart from the physical absence from gang activity during the day that unemployment or schoolgoing entailed, it was difficult to hold down a steady job and retain respect within a *tsotsi* gang.

STYLE AND RITUAL

Movies, comics, magazines, and cheap novels were the key sources for the *tsotsi* aesthetic. For permanently urbanized African youths there was an almost complete absence of alternative imagery. Rural and "traditional" imagery had very little impact on them. Most had lived in the cities all their lives and had lost contact with a rural lifestyle. Those elements of rural style and ritual that did seep through to them via their parents or grandparents were generally rejected in their struggle to assert an urban identity. Traditionalism was seen as naive, old-fashioned, and inappropriate to modern urban street life. This set the *tsotsis* starkly apart from groups such as the migrant *amalaitas*, who drew heavily on traditional images and participated in rituals such as circumcision. Because of racial discrimination and economic deprivation, township youths were denied access to fashionable white middle-class style and culture. As Anthony Sampson puts it: "Gangster films, street-corner gambling, drinking to get drunk, were open to all. Theatres, decent houses, libraries, travel abroad, were for Europeans only."[107] And so they had to draw on images which were familiar, affordable, accessible, appropriately urban, and exciting. It is not surprising, then, that movies, in the absence of alternatives, became such a powerful aesthetic influence on township youths during the 1940s and 1950s.

By the late 1930s, movies were easily accessible to township youths. The Institute of Race Relations began, even at this stage, to be concerned about the influence of movies on youths, singling out popular shows of the time such as *Murder in Trinidad*, *Road House*, and *Charlie Chan in Paris*.[108] In 1940 Lucas Nkosi of the Orlando Boys' Unit, in a survey of Orlando youth gangs, expressed similar concerns. Gang members, he observed, would go to movies whenever they had money. Afterwards they would act out the stories for other members who were unable to afford the entrance fees.[109] Municipal authorities also recognized the problem but, until the mid-1950s, argued that, as long as movies with specifically immoral messages were banned, the popularity of movies amongst township youths need not be discouraged. They preferred to have the youths in cinemas than out on the streets. In 1954 an irate doctor wrote a letter to *The Star* complaining, "We are helping to feed the fires of crime by our indifference to what is a canker in our society—the showing of crime films to the less educated class of our population." But W.J.P. Carr, the manager of Johannesburg's Non-European Affairs Department, replying to the letter writer, was not worried. The upholders of law and morality always came out on top in these movies, he felt, and the good, law-abiding people were always the heroes. He expressed confidence that the movies shown in the townships could have only a good influence.[110] Carr's department even employed mobile film units in the West Rand townships, both to help keep youths off the streets and to encourage the right kind of morally sound movies. By 1954 there were nine cinemas dotted around the townships as well as four Non-European cinemas in Johannesburg and two in Fordsburg. In addition to these, three mobile NEAD film units were in operation, attracting about 30,000 African viewers every week.[111] What Carr and his department failed to understand, of course, was that African youths tended to identify with the villains. Even though they invariably lost out by the end of the movie, it was the bad guys who provided the source of imagery and style. Anthony Sampson's account of watching *Street with No Name* in Sophiatown is again revealing. "Stiles wore a long overcoat, sniffed a Benzedrine inhaler and occasionally bit an apple. Beside him slouched his henchman, wearing a belted raincoat with slits at the back. 'When this film first came out,' Can [Themba, who accompanied Sampson,] whispered, 'the sales of Benzedrine rocketed. Everybody munched apples. All the *tsotsis* wore those raincoats.'"[112]

Movies were always influential in informing style in the dominant South African culture as well, but, by modeling themselves on the thugs and gangsters rather than on the good guys and the cops, *tsotsis* inverted conventional symbolism and morality.

Aside from movies, magazines, comics, and cheap books provided a rich source of imagery for the largely semiliterate *tsotsis*. *Zonk* and *Drum*, magazines that targeted a young township audience, ran regular, well-illustrated features on American fashion and on local music, sport, and gang activity. The magazines were widely available and widely read by young people in the townships.[113] *Drum* itself had an ambivalent admiration for gangsters and gang style. While the editors tried to convey a young, hip image, they were steeped in middle-class morality. The moral noises, however, were largely lost in the magazine's celebration of urban fashion. This was essential for it to retain its niche market.[114] For younger *tsotsis*, Marvel Comics were particularly popular; the young *tsotsis* used to compete over their comic collections. Once they became a little older, more literate *tsotsis* graduated to American paperback thrillers in the James Hadley Chase mold.[115]

Tsotsi dressing style was distinctive and it was a central element of subcultural identification. *Tsotsis* were extremely self-conscious about their clothes. In 1945 a *Bantu World* reader referred to *tsotsis* sarcastically as "a group of well dressed gentlemen";[116] another reader called them "gentlemen of leisure."[117] Jazz musician Hugh Masekela, recalling his days as a stylish township youth in the 1950s, commented in a *Drum* interview: "In those days, a man was known and recognised by the label that was attached to his clothes. We used to spend hours cleaning our shoes, and then go to the cinema very early, just to show off."[118] Before attempting to describe *tsotsi* clothing style, two important observations need to be made. First, style was not static. Within the broader parameters of *tsotsi* style, details shifted: certain elements of style went through waves of fashionability, usually brought about by a particularly popular movie. For example, *tsotsis* liked to chew on something to round off their stylistic effect, but whether it was apples or toothpicks or chewing gum was influenced by the particular fad of the day.[119] Second, although *tsotsis aspired* to high style, most were unable to afford it. For the average *tsotsi*, a stylish item of clothing, whether it was a pair of trousers, a hat, a jacket, or a smart pair of imported shoes, was a treasured possession that was worn frequently. *Tsotsis* often managed to pull off an acceptably stylish image with very little; only the big, successful gangsters could afford polish and variety.

The key to subcultural style lay in imitating American fashion. "Anything American was something to imitate," in the words of Motjuwadi.[120] The Americans gang of Sophiatown perfected American style, and they consequently became a role model for other *tsotsis*. The most important source of American fashion was, of course, Hollywood. *Tsotsis* were heavily influenced by cowboy, gangster, and black American jazz movies.[121]

The central element of clothing style was the *tsotsi* trousers. The bottoms were extremely narrow, resting either at the ankles or around the shoes. One variation was called "the bottom"; it had a normal width most of the way down and then tapered sharply to a very narrow bottom.[122] *Tsotsis* "used to clip the bottoms to make the bottoms narrow."[123] According to ex-*tsotsi* Henry Miles, "some people wore their pants so narrow you had to use vaseline on your legs to pull [the pants] down."[124] Stan Motjuwadi recalled, however, that the bottoms gradually widened during the late 1950s in accordance with American fashions; "they became less and less zooty" by the end of the decade.[125] If a township male adolescent wanted to identify with the *tsotsi* subculture he would be under great pressure at least to get hold of a pair of *tsotsi* trousers. Norris Nkosi tells the story of how, as a young teenager in 1949, he pleaded with his mother to buy him a pair of *tsotsis*. She refused, arguing that he was too young to wear long pants, let alone identify himself with *tsotsi* youths. In desperation, he used to steal his brother's pair to wear after school. Equipped with his *tsotsis*, he would join his friends selling things and picking pockets on the trains.[126] Whereas the trousers were the item that established identity, there was a cluster of style variations that could be added to the trousers. The most common of these modeled itself on the American gang henchman. According to *Drum*, the average *tsotsi* wore "tight-fitting zoot trousers, wide-brimmed hats, loud shirts and ties."[127] In another description of a *tsotsi*, "Spike was wearing the *tsotsi* rig, with very narrow 'sixteen-bottom' trousers, a long floppy coat, a bright scarf tucked into it and a slouch hat."[128] Another variation was the cowboy look: black zoot trousers, black shirt, and cowboy hat.[129]

Probably the next most important item on the agenda was the hat. In hatware the style was less precise, but generally a broad-brimmed hat such as a Stetson or a peaked cap was preferred. *Tsotsis* liked to wear hats low over their eyes. Shoe styles were also diverse. The more stylish gangsters bought expensive imported shoes, usually with pointed toes. For the small-fry *tsotsis*, simple *takkies* (cheap sports shoes) were popular, worn with turned-up tongues.[130]

Style was also reflected in the choice of personal and gang names. Nicknames were powerfully influenced by the movies so that names such as "Stiles" and "Zorro" were popular. If a boy's real name was Humphrey, he would almost inevitably be called "Bogart," James would be called "Jesse James," and John would be called "Dillinger."[131] Gang names often suggested an identification with society's "natural" enemies in order to be as offensive as possible to the white middle-class establishment. Names such as "Gestapo," "Berlins," and "Germans" went beyond the pale in identifying with the Nazis; the "Mau Mau" gang rose up at the height of white hysteria about the violent Kenyan rebellion; the "Apaches" made it clear whom they backed in the tussle between cowboys and Indians; the "Satan Boys" and "Gas Devils" aligned themselves against God. The "Benzine Boys," famed for setting fire to their victims after dousing them in benzine, and the "Slagpaal" ("abattoir") gang used names with provocative connotations of brutal violence. The "Dead End Kids" boasted of their delinquency and lack of social mobility.

Smoking dagga, drinking alcohol in quantity, and gambling, although by no means unique to the *tsotsis*, were further important antisocial rituals that helped to define the subculture. They were rituals that flew in the face of clean-living, cautious, adult middle-class respectability. Youths who could not demonstrate a familiarity with these rituals were considered "square."[132]

Perhaps the most distinctive feature of the *tsotsi* subculture was its own language, *tsotsitaal*. The language was an urban hybrid based largely on Afrikaans but with large Xhosa/Zulu and English inputs. The meanings of many of the words were shifted from those of the original language and the syntax was inconsistent, generally oscillating between that of Afrikaans and that of Xhosa/Zulu.[133] The extensive use of Afrikaans in *tsotsitaal* was probably linked to the residential proximity of coloreds and Africans in crucial style-generating townships such as Sophiatown and Marabastad (in Pretoria). As I show later, Zulu gradually superseded Afrikaans as the street language basilect on the Rand after the destruction of the Western Areas townships.

Although Afrikaans was a language symbolically associated with repression, it was also a useful cultural resource that helped to bridge language divisions in a linguistically diverse urban milieu. *Tsotsitaal* was more than simply a medium for communication; it was an important element of cultural style. It was the lingua franca of township youths. The language reinforced *tsotsi* identity. South African linguist C. T. Msimang comments: "There is no doubt . . . that *tsotsitaal* is used as a register. It is abandoned where the *tsotsi* wants to maintain the distance between himself and members of the out-group; and he will use it to maintain identity and solidarity with members of the in-group. Distance is maintained in order to snub members of the out-group as well as to endorse his attitude towards them."[134]

Different levels of proficiency in the language indicated different levels of urban and subcultural familiarity. A well-established *tsotsi* had to be able to do more than "get by" in *tsotsitaal*. Subcultural status was attached to speaking the language with flair and dexterity, to familiarity with the latest linguistic nuances and innovations.[135] *Tsotsis* from Sophiatown and Alexandra apparently looked down upon *tsotsis* from Orlando because the latter spoke a *tsotsitaal* that was considered old-fashioned. The Orlando *tsotsitaal* had a far greater Zulu content. Nevertheless, the Sophiatown and Orlando versions of the language were mutually intelligible, if only with difficulty. So *tsotsis* would use *tsotsitaal* to compete with each other for subcultural status but, at the same time, the language delineated the boundary between the in-group and the out-group.

The *tsotsi* subculture, through its value system, style, and ritual, aggressively rejected any kind of cultural consensus in society. *Tsotsi* values, such as brazen rejection of the law and glorification of violence, criminality, and hedonism, were defined in direct antagonism to values broadly accepted by the society around them. *Tsotsi* style and ritual often drew on imagery familiar to middle-class and urban adult working-class culture but inflected and subverted the symbolic structure of those images. At the same time, the subculture provided an alternative, insulated system in which young ghettoized males had a real chance of acquiring prestige and fame.

NOTES

1. C. V. Bothma, " 'n Volkekundige Ondersoek na die Aard en Ontstaans oorsake van Tsotsi-groepe en hulle Aktiwiteite soos Gevind in die Stedelike Gebied van Pretoria," M.A. thesis, departement van Bantoetale en Volkekunde, University of Pretoria, July 1951, p. 38.

2. Bothma, "'n Volkekundige Ondersoek," p. 30. Interestingly, this confusion is apparent in a memorandum on *amalaita* gangs by S. S. Tema in 1935. He fails to distinguish between the embryonic *tsotsi* gangs and the *amalaitas*; Joint Council Collection, Historical Papers Library, University of the Witwatersrand, Johannesburg, A1433, "The

Amalaita menace," by S. S. Tema, 18 July 1935. The Ninevites, who operated on the Witwatersrand between 1890 and 1920, also represented a very different tradition of gangsterism. They were a specific band of brigands, tightly controlled by one powerful leader, rather than a generic phenomenon. The Ninevites were not exclusively youths, they had strong rural connections, and, rather than being rooted in urban neighborhoods, they roved on the fringes of the urban complex. See Charles Van Onselen's *Studies in the Social and Economic History of the Witwatersrand 1886–1914*, Johannesburg, 1982, vol. 2, *New Ninevah.*

3. For a more detailed account of the *amalaitas*, see P. La Hausse, "'Mayihlome!': Towards an Understanding of Amalaita Gangs in Durban, c 1900–1930," in S. Clingman (ed.), *Regions and Repertoires: Topics in South African Politics and Culture*, Johannesburg, 1991. See also Bothma, "'n Volkekundige Ondersoek," pp. 27–30. On the issue of *amalaita* rural consciousness and circumcision, see Peter Delius, "Sebatakgomo: Migrant Organisation, the ANC and the Sekhukhuneland Revolt," *Journal of Southern African Studies*, 15, 4, 1989, pp. 389–392.

4. For the most up-to-date analysis of the *indlavini*, see William Beinart, "The Origins of the Indlavini: Male Associations and Migrant Labour in the Transkei," *African Studies*, 50, 1991.

5. Absolom Vilakazi, *Zulu Transformations,* Pietermaritzburg, 1962, pp. 76–78.

6. Bothma, "'n Volkekundige Ondersoek," p. 30; see also *Bantu World* (*BW*), 2 June 1945, Readers' Forum, letter from W. N. Nzima of Lady Selbourne.

7. Interview, Mattera (b); see also *BW*, 2 June 1945, letter from W. N. Nzima.

8. West Rand Administration Board Archive, Intermediary Archive Depot, Johannesburg (IAD WRAB) 351/3, "A Preliminary Survey of Juvenile Gangs in Orlando," L. J. Nkosi of Orlando Boys' Unit, February 1940.

9. IAD WRAB 351/2, letter from Orlando Residents' Association to the Manager NAD Johannesburg, 27 January 194[2].

10. IAD WRAB 351/2, letter from the Manager NAD Johannesburg to Senior Superintendent, Orlando, 24 September 1942.

11. IAD WRAB 351/2, letter from G. S. Mabeta (Western Native Township resident) to the Manager NAD Johannesburg, 29 December 1943.

12. IAD WRAB 351/3, letter from Magistrate W. L. Marsh to Social Research Officer NAD, 14 March 1942 (see also enclosed letter from L. T. de Jager, Probation Officer); IAD WRAB 351/3, letter from Native Commissioner to the Manager NAD Johannesburg, 11 February 1942.

13. IAD WRAB 351/3, letter from Superintendent, West Native Township, to the Manager NAD Johannesburg, 7 March 1942.

14. IAD WRAB 351/3, letter from Lieutenant-Colonel Horak, Deputy Commissioner of Police commanding Witwatersrand Division, to the Manager NEAD and NAD Johannesburg, 12 March 1942.

15. *BW*, 2 June 1945, letter from W. N. Nzima.

16. C. T. Msimang, "Impact of Zulu on Tsotsitaal," *South African Journal of African Languages*, 7, 3, July 1987, p. 82; Bothma, "'n Volkekundige Ondersoek," p. 49.

17. Bothma, "'n Volkekundige Ondersoek," p. 50.

18. See Msimang, "Impact of Zulu," p. 86.

19. Interviews: Norris Nkosi, Nhlapho, Peggy Bel Air, Miles (a) and (b), Motjuwadi, Mdlalose.

20. Bothma, "'n Volkekundige Ondersoek," p. 29.

21. Interview, Peter Magubane.

22. Interviews: Nkosi, Motjuwadi; see also Bothma, "'n Volkekundige Ondersoek," p. 39.

23. Interview, Nkosi.

24. Interview, Miles (a).

25. Interview, Motjuwadi.

26. Interview, Miles (a).

27. Interview, Nkosi.

28. Interviews: Mdlalose, Motjuwadi.

29. *BW*, 7 April 1945, letter from J.D.N. of Benoni.

30. *BW*, 2 June 1945.

31. *BW*, 7 July 1945; see also *BW*, 28 April 1945, letter from Mr. Pooe of Sophiatown.

32. Interviews, Miles (a) and (b).

33. Interview, Peggy Bel Air.

34. Interviews: Mdlalose, Nhlapho, Magubane.

35. Interviews: Nkosi, Magubane, Motjuwadi.

36. Interview, Nkosi.

37. Interview, Motjuwadi.

38. Interview, Motjuwadi.

39. Interview, Nkosi.

40. Interviews, Miles (a) and (b).

41. Interview, Motjuwadi. Although most *tsotsi* crime took place in the townships or on daily commuter transport, most gangs, as I argue in chapter 1, avoided carrying out their criminal activities in neighborhoods where they were known.

42. Interview, Nkosi.

43. Interviews: Peggy Bel Air, Motjuwadi, Mattera (b), Magubane.

44. See Clive Glaser, "The Mark of Zorro: Sexuality and Gender Relations in the Tsotsi Youth Gang Culture on the Witwatersrand," *African Studies*, 51, 1, 1992, for a more thorough exploration of sexual violence in the subculture.

45. Interview, Miles (a).

46. Interviews: Nhlapho, Motjuwadi, Nkosi, Mattera (b), Miles (a), Kuzwayo.

47. Interview, Mattera (b).

48. Bothma, "'n Volkekundige Ondersoek," p. 39. Henry Miles uses the term frequently.

49. Bloke Modisane, *Blame Me on History*, London, 1963, pp. 67–68. Modisane spent his teenage years in Sophiatown in the 1940s. He became a writer for *Drum* during the 1950s before going into exile in the early 1960s.

50. Interview, Miles (a).

51. Interview, Motjuwadi; IAD WRAB 351/3, "A Preliminary Survey of Gangs in Orlando" by L. J. Nkosi of the Orlando Boys' Unit, February 1940.

52. Interview, Mdlalose.

53. Bothma, "'n Volkekundige Ondersoek", pp. 31–32.

54. See Chapter 5.

55. For the full list, see Clive Glaser, "Anti-Social Bandits: Juvenile Delinquency and the Tsotsi Youth Gand Subculture on the Witwatersrand, 1935–1960," M.A. thesis, University of the Witwatersrand, 1990, pp. 98–102.

56. *BW*, 26 May 1945, letter from T. B. Masekoameng of Brakpan.

57. *BW*, 2 June 1945, letter from W. N. Nzima.

58. Interviews: Manana, Thabethe, Nkosi, Nhlapho, Mdlalose.

59. Interviews: Nkosi, Mdlalose, Motjuwadi, Miles (a), Manana.

60. See especially the following: IAD WRAB 351/1, extract from minutes of Jabavu AB meeting, 8 September 1955; IAD WRAB 351/1, minutes of conference between Deputy Commissioner, SAP, Witwatersrand, Area Officers, members of the Non-European Affairs Committee and members of the AB, Johannesburg, 14 December 1955; IAD WRAB 351/2, extract from minutes of West Native Township AB meetings, 7 August 1956 and 15 August 1956; IAD WRAB 351/3, letter from W.J.P. Carr, Manager, NEAD Johannesburg, to NEAD, 1 October 1957, in which Carr informs NEAD of a meeting scheduled for 4 October 1957 with the Executive of the Joint AB (the only item on the agenda is "Suggested Steps to Deal with Young 'Tsotsies' in the Townships"); IAD WRAB 351/3, extract from minutes of Moroka AB meeting, 21 December 1957; IAD WRAB 351/3, extract from minutes of Moroka AB meeting, 8 February 1958; IAD WRAB 351/3, extract from minutes of Orlando AB meeting, 9 December 1958. The issue of civil guards is dealt with in chapters 8 and 11.

61. *BW*, 29 October 1955, editorial.

62. *The Star*, 21 January 1957.

63. Moses Dlamini, *Robben Island: Hell Hole*, Nottingham, England, 1984, p. 99; the whole career of Abel is interesting as a case study of a *tsotsi* (pp. 88–99). The relationship between gangs and political movements is explored in depth in chapters 4 and 7.

64. Interview, Moloi.

65. Interview, Motjuwadi.

66. Interview, Miles (a) and (b).

67. Interviews: Mdlalose, Nkosi.

68. Interview: Motjuwadi.

69. Interview, Thwala. Gertrude Thwala, as a teenage girl in Orlando during the 1950s, observed the gangs from the outside. Nevertheless, through familial contacts and fear of victimization, gangs were a constant presence in her life.

70. Interview, Peggy Bel Air.

71. Interview, Magubane. See also IAD WRAB 351/1, letter from Abner Sekoane to W.J.P. Carr, Manager NAD Johannesburg, received 18 September 1959.

72. IAD WRAB 351/1, "Some Aspects of Urbanized Native Life in the Cities." 1 November 1957.

73. Ellen Hellman Papers, Historical Papers Library, University of the Witwatersrand, Johannesburg, EHP, File 51, "The Sociological Background to Urban African Juvenile Delinquency," 16 August 1953, p. 1 and p. 8.

74. *Drum*, October 1951.

75. See, for example, *Golden City Post* (*GCP*), 27 March 1955; *GCP*, 30 December 1962; *Drum*, May 1953.

76. EHP, File 51, "Bantu Youth in Our Cities," 26 April 1951, p. 15.

77. Complaints about parental compliance are a prominent theme in minutes of Advisory Board meetings, IAD WRAB, 351/1. This issue also came up in interviews with Moloi and Mattera (a). See also Can Themba's journalistic writing on the subject in *The World of Can Themba*, (Essop Patel, ed.), Johannesburg, 1985, p. 124, and Moses Dlamini, *Robben Island,* 1984, pp. 89–99.

78. Anthony Sampson, *Drum: A Venture into the New Africa* (London, 1956), pp. 101–102.

79. IAD WRAB 351/3, Lucas Nkosi, "The Nsibanyoni Gang," April 1940.

80. Interviews: Moloi, Norris Nkosi, Miles (a) and (b). See also EHP, File 51, C.V. Botha (*sic*), quoted in Hellmann, "The Sociological Background to Urban African Juvenile Delinquency," memorandum, 16 August 1953, and comments by Captain R. De Villiers in *The Star*, 21 January 1957.

81. IAD WRAB, 351/1, Extract from the minutes of a conference between the Witwatersrand Deputy Commissioner of SAP, Area Officers, Members of the Non-European Affairs Committee, and Advisory Board members, 14 December 1955.

82. *GCP*, 13 November 1960.

83. See, for example, *GCP*, 23 August 1959.

84. *The World of Can Themba*, "Terror in the Trains," p. 112.

85. Interviews: Motlana, Mattera (a), Motjuwadi, Magubane.

86. Interview, Mattera (a).

87. Territorial fights were highlighted by virtually all my informants. There are also numerous references to gang fights in *Drum*, *GCP*, and *BW*.

88. Interviews: Moloi, Motjuwadi. See also Modisane, *Blame Me on History*, pp. 67–68.

89. IAD WRAB 351/2, Juvenile Court statistics, 1949–1960 (figures not available for the 1940s).

90. Interviews: Mattera (a), Peggy Bel Air.

91. *Drum*, April 1955. See also *GCP*, 8 May 1955.

92. *GCP*, 26 July 1959

93. *Drum*, November 1951.

94. *GCP*, 7 September 1958.

95. *GCP*, 23 August 1959.

96. *Drum*, November 1951.

97. Dlamini, *Robben Island*, pp. 89–90.

98. Interview, Moloi.

99. *Drum*, November 1951.

100. G. Viljoen, *Report of the Commission of Enquiry into the Penal System of the Republic of South Africa*, Pretoria, 1976, RP 78/1976, 1951, pp. 6–7; M. C. Botha, *Verslag van die Interdepartementele Komitee insake ledige en niewerkende Bantu in die Stedelike Gebiede* (Report of the Interdepartmental Committee into Idle and Unemployed Bantu in the Urban Areas), 1962, introduction and par. 66, 75.

101. IAD WRAB, 285/7, extract from minutes of a meeting between NEAD and Native Youth Board deputation, 28 September 1950.

102. *Drum*, November 1951. For a string of references to the *tsotsi* "non-work ethic" see *BW*, Readers' Forum, April–June 1945.

103. Interview, Moloi.

104. *Drum*, November 1951.

105. See, for example, IAD WRAB, 351/1, extract from meeting of Mofolo Advisory Board, 5 December 1957; IAD WRAB, 351/1, letter from resident of Orlando East II, W. S. Ndlovu, to manager Johannesburg NEAD, 6 July 1959.

106. Godfrey Moloi (Otto Town Gang), Peggy Bel Air (Americans), and Norris Nkosi (Spoilers) all described themselves as unusual *tsotsi* gangsters in that they all attended school while they were active gang members. The fact that they all completed their schooling probably goes some way to explain their relative success and prominence in

later life. Although fully fledged gang members, they tended to be cerebral enough to keep out of more serious danger. As Nkosi wryly commented: "We used to push the illiterate ones in front of us with the guns." They survived their violent gang years and received the benefits of both an education and a wide range of old gang connections. Mdlalose, Magubane, and Nhlapho all had strict parents who kept them at school until matriculation but, although they adhered to many elements of *tsotsi* style, they were never gangsters.

107. Sampson, *Drum*, p. 99.

108. South African Institute of Race Relations Collection, Historical Papers Library, University of the Witwatersrand, Johannesburg (SAIRR) B23, memo on Native Juvenile Delinquency, 1938.

109. IAD WRAB 351/3, L. Nkosi, "A Preliminary Survey of Juvenile Gangs in Orlando," February 1940, and "The Nsibanyoni Gang," April 1940.

110. *The Star*, 15 January 1954. See also Dlamini, *Robben Island*, p. 88.

111. IAD WRAB 301/1, NEAD Cinema Branch, cinema show returns, March 1954.

112. Sampson, *Drum*, p. 102.

113. Interview, Miles (a) and (b). Interestingly, Miles comments that other African township fashion, outside South Africa, was well represented in *Zonk* and *Drum*. See Erwin Manoim, "The Black Press in South Africa 1945–1953," M.A. thesis, University of the Witwatersrand, 1983, pp. 62–94.

114. See M. Fenwick, "'Tough Guy, eh?': The Gangster-Figure in Drum," *Journal of Southern African Studies*, 22, 4, December 1996.

115. Interviews: Miles (a), Moloi. Willard Motley's *Knock on Any Door* was apparently popular with literate *tsotsis*; see Sampson, *Drum*, p. 100; and Dlamini, *Robben Island*, pp. 89–90.

116. *BW*, 16 June 1945, letter from Sgt. Rameetse.

117. *BW*, 12 May 1945, letter from Daniel Ntaopane of Johannesburg.

118. *Drum*, June 1983, interview with Hugh Masekela.

119. Interview, Miles; Sampson, *Drum*, pp. 101–102.

120. Interview, Motjuwadi. This point was made by several interviewees.

121. Motjuwadi, in particular, emphasised the influence of black American movies.

122. Bothma, "'n Volkekundige Ondersoek," p. 46.

123. Interview, Nkosi.

124. Interview, Miles (a).

125. Interview, Motjuwadi.

126. Interview, Nkosi.

127. *Drum*, October 1951.

128. Sampson, *Drum*, p. 98.

129. See the description of Abel in Dlamini, *Robben Island*, pp. 89–90.

130. The description of clothing style is a composite picture drawn from a number of interviews. See also Bothma, "'n Volkekundige Ondersoek," pp. 46–47, for a detailed description of *tsotsi* clothing style in Pretoria around 1950.

131. Interviews: Moloi, Nkosi.

132. In *Drum*, November 1951, a *tsotsi* recalled how, as a fourteen- or fifteen-year-old mugger, "Always we had something to drink or smoked dagga to give us a big heart." See also *BW*, 2 March 1940, in which a connection is drawn between dagga,

alcohol, and juvenile delinquency; *BW*, 17 August 1946, letter from W. B. Mkhasibe; *BW*, 7 April 1945, letter from J.D.N.; *BW*, 28 April 1945, letter from Mr. Pooe of Sophiatown; *BW*, 14 August 1954, p. 1, article on Germiston's Fast Elevens gang; SAIRR B23, memo on Native Juvenile Delinquency, 1938; IAD WRAB 351/3, L. Nkosi, "A Preliminary Survey of Juvenile Gangs in Orlando," February 1940, and the "Nsibanyoni Gang," April 1940; Sampson, *Drum*, p. 99; Bothma, " 'n Volkekundige Ondersoek," pp. 47–49; interview, Miles. Miles points out, interestingly, that the Spoilers of Alexandra made a great deal of their money through illegal liquor and dagga sales. For gambling specifically, see *Drum*, October 1951; *Drum*, November 1952; *GCP*, 31 July 1955; interviews: Moloi, Mdlalose, Mbawu, and Ngwenya. It is clear that the running of gambling "schools" was a profitable part of the operations of many of the bigger gangs.

133. See B. V. Khumalo, "Sources and Structures of Tsotsitaal," B.A. Honours dissertation, University of the Witwatersrand, April 1986, p. 11.

134. Msimang, "Impact of Zulu on Tsotsitaal," p. 84.

135. Interviews: Nkosi, Motjuwadi, Mdlalose.

4

"Irresponsible Youths": Students, *Tsotsis*, and Africanists, 1944–1960

During the late 1940s and 1950s, while the style-conscious *tsotsi* gangs were at their most prominent, South Africa experienced a phase of political foment. The Congress movement, under the influence of a new generation of young leaders, spearheaded numerous militant campaigns in the 1950s that appealed increasingly to the African youth, yet the relationship between *tsotsi* gangs and organized youth politics was complex and ambiguous. While *tsotsis* generally found the intellectual, nonviolent political methods of the Congress movement alien and incomprehensible, they nonetheless shared its militant rejection of the political status quo. *Tsotsi* gangs were likely to participate spontaneously in political upheavals but lacked the discipline and vision to sustain their participation. In part, this was due to the fundamental incompatibility of Congress-style politics with gang culture and the failure (and unwillingness) of most Congress politicians to tune into the cultural wavelength of the gang world.

From the mid 1930s to the mid 1940s, urban youths were conspicuously absent from African resistance politics. The establishment of the Congress Youth League (CYL), which was dominated by youthful, militant Africanist intellectuals, marked the beginning of a conscious attempt to mobilize African youth politically. But, despite the anger and energy of the *tsotsi* gangs, organized youth politics was confined almost entirely to a small student elite until the late 1950s, at which point the breakaway Pan Africanist Congress (PAC) began to experiment with the mobilization of the *tsotsi* constituency. Strategic disagreement over the mobilization of the urban youth was, I will argue, one important ingredient of the PAC's dissatisfaction with the ANC.

This chapter begins by tracing the emergence of the Congress Youth League, the first formal political organization of African youth, and then analyzes the Pan-Africanist split of the late 1950s from the perspective of youth mobilization. Finally, it assesses the participation of *tsotsi* gangs in the March 1960 anti-pass campaign, as well as the reaction of both the state and the PAC to gang involvement.[1]

THE CONGRESS YOUTH LEAGUE

In 1944, around the time the term *tsotsi* came into use, the Congress Youth League (CYL) was established under the guidance of Anton Lembede and A. P. Mda. Lembede promoted a form of African nationalism that excluded whites and Indians and rejected "imported" political philosophies, such as communism. The new body's twin aims were to mobilize the African youth and to radicalize the ANC from within. High school students were the Youth League's key constituency. Many of the original Youth Leaguers, including Lembede and Mda themselves, became politicized as school students. Congress Mbata, William Nkomo, and Peter Raboroko, founding members of the CYL, were all prominent in the Transvaal Student Association (TSA) prior to the formation of the CYL.[2] The TSA was more of a social organization than a political one during the 1930s and 1940s. Nevertheless, a great deal of political discussion took place in the TSA and it is likely that the political ideas of the CYL were formulated in this group. The Youth Leaguers were familiar with the mood and internal workings of student associations and ~~most CYL activists joined when attending school~~ schools. They understood that students were receptive to political ideas. The CYL used this familiar network to reproduce itself; most of the "second generation" CYL activists who operated in the 1950s were influenced by and incorporated into the CYL while attending school. CYL meetings on the Witwatersrand were well attended by students throughout the 1940s and 1950s. Orlando High School, with a conspicuously politicized stratum of senior students, was a strong support base for the CYL.[3]

Teachers represented an important component of the CYL in the Transvaal. A number of prominent Leaguers were teachers at one stage in their careers. Oliver Tambo and Godfrey Pitje were teachers before they became lawyers; Robert Sobukwe, Zeph Mothopeng, and Es'kia Mphahlele were all teachers on the Rand during the 1950s. Despite teachers' vulnerability as employees of the Transvaal Education Department, the CYL often used teachers to penetrate the high schools. Teachers were generally apolitical during the 1940s and 1950s, but there was usually a small core of politicized, CYL-sympathetic teachers at every school on the Rand. At Orlando High in the early 1950s, for instance, Mphahlele recalls that four teachers out of a staff of thirty-five were politicized; two of the four were signed-up CYL members. Although numerically small, this core of politically conscious, articulate teachers raised political issues in the classroom and was influential among the students.[4]

Although the teacher–pupil interaction was important, the CYL did most of its organizing among school students outside of the school environment. School authorities were hostile to political penetration and had the power to expel students or teachers involved in politics. The CYL generally organized through student associations during the holidays. CYL activists would try to form little pockets of CYL supporters and then encourage them to form autonomous branches. There was a great deal of activity at the branch level on the Rand between 1949 and 1952. Once a core group of about ten new activists had been established, it was considered large enough to form a new branch. This would involve electing its own secretary and treasurer and acting autonomously from other branches.[5]

Outside of urban schools, Fort Hare University, which attracted many of the best African students from around the country, was the CYL's only significant area of operation. Apart from the liberal English-speaking universities, which took in small numbers of black students, Fort Hare was the only tertiary institution in South Africa that accepted Africans during the 1940s and 1950s. It was not surprising, then, that Fort Hare generated a high proportion of the CYL leadership.

The CYL succeeded in winning substantial support from African high school and university students but at no stage did it identify *tsotsis* or uneducated youths as potential recruits. *Tsotsis* themselves were not attracted to the CYL's disciplined and rather elitist style of politics. Throughout the 1940s and most of the 1950s, apart from young educated professionals and senior school students drawn to the CYL, township youths in Johannesburg kept their distance from political organization.[6] Even once the CYL's influence had spread, "older people" dominated ANC rallies at Freedom Square in the 1950s. It was unusual to find anyone less than twenty years old attending ANC rallies or meetings. Even the senior school students tended to be twenty or older. The CYL leaders were generally in their late twenties or early thirties. To the *tsotsis*, the ANC seemed intellectual, respectable, and remote. The gangs were absorbed in their own style, ritual, and rivalry.[7]

The CYL, like its parent body, the ANC, found *tsotsi* culture threatening and destructive throughout the 1940s and 1950s. *Tsotsis* were seen as violent, irresponsible, and uncontrollable.[8] Nevertheless, the ANC did identify the *tsotsis* as victims of "the system" and of socioeconomic hardship. There were a number of ANC activists, notably Robert Resha, P. Q. Vundla, and

Nelson Mandela, who made a great effort to "rehabilitate" individual *tsotsis* and involve them in constructive political activity. Some *tsotsis*, particularly in Sophiatown, did join the local CYL branch. It is important to draw a distinction between mobilizing and rehabilitating. With hardly any exceptions, only individual youngsters who shed their *tsotsi* identity were drawn into organizational structures. As a constituency, the *tsotsis* were regarded more as a menace to the community than as a potential support base. In fact, the ANC was sympathetic towards, and often even helped to organize, local civil guards dedicated to combating *tsotsi* crime.[9]

Although the majority of township youths had no interest in political organizations, it would be incorrect to assume that *tsotsis* lacked political consciousness. Through everyday experiences of poverty, discrimination, blocked social mobility, and police harassment, *tsotsis* developed an antipathy to the establishment and to institutions of authority. Above all, *tsotsis* were politicized by the pass laws. Young men, more than any other section of the township community, were victimized by pass law implementation. Police used the pass laws to screen out urban "undesirables," which included the unemployed and the criminal elements. Any African, whether born in the city or not, could be deemed a "vagrant" and expelled to the countryside. The procedure for registering as a legal urban resident was complicated and humiliating; thousands of *tsotsis* ducked registration altogether, preferring to live illegally in the cities, thus leaving themselves all the more vulnerable to "endorsement out."[10]

Tsotsis demonstrated their anger through style and ritual; an anger directed at both the dominant white middle-class culture and, as they saw it, the passive, acquiescent culture of their parents. Apart from its antiestablishment style and language, the *tsotsi* subculture separated itself from mainstream society by embracing criminality, rejecting the work ethic, and glorifying violence. Their primary concern was to survive on the streets, to forge personal power and status within their subculture. If they were making a political statement, it was unarticulated and inconsistent. For *tsotsis*, the police were the universal enemy and, in this respect at least, their interests overlapped with those of the ANC. Police raids in the townships, whether for passes or illegal beer-brewing, were treated by the *tsotsi* gangs as territorial invasions. They were often prepared to meet police incursions with physical resistance.

In the late 1940s and throughout the 1950s there were numerous violent *tsotsi*–police clashes on the Witwatersrand. *Tsotsi* resistance reflected not an organized political response but a spontaneous anger against the enforcement of laws that impinged on their freedom and movement within their own territories. In 1949, *tsotsis* were at the forefront of riots in Krugersdorp and Newclare, which were sparked off by police entering townships to deal with pass and beer brewing offences. There was another running battle between *tsotsis* and police, which lasted for a day and a night, in Newclare in February 1950.[11] During the Sophiatown removals there were several violent engagements between street gangs and police.[12] In one incident in Moroka in 1958, *tsotsis* even invaded the local police station to release a fellow gang member arrested for assault.[13] In April 1959 Orlando *tsotsis* threatened to break up the opening ceremony for the new Orlando Stadium, apparently because control of the stadium was given to the Johannesburg Bantu Football Association rather than to the local soccer organization.[14] To the *tsotsis* this represented an invasion of local "sovereignty."

The *tsotsi* element did occasionally participate randomly in ANC campaigns during the 1950s but, with possible exceptions during the Sophiatown removals and the Bantu Education boycott in Benoni and Brakpan, gangsters were never actively recruited to do so. Despite the alien methods of the ANC, *tsotsis* often felt sympathy for many of the organization's campaigns. The gangs would intervene in an uncoordinated and undisciplined way to further the interests of campaigns as they saw fit. Occasionally, gangs would take an interest in local political struggles because of personalized connections between gang leaders and activists. The gangs provided an element of physical intimidation from which the ANC, with its principled adherence to nonviolence during the 1950s, shied away. They often took it upon themselves to enforce boycotts and stayaways. Former CYL leader Godfrey Pitje recalls, for instance, that during the Western Areas tram boycotts, *tsotsis* "could be trusted to board a tram and beat up those who were on the tram and in that way help to make the tram boycotts more effective."[15]

In one isolated instance in 1955 an ex-*tsotsi*, who had been rehabilitated by the Benoni CYL, used his extensive subcultural contacts to draw gangs effectively into the local Bantu Education boycott.[16] There were other random incidents with regard to *tsotsi* harassment during the education boycotts.[17] As outsiders of the school system, scornful of the status attached to education, *tsotsis* were always likely to be enthusiastic enforcers of the boycott.

Despite the fact that the ANC had a history of supporting the Sophiatown civil guard movement, *tsotsis* and the ANC found themselves on the same side in opposition to the Sophiatown removal. The ANC had its own political motivations but, far more immediately, the fiercely territorial gangs understood that removal would lead to their disintegration. From around 1953, when the removal was first announced, until the end of the decade, gangsters were involved in street battles with the police and removal teams.[18] The ANC, finding itself loosely allied to the gangs, struggled to restrain local youths from resorting to armed resistance. In February 1953, when the

Sophiatown removal had become a very real prospect, a revealing lead story appeared in *Bantu World*:

> There is an arsenal of machine-guns, rifles and revolvers in the Western areas. There are people who are prepared to use them but the African National Congress will have nothing to do with them. For the past couple of weeks, Sophiatown has been a battleground for the souls of the youth. The violent section have demanded action.
>
> But Congress has fought for non-violence and the people have followed its lead. The battle was fought again over the weekend. Young men poured into Sophiatown from all over the Reef. They gathered in secret in many rooms. The wordy battle raged for hours. They demanded violent action to check the Removal. Congress people pleaded with them to stick to the non-violent line. Meanwhile big forces of police patrolled the streets, the railway stations of the Western Areas, the bus stops and the street corners. The weekend passed without violence.[19]

The police also feared the militancy of the Sophiatown youth. In late March 1958, for instance, they organized a systematic pass swoop on local teenage boys, which many residents suggested was a preemptive attempt to disorganize a meeting scheduled for Freedom Square on 14 April. Sophiatown teenagers had been marching from street to street shouting slogans and calling people to the meeting.[20] The ANC could not subject the local gangsters to organizational discipline. Cultural and strategic tensions ran deep between the ANC and the gangs. The loose Sophiatown alliance was strictly temporary. The gangs, in their own way, were politicized but they were indifferent to conventional political practice. To them, the ANC remained a respectable organization "for older people."

THE AFRICANIST SPLIT

At the Bloemfontein Conference of 1949 the CYL effectively seized control of the ANC. Many key CYL figures, most notably Mandela, Oliver Tambo, and Duma Nokwe, moved into senior positions in the parent body. This mini-coup from within succeeded in dynamizing the ANC substantially. The organization's new militancy was reflected in the adoption of the CYL-sponsored Programme of Action. This document mapped out the strategy of nonviolent defiance that characterized the ANC throughout the 1950s. As it moved into the mainstream of the ANC, the CYL leadership toned down much of its militancy and, crucially, accepted the ANC's line of nonracialism and its controversial alliance with the South African Communist Party (SACP). By 1949 Lembede, the ideological father of the CYL, had died, and Mda was suffering from persistent ill-health that kept him out of active politics. The CYL gradually lost its distinctiveness and direction. Its official policies came into line with those of the ANC and it was effectively relegated to a youth recruitment wing of the parent body.

During the early 1950s the CYL began to split between those members loyal to the ANC leadership and those loyal to what they saw as the original principles and spirit of the Youth League. The latter group maintained a stronghold in the Orlando East branch, led by Potlako Leballo. The Africanist faction argued against cooperation with non-Africans and agitated for more adventurous forms of political mobilization. The CYL dissenters linked up to a wider Africanist faction, which, by 1953, was coordinated by a secret Central Committee under the chairmanship of the charismatic veteran Alexandra activist, Josias Madzunya. In 1955 both Madzunya and Leballo, were expelled from the ANC, and the Orlando East CYL branch was suspended. Madzunya, Leballo and their followers were considered to be irresponsible and racially exclusivist. Africanists, mostly Youth Leaguers, rallied behind their expelled leaders, and the breakaway, which eventually led to the formation of the Pan-Africanist Congress (PAC), was set in motion. Around 1957 Robert Sobukwe, a highly articulate and dedicated follower of the old Lembede school, returned to Johannesburg after having taught in Standerton for several years. He quickly eclipsed both Madzunya and Leballo in popularity and became the PAC's first president when the new organization was officially inaugurated in April 1959.[21]

The PAC began an intensive recruitment drive immediately after its inception. By August 1959 it claimed a signed-up membership of 25,000, of which roughly half came from the Transvaal.[22] Unlike the ANC, the PAC was essentially an organization for young men. The average member, from rank-and-file through to leadership level, tended to be at least ten years younger than the average member of the ANC. On the Witwatersrand, young men seemed to join enthusiastically in large numbers.[23] *The Africanist*, the PAC mouthpiece, proclaimed this proudly: "The most striking thing about the [inaugural] Convention was the youthfulness of its composition. . . . Someone remarked apropo[s] the youthfulness of the delegates that there was in fact no need for a youth league in the PAC; because the movement as such was a movement of the youth."[24]

On a formal level, the PAC's most important recruitment grounds were the urban high schools. Continuing in the tradition of the CYL, the PAC identified school students as their key constituency. School students were disciplined, enthusiastic, and relatively easy to organize. In Johannesburg, the PAC had its strongest support base at Orlando High School, where students had been sympathetic to the Africanists since the mid-1950s.[25]

Beyond the schools, the PAC did break new ground. For the first time, a resistance movement made a substantial impression on the Witwatersrand's *tsotsi* constituency. *Tsotsi* participation in PAC structures was not as tangible as that of the students; it tended to be fluid and informal. Nevertheless, support for the movement was widespread and actual recruitment was not insignificant. This applied as well to the period in 1958–1959 following the Africanist split but prior to the formal establishment of the PAC. Gail Gerhart goes so far as to suggest that "if any single group could be described as PAC in orientation, it would be the broad category of Africans known in some contexts as 'location boys' and in others as *tsotsis.*"[26] The PAC actively encouraged this. The *Africanist* announced proudly that a large number of the "youthful delegates" to the inaugural conference were "illiterate and semi-literate." In a July 1959 speech. Sobukwe emphasized that one of the "basic assumptions" of the PAC was that "the illiterate and semi-literate masses of the African populace are the key, the core and the cornerstone of the struggle for democracy in this country."[27]

Tsotsis were attracted to the PAC's emphasis on "action" and confrontation. Although the PAC officially rejected violence, there was unstated sympathy, even admiration, for violent resistance in the organization's rhetoric. Unlike the ANC, the PAC did not make a point of emphasizing nonviolence.[28] PAC rhetoric appealed to the aggressively antiestablishment *tsotsi* subculture. Although *tsotsis* did not necessarily identify with the intellectual concept of Africanism, they shared the PAC's hatred of white middle-class values and white structures of authority. There was an appealing simplicity in the PAC's analysis of oppression in clear African versus "settler" terms. As Gerhart puts it, the PAC "shared the same sense of urgency and frustration, the same explosive anger as the younger generation."[29]

The PAC's confrontational rhetoric and its tacit sympathy for violence tapped into the raw machismo of the *tsotsi* subculture. The PAC saw politics as a man's game with little of a role for women other than to support their men; its membership was almost exclusively male and it considered a woman's league unnecessary.[30] This matched the pattern of urban gang membership and it made sense to the *tsotsis*. It was also clear that, unlike the ANC, the PAC was prepared to break the law without too many qualms. According to Gerhart, the PAC, short of finances, quietly encouraged *tsotsi* members and sympathizers to steal printing equipment or cars to further organizational objectives.[31] For the *tsotsis*, of course, this was easy to understand. Perhaps the most appealing aspect of the PAC was its concentration on the pass law issue. As I have pointed out, the "dompas," with all its humiliating connotations and associated terrors of eviction, was a longstanding thorn in the side of urban youth. Although other organizations had tackled the pass issue, none had focused on it with quite the intensity of the PAC.[32]

The recruitment of street youth by Africanists began even before the formation of the PAC. Throughout the late 1950s, marginalized Africanist activists, particularly in Orlando and Alexandra, were making an impression on the lumpen youth constituency. From the time of the Africanist breakaway in late 1958, Africanist and later PAC activists conducted intensive door-to-door campaigning. They went scouting on the weekends, attempting to politicize school students and gangsters alike. In 1959 the Orlando branch of the PAC called two warring local gangs to a meeting in an attempt to bring about a truce and politicize the youths.[33] Ben Mapisa, a well-known local boxing instructor who ran a gymnasium in Orlando, would call gangs together and try to redirect their energies towards politics. As a boxer, Mapisa had street credibility and he was apparently successful in recruiting many gangsters from the local Otto Town and Boom Town gangs. Initially a member of the Orlando CYL, Mapisa later became a "scout" for the PAC in 1959.[34] Robert Sobukwe, with his fiery, articulate speeches and uncompromising militancy, quickly established a following among African youth on the Rand by 1958. He addressed numerous meetings in 1959 and early 1960; youngsters flocked to hear him speak in a way they never had for ANC leaders.[35] Josias Madzunya, arguably the most influential figure in the Africanist movement of the late 1950s, was known to have a particular rapport with the unemployed street youth of Alexandra. As a hardliner sympathetic to violent methods, Madzunya apparently advocated physical resistance during the Sophiatown removals. He could often be seen recruiting youths on the street corners.[36]

Support for the PAC rose dramatically during 1959 and especially in early 1960. In February 1959, *The World* reported a significant shift away from the ANC toward the Africanist movement in the Soweto area. Africanist support was said to be strong in Dube, Mofolo, Orlando West, Phefeni, and Mzimhlophe as well as in Alexandra.[37] During the March 1960 anti-pass campaign and its immediate aftermath, the PAC support base swelled to such an extent that journalists Anthony Sampson and Benjamin Pogrund both suggested that it might supersede the ANC as the premier African resistance organization in South Africa. They argued that the PAC's decisiveness and the willingness of its leadership to take personal risks accounted for this buildup of sympathy.[38]

In March 1960 the PAC threw itself headlong into an all-or-nothing anti-pass campaign. It was not entirely a historical accident that the Sharpeville massacre took place where it did. Sharpeville activists had organized systematically and cautiously during 1959 and early 1960 to set up probably the best-organized PAC branch in the Transvaal. The township, near Vereeniging and about an hour's drive south of Johannesburg, had a massive population of angry unemployed youths, which provided fertile ground for PAC activity.[39] On 21 March, the day of the massacre, the leadership ensured exemplary discipline among its followers as they massed at the local police station to hand in their passes. At other centers in the Pretoria–Witwatersrand–Vereeniging (PWV) urban complex the crowds were smaller, and activists were systematically arrested with relatively little commotion. The Sharpeville police, faced with a particularly large crowd, panicked and opened fire, sparking off a wave of unrest throughout the country. On the same day, in the African township of Langa, outside Cape Town, another large anti-pass demonstration was quelled by a violent police reaction. In Langa the PAC mobilized substantial support among migrant laborers who had in preceding years suffered from unusually harsh implementation, even by South African standards, of the pass laws.[40] During the angry days of unrest that followed, sympathy for the PAC was high but, on the Witwatersrand at least, the organization found it had little control over its youthful followers. One of the reasons for this was that virtually all the key leaders who might have been able to rein the youth in, including Sobukwe himself, were detained in the very early stages of the campaign.

High school students played a prominent role in the initial, disciplined phase of the anti-pass campaign. In Soweto they made up a large portion of the rank and file who marched behind Sobukwe. They seemed to disperse in disarray once the leadership had been detained. In the more violent post-massacre phase, the *tsotsis* became far more prominent. It is possible that students were among the stone-throwing, intimidatory youths but no evidence points directly to their involvement.

In the wake of the Sharpeville and Langa shootings, the ANC was forced to take a bolder stand; it temporarily joined forces with the PAC to co-sponsor the March 28 stayaway. On the Rand, *tsotsis* used force to police the strike. Lodge describes the turmoil of that day:

> Despite the ANC's insistence on the peaceful conduct of the stay-away, in the late afternoon of the 28th violence broke out in many parts of Soweto as "tsotsi" gangs attacked homecoming workers who had ignored the strike call. Large groups of teenagers gathered outside the railway stations and manned roadblocks to stone alighting passengers. . . . As the Tsotsis' attacks continued into the night the railway service was suspended.[41]

In the late afternoon of 28 March, two African policemen were trapped and assaulted by a crowd of "blood-boiled, furious" youths in Meadowlands. Their passes were burnt and one of them was stabbed to death after being chased through the streets. The crowd then proceeded systematically to attack the municipal offices in each of Meadowlands' six zones. Throughout the night and early morning, offices were ransacked, windows were smashed, and buildings set ablaze with paraffin. As one witness described it, "curtains were burnt, the flames went up and the crowd shouted 'Hooray'" before proceeding to the next municipal office. Of the thirty-one who were later brought to trial, twenty-five were twenty-one years old or less; seventeen of them, more than half, were between eleven and sixteen. Only four were female. The crowd swelled as it moved through Meadowlands. Many people were playing football in the early evening when they saw the stone-throwing crowd and, recognizing neighborhood friends among the faces, joined in. The youths used distinctively Africanist slogans. One witness recalled that on the way to the municipal offices "the crowd was shouting Mayibuye i Afrika." One of the accused was heard to call out, "Strike, Afrika!" At another point the crowd was shouting, "We are going to burn the office down. . . . Let Afrika come back." According to several witnesses, *tsotsis* were prominent among the youths, some of whom seemed more interested in stealing than in making a political point. The crowd's rage was directed primarily at passes and at the policemen who were perceived to be enforcing the pass laws. The youths referred to the policemen by the derogatory *tsotsitaal* term, *gatters*.[42]

On the same day, cars were stopped and stoned and passes were burnt by crowds of youths in Zola and Jabulani. One driver was killed. The trial record suggests that the participants were a little older here, generally in their twenties. As in Meadowlands the crowd shouted "Afrika!" repeatedly. In an affidavit, William Carr described his own visit to Zola on the afternoon of 28 March:

> In front of the municipal offices I found a fairly large crowd of Bantu males, some of whom were interfering with passing traffic, stopping motor-cars and pulling drivers and passengers out of their cars. They took reference books away from these Natives and one of them . . . was carrying a wire hook on which was impaled about 10 reference books which had been mutilated and partially burnt. This man, together with several others, approached my car and demanded to know what I was doing in the location. They then recognised me and the one man who was wearing a small pointed beard on his chin ordered me to leave the location immediately "if I knew what was good for me."[43]

The annual *Survey of Race Relations* argued that the March 28 "stay-at-home" had been effective partly because of "the *tsotsi*-types" who "play a self-chosen intimidatory role." Many township residents who ignored the strike call "were assaulted and injured by elements from the 'anti-work' group."[44]

March 31 was also a tumultuous day in Soweto. The ANC had originally called the stayaway for this day but at the last minute had changed its call to 28 March. In what *The World* called "the stay-at-home muddle," bands of youths, clearly failing to register the change of date, conducted a "reign of terror on workers." Workers returning home were stoned and assaulted. Cars and buses were stopped and damaged. Workers were forced to move in large groups for self-protection. The Apache gang both robbed workers and burned their pass books.[45]

The political activity of gangs became increasingly blurred with ordinary criminality. Waves of *tsotsi* crime were common in the townships but, for the first time, the criminal and the political became intertwined. On 3 April the *Golden City Post*, under the headline "BOY THUGS TAKE OVER from political leaders in the Townships," reported on "vicious young thugs cashing in on the crisis . . . in the past few days." *Tsotsis* had been responsible for numerous assaults and rapes. "Taking advantage of the confusion arising out of the crisis, and the fact that many houses have been left unprotected, they have used Pan Africanist and A.N.C. slogans as 'fronts' for their activities as they continue to rob and pillage on the majority of the Reef's larger towns." The "notorious" Berlins and Apaches of Orlando East were prominent in the violence. In Alexandra a gang of *tsotsis* called the Red Knife Boys attempted to burn down the offices of the Peri-Urban Health Board. According to the *Post*, most of the youths involved in the violence of the previous days did not possess pass books.[46] On 4 April, as the ANC packed up its Johannesburg office in the face of impending banning orders, an ANC spokesman insisted that the Congress would never tolerate violence. He said that the *tsotsis* were the main cause of the violence of the previous few days.[47]

As early as 1950, the South African state feared the potential politicization of the *tsotsi* constituency. *Tsotsi* gangs were perceived as a major social control issue throughout the 1950s.[48] The urban youth, particularly the *tsotsi* element, appeared to be the primary target of the post-Sharpeville state of emergency. The PAC itself recognized this. In an internal organizational memorandum, dated 8 August, the writer observed: "The government took the line that the massive demonstrations were organised by the tsotsis. The [PAC] task force was described as a tsotsi element and over 1800 people were locked up in the first few days."[49] Between April and July, police conducted a series of massive swoops in the townships, not for pass offenses but, according to the Deputy Commissioner of Police for the Witwatersrand, "to clean up out-of-works, criminals and loafers." By 17 July the *Golden City Post* reported that about 15,000 youths, a very large proportion of them under the age of twenty-one, were being held in the giant Modder B jail, a converted mine compound on the outskirts of Johannesburg. Youths were delivered to the jail by the truckload, thoroughly screened by a special enquiry presided over by three magistrates, and generally released. Every day about a hundred were brought in and the same number released. Many were sent to farm jails or endorsed out of the urban area. Most youths were detained under Section 4 of the Emergency Regulations and often held for weeks without being charged. Common criminals and pass offenders were apparently separated from the political detainees.[50] It seems clear that this massive clampdown on township youth, although not always directed at people who were overtly political, was closely linked to the political control objectives of the state of emergency. The timing of this clampdown also suggests that the state perceived the extent to which the PAC had galvanized the wider urban youth constituency.

During March and April 1960 the Johannesburg townships had their first experience of what became known as the *com-tsotsis* during the 1980s. *Tsotsis* were attracted to the PAC's style of politics during 1959–60 and responded in large numbers to the anti-pass campaign. But, particularly after the early detention of a number of key PAC leaders with credibility on the streets, *tsotsis* became extremely difficult to control. Nonviolence, accountability, and coordinated political action did not come naturally to the *tsotsi* constituency. The gangs saw no serious contradiction between their usual criminal activity and their political motivations. They reacted spontaneously to various political calls but operated without consulting the activists. Administrative buildings, white-owned property, and individuals who broke stayaway calls were all considered fair game for robbery and pillage. By April the PAC leaders, who had initially seemed to embrace these youths enthusiastically, were forced to condemn the *tsotsi* activity. PAC spokesman William Jalobe stated publicly: "We strongly condemn the fact that irresponsible youths are using violence on innocent people."[51]

By the middle of 1960 the PAC and the ANC had been decimated. In August, Benjamin Pogrund of the *Rand Daily Mail* reported that "[t]he A.N.C. and P.A.C. today are mere shells of the organisations which existed at the start of the State of Emergency on March 29." State repression involved "sudden arrests of several thousand leaders, organizers and officials throughout the country; the banning of the organisations themselves and their allied newspapers; the mobilisation of the armed forces; military cordons around residential areas; and the summary arrest and indefinite detention of those who might, after all this, still consider continuing their normal political activities."[52] The urban youth on the Rand remained sympathetic towards the banned organizations during the early 1960s. There was a great deal of interest in the emerging "armed wings" of the PAC and the ANC, *Poqo* and

Mkhonto we Sizwe. Throughout the early 1960s a steady trickle of youths made the decision to leave the country and join the exile movements.[53] Internally, however, both the PAC and the ANC were reduced to little more than symbols of resistance. As I show in chapter 5, most of Johannesburg's better-known youth gangs from this period, as a result of politically motivated police clampdowns and ongoing residential relocation, splintered and disappeared.

NOTES

1. This chapter is adapted from my article, "'When Are They Going to Fight?' Tsotsis, Youth Politics and the PAC," in P. Bonner, P. Delius, and D. Posel (eds.), *Apartheid's Genesis 1935–1962*, Johannesburg, 1993. The emphasis in this chapter, however, tends more towards the 1960 eruption itself, and I use additional primary sources, notably trial records from the Witwatersrand Legal Division.

2. Interviews: Mbata (Carter and Karis), Nkomo (Carter and Karis).

3. Interviews: Pitje, Mphahlele.

4. Interviews: Pitje, Mphahlele, Motlana, Mbata (Carter and Karis).

5. Interviews: Mphahlele, Motlana.

6. For a more detailed account of CYL recruitment and organizational strategy, see Clive Glaser, "Students, Tsotsis and the Congress Youth League 1944–1955," B.A. Honours dissertation, University of the Witwatersrand, October 1986. It appears in a condensed version as "Students, Tsotsis and the Congress Youth League: Youth Organisation on the Rand in the 1940s and 1950s," *Perspectives in Education*, 10, 2, 1988–1989.

7. Interviews: Moloi, Magubane, Twala, Norris Nkosi, Peggy Bel Air, Miles (a) and (b), Mdlalose, Mbawu and Ngenya. See also interview, Mattera (Lodge).

8. Interviews: Motlana, Mphahlele, Pitje. All were members of the CYL during the late 1940s and early 1950s.

9. Interviews: Mattera (a), Motlana, Nhlapho. See Clive Glaser, "Anti-Social Bandits: Juvenile Delinquency and the Tsotsi Youth Gang Subculture on the Witwatersrand, 1935–1960," M.A. Thesis, University of the Witwatersrand, 1990, pp. 200–203.

10. Interviews: Kuzwayo, Motjuwadi; West Rand Administrative Board Archive, Intermediary Archive Depot, Johannesburg (IAD WRAB) 219/3, Minutes of first AGM of the Johannesburg Planning Council for Non-European Social Welfare, 26 March 1957. See also Michael Dingake's account of the Sophiatown gangster, Vivian Dladla, in *My Fight against Apartheid*, London, 1987, pp. 29–30; and *Golden City Post* (*GCP*) features on youth labor camps on 1 September and 8 September 1957, which examine the precariousness of township youths' urban status.

11. J. de Villiers Louw, *Report of the Commission Appointed to Enquire into Acts of Violence Committed by Natives at Krugersdorp, Newlands, Randfontein and Newclare*, UG 47/1950, Pretoria, 1950; *Bantu World* (*BW*) 4 February 1950.

12. Interviews: Mattera (Lodge), Mattera (b). See also *BW*, 19 February 1953.

13. IAD WRAB 351/3, letter from Senior Superintendent of Moroka/Jabavu to the Manager, Johannesburg NEAD, 22 January 1958.

14. *BW*, 25 April 1959, headline article.

15. Interviews: Pitje, Magubane, Mattera (b), Mattera (Lodge), Motjuwadi, Mphahlele, Motlana. See Glaser, "Students, Tsotsis and the Congress Youth League," *Perspectives in Education*, 10, 2, 1988–1989, for a more detailed analysis of the relationship between gangs and the CYL. See also lead story in *BW*, 19 April 1958, which focuses on *tsotsi* stay-at-home enforcement in the Western Areas.

16. See P. Bonner, "Family, Crime and Political Consciousness on the East Rand 1938–1955," *Journal of South African Studies*, 15, 1, 1988. It is worth noting that the boycott was particularly successful in Benoni. See *GCP*, 17 April 1955.

17. See, for instance, IAD WRAB 351/1, minutes of conference attended by the Deputy Commissioner of the SAP Witwatersrand, Area Officers, members of the NEAD Committee, and members of the Advisory Board, Johannesburg, 14 December 1955.

18. Interviews: Motlana, Mattera (b).

19. *BW,* 19 February 1953, lead story.

20. *The World*, 29 March 1958.

21. For a more detailed account of the CYL in the 1950s and the emergence of the Pan Africanist movement, see Gail Gerhart, *Black Power in South Africa*, Berkeley, 1978, pp. 138–172; and Glaser, "Students, Tsotsis and the Congress Youth League," Hons. dissertation, pp. 9–58. On the role of the Central Committee and Josias Madzunya, see Tom Lodge, "Insurrectionism in Southern Africa: The Pan Africanist Congress and the Poqo Movement 1959–1965," D. Phil. thesis, University of York, England, April 1984, pp. 124–125. Madzunya was a particularly prominent figure in Johannesburg politics in the second half of the 1950s. Among other things, he masterminded the successful Alexandra bus boycott of 1957 and, despite official expulsion, made a bid for the Transvaal ANC leadership in 1958. He received much attention in *The World* newspaper, particularly during 1958. For a good example, see 4 October 1958.

22. *The Africanist*, November 1959.

23. Gerhart, *Black Power*, p. 221; Lodge, "Insurrectionism in South Africa," p. 206; interviews: Mbawu and Ngwenya, Motjuwadi, Norris Nkosi, Thloloe (Lebelo). Joe Thloloe was a PAC organiser on the Rand in 1959–1960.

24. *The Africanist*, editorial, May/June 1959.

25. Moses Dlamini, *Robben Island: Hell Hole*, Nottingham, England, 1984, p. 143; interview, Tlholoe (Lebelo). See also Lodge, "Insurrectionism in South Africa," pp. 336–341, pointing to effective PAC cells in the Pretoria schools of Kilnerton and Atteridgeville that survived even the banning of the PAC.

26. Gerhart, *Black Power*, pp. 223–224. Lodge, "Insurrectionism in South Africa," pp. 15–16, directly disputes Gerhart's claim. He insists that the PAC established a mass following only in the Western Cape. But his own thesis fails to support this argument. If anything, his evidence adds weight to the claims of many of my informants that the PAC commanded widespread sympathy and support among the Transvaal urban youth. See, for instance, "Insurrectionism," pp. 205–207 as well as the chapters on Pretoria and Sharpeville. See Glaser, "Anti-Social Bandits," pp. 214–215, in which I assess this mini-debate. Interviews: Norris Nkosi, Peggy Bel Air, Mbawu and Ngwenya, Motjuwadi, Tlholoe (Lebelo).

27. *The Africanist*, editorial, May/June 1959, pp. 1–2. Institute of Commonwealth Studies, London (ICS): Political Parties Collection: Pan Africanist Congress (henceforth, ICS PAC), Robert Sobukwe, speech entitled "State of the Nation," July 1959.

28. See Gerhart, *Black Power*, p. 220; and B. Pogrund, *How Can Man Die Better: Sobukwe and Apartheid,* Johannesburg, 1990, p. 96.

29. Gerhart, *Black Power*, p. 222.

30. Gerhart, *Black Power*, p. 221. See also Pogrund, *Sobukwe and Apartheid*, p. 96. Pogrund recalls that there were virtually no women at the inaugural congress of the PAC in stark contrast to ANC gatherings.

31. Gerhart, *Black Power*, p. 223.

32. During Philip Kgosana's trial in 1960, Albie Sachs, as defense lawyer, asked key "expert" state witness, Lieutenant Sauerman, if the PAC was the only organization that criticized and campaigned against passes. Sauerman answered: "No, not only them, but to the best of my knowledge . . . no other organisation has ever taken it so far as they have." See ICS: Albie Sachs Papers (Legal cases and political trials 1956–67), Folder 31/1, PAC/Kgosana Trial June–December 1960, vol II, p. A486.

33. Interviews: Norris Nkosi, Tlholoe (Lebelo).

34. Interviews: Norris Nkosi, Ndaba.

35. Interviews: Nkosi, Peggy Bel Air, Motjuwadi, Mbawu and Ngwenya. See also Gerhart, *Black Power*, pp. 182–193.

36. Interviews: Thabethe, Tlholoe (Lebelo). For more on Madzunya's role in the Africanist camp, see Lodge, "Insurrectionism in South Africa," pp. 124–125; and Carter and Karis Collection, Historical Papers Library, University of the Witwatersrand, Johannesburg, Reel 11A, biographical notes on Josias Madzunya. See also numerous scattered references to Madzunya and his politics in *The World*, particularly during 1958.

37. *The World*, 21 February 1959.

38. *The London Observer*, 24 April 1960, "This Isn't the Gale Yet," by Anthony Sampson; *Rand Daily Mail (RDM)*, 24 August 1960, "Now They Work Underground," by Benjamin Pogrund. See also E. A. Brett, "African Attitudes," *South Africa Institute of Race Relations Fact Paper*, 14, Johannesburg, 1963, for an interesting comparison of ANC and PAC support in the PWV area in 1960–1961. The survey is obviously thin and technically dubious but nevertheless suggestive of the dramatic rise in PAC support during 1960.

39. See Lodge, "Insurrectionism in South Africa," pp. 133–136.

40. See Lodge, *Black Politics in South Africa since 1945*, Johannesburg, 1983, pp. 210–223, for a detailed account of events in Langa. The dynamics in Langa seemed to differ from the Witwatersrand in many respects. Not only were migrants far more prominent in Langa, but there was little evidence of gang participation, and PAC leaders, most notably Philip Kgosana, were able to maintain more disciplined control over their followers in the days after the massacre.

41. Lodge, "Insurrectionism in South Africa," p. 173. See also *RDM*, 29 March 1960. Lodge, "Insurrectionism," p. 336, also points to a similar wave of violence in Pretoria on 28 March.

42. Criminal Cases of the Witwatersrand Legal Division, Central Archive Depot, Pretoria, trial records, (henceforth CAD WLD) 437/60, State vs Joseph Mothlamme and thirty others, 1 October 1960.

43. CAD WLD 504/60, 6 June 1960.

44. Muriel Horrel (ed.), *Survey of Race Relations in South Africa*, 1959/60, p. 61, and 1961, pp. 38–39. The survey argued that an attempted stayaway on 28 March 1961 failed partly because of the absence of the *tsotsi* element that had been so prominent in

1960. "In this case the police had rounded up unemployed Africans who might have acted in this way."

45. *The World*, 9 April 1960, "Pictures of the Day the Gangs Ran Rriot in the Townships."

46. *Golden City Post (GCP)* 3 April 1960, p. 1.

47. *The Star*, 4 April 1960.

48. See the de Villiers Louw Report, UG 47/1950. See also John Hyslop, "'A Destruction Coming in': Bantu Education as Response to Social Crisis," in P. Bonner, P. Delius, and D. Posel (eds.), *Apartheid's Genesis 1935–1962*, Johannesburg, 1993. Hyslop suggests that the Bantu Education system was set up largely as a solution to the problems of social control of urban youth.

49. ICS PAC M859, letter from "Son of Africa" to "Sons of Africa" re: "Conditions in S. A. after the Pass Campaign," 8 August 1960 (writer unidentified).

50. *GCP*, 17 April, 17 July and 31 July 1960. See also *GCP*, 3 July, 10 July, and 7 August 1960; and *The World*, 16 April 1960. Lodge points to similar operations carried out in Pretoria's townships throughout 1960 and 1961. See Lodge, "Insurrectionism in South Africa," p. 341.

51. *GCP*, 3 April 1960. Philip Kgosana, in his early twenties, was probably the most important figure in the PAC's anti-pass campaign in the Western Cape. From exile in Addis Ababa in 1963 he argued that in 1960 the Western Cape branch of the PAC had been much better organized than in the branch in Johannesburg "where the discipline was so lacking . . . with its large criminal element" that was so difficult to control. See Carter and Karis Collection, Reel 11A, Kgosana in conversation with Bob Hess, Addis Ababa, 15 August 1963.

52. *RDM*, 24 August 1960.

53. Interviews: Norris Nkosi, Mattera (b), Motjuwadi. Michael Dingake, in his autobiography, *My Fight against Apartheid*, p. 68, recalls that 1962 was a particularly good year for *Mkhonto* recruitment.

5

"IDLE AND UNDESIRABLE": RELOCATION, GANGS, AND YOUTH IDENTITY IN SOWETO DURING THE 1960S

In the early 1950s, aside from live-in servants in white areas, most of Johannesburg's black population lived either in freehold townships close to white suburbs or in Orlando and adjacent southwestern townships. The two most populous freehold townships were Alexandra to the north of the city and Sophiatown to the west. Both areas had been settled since the early part of the century and became densely populated during the 1930s as inner-city black slums were systematically cleared. Alexandra and Sophiatown were popular options because they were relatively close to town and still offered possibilities of freehold rights. Clustered around Sophiatown were the smaller black suburbs of Western Native Township, Newclare, and Martindale. Together these western freehold townships were known as the Western Areas.

Orlando was established in 1936. Situated to the southwest, beyond the city limits, it accommodated 80,000 residents. In response to the massive housing shortages and squatter movements of the 1940s, new housing estates, as well as temporary shelters and site-and-service schemes, were established in nearby Dube, Mofolo, Jabavu, Moroka, and Pimville. Orlando and the adjacent settlements formed the core of what later became known as Soweto.

Between 1954 and 1960 the Western Areas were cleared. During the early 1960s, residents from a section of Alexandra were also removed. As they were evicted from their old homes, they were mostly resettled by the Native Affairs Department in two new townships on either side of Orlando: Meadowlands and Diepkloof. Simultaneously, the Johannesburg City Council es-

tablished a cluster of new townships further to the west and south in response to the pressing housing needs of the more recently urbanized. In the
late 1950s this entire urban complex acquired the official name of Soweto,
a shortened version of Southwestern Townships.

Following the turbulence of the late 1950s and the 1960 state of emergency, Soweto gradually replaced the destroyed Western Areas freehold townships as the heartland of African youth gang culture in Johannesburg. During the late 1940s and 1950s, gangs had proliferated in the old core of Soweto
but they had generally lacked the power, prestige, and style of the major
Sophiatown or Alexandra gangs.

As in previous decades, patterns in local employment, education, and
housing intimately shaped the contours of youth identity in Soweto during
the 1960s. In a context of expanding adult employment opportunities in
Johannesburg, unemployment remained extremely high amongst urbanized
youth. At the same time, the state maintained an attack on the urban residential status of young unemployed men, who were increasingly catego-
rized as "idle and undesirable." On the education front, the provision of
mass primary schooling by the Department of Bantu Education ensured that
school became a more significant counterweight to street life in the 1960s.
The most striking changes, however, occurred in the field of housing and
urban planning. The destruction of old neighborhoods and the rapid establishment of new formal residential areas had direct implications for the youth
gang subculture. Neighborhood networks were uprooted and dislocated during the forced Western Areas resettlement from the mid-1950s to the early
1960s. Dislocation also occurred when squatter communities moved voluntarily into new formal housing estates. It took time for neighborhood networks and, by extension, prominent youth gangs to regenerate. Nevertheless, youth gang culture, albeit in a fairly muted and unspectacular form,
continued into the 1960s, especially in the older areas of Soweto.

HIGH APARTHEID AND URBAN ADMINISTRATION

The 1960s were characterized simultaneously by "high apartheid" and by
high economic growth. State repression in the early 1960s restored political
stability, and foreign investment flowed into South Africa. Between 1963
and 1968 the economy realized an average Gross Domestic Product growth
of 6.4 percent per annum.[1] The manufacturing and construction sectors, centered in the urban areas, grew impressively and underpinned the boom.[2] By
1970 the manufacturing sector employed almost 1.1 million people, more
than double the 1951 total.[3] Despite the growing demand for labor, real
wages for Africans in the manufacturing sector increased only marginally
during this period because levels of skill were low, workers were not union-

ized, and their urban residential status was often unstable. Nevertheless, it has been argued that standards of living for urban Africans did improve because of the increase in sheer numbers employed in the better-paid manufacturing sector. Also the average number of employed people per household increased significantly.[4]

In 1958 H. F. Verwoerd, an advocate of tougher influx control and ethnic balkanization, succeeded to the premiership after having directed the Native Affairs Department (NAD) since 1952. From the outset he was determined to streamline the "practical," piecemeal approach to urbanization, which, he argued, was riddled with loopholes. The concept of ethnic self-determination gave the Verwoerdian faction its ideological and strategic coherence.[5] During the 1960s the bantustan system became the cornerstone of apartheid policy. This was a clear departure from the politics of the 1950s. The government attempted to deny South African citizenship to all Africans resident in "white areas," insisting that they be classified as citizens of one or another of the ethnic "homelands." The central premise of the separate development strategy was that political stability and control could best be achieved by restricting the urban African population to a minimum. Verwoerd's policies were popularized as a counterattack against late 1950s African militancy.

During the 1950s the NAD had accepted that unemployed Africans with the correct documentation could remain in the cities; in the decade that followed, the NAD, renamed the Bantu Affairs Department (BAD), attempted to institute a system whereby "all Africans, irrespective of their place of birth or length of employment, were entitled to remain in the white areas only as long as they ministered to white needs." The BAD continued to emphasize the Urban Labour Preference Policy (ULPP); as far as possible it wanted to absorb available urban labor before granting additional entry permits to migrant workseekers.[7] There was strategic continuity in the early years of the Vorster administration, following Verwoerd's assassination in 1966. In fact, even more strenuous efforts were made to reverse the flow of Africans to the cities during the late 1960s.[8]

Although the BAD was forced into compromises and never achieved anything close to its stated objectives, influx control was administered far more rigidly in the 1960s than before. The BAD was given wide jurisdiction for the "removal of idle or undesirable Black persons" from the urban areas. An "idle" person included anyone who was unemployed or who had been discharged from a job due to his own misconduct. An unemployed person was defined as one who had refused three offers of "suitable" legal employment within 122 days.[9] According to the Black Sash, a prominent anti-apartheid welfare organization, the two categories of people most vulnerable to endorsement out were, first, young men and, second, wives who had joined their husbands in the city. In 1965 the organization's Johannesburg advice office commented that "it is very difficult for young men to enter proscribed areas, regardless of family ties." In 1968 great concern was expressed about "the number of youngsters (especially boys), children of old Johannesburg residents, who on reaching the age of 16 cannot get themselves registered. They have usually some technical infringement of the pass laws and so do not comply with the conditions necessary for permission to remain here." During 1969 the office reported that "there has been a preponderance of teenage boys and young men whose problems are insurmountable."[10]

The convergence of rapid growth, tightened influx control, and the Urban Labour Preference Policy ensured virtually full adult employment in Johannesburg during the 1960s. For those who were prepared to do unskilled and semiskilled work for poor wages, there was employment aplenty.[11] In 1969 the *Survey of Race Relations* reported an acute labor shortage and business fears of wage inflation.[12] For all this, Soweto continued to be dogged by a serious *juvenile* unemployment problem throughout the 1960s. There were three reasons for this, all reflecting basic continuity from the 1950s.[13] First, numerous urban employers preferred to risk employing illegal workers from the countryside rather than take on city youths, whom they perceived as unreliable and defiant.[14] Second, and related to the first, was the scorn for regular, arduous, poorly paid employment prevalent in township youth culture. Third, the pass laws, which put the onus of proof of urban status on the individual rather than the state, deprived many city-born youths of the right to reside and work in town. It was common for youths in this position to avoid registration altogether and live illegally in the city, often turning to crime for survival.[15] It is difficult to find reliable employment figures for Johannesburg broken down by age after 1960. But records of the local Non-European Affairs Department's juvenile employment section suggest that well over half and possibly as much as two-thirds of the African male population of Johannesburg between the ages of sixteen and eighteen were registered as unemployed by 1967.[16] The limited employment prospects for youths, in a context of economic boom, must have reinforced their sense of social marginalization. Most of their parents, albeit ground down by low wages and long hours, occupied a relatively secure niche in the urban setting. But, as in the 1950s, thousands of young urban males, unemployed and often under threat of removal, were attracted to criminal options.

The Bantu Education system, though introduced in the mid-1950s, entrenched itself as an institution during the 1960s; it provided schooling for greater numbers but at lower standards and under tighter centralized control. During the 1940s and 1950s, African schoolgoing children were a relatively small constituency in Johannesburg's townships. In the 1960s, schooling became an increasingly common township experience.

Jonathan Hyslop identifies two broad phases in Bantu Education policy between 1955 and 1971. During the first phase, 1955–1962, the Department of Bantu Education (DBE) concentrated on cramming as many youths as possible, in both rural and urban areas, into the first four years of schooling. The government had both economic and social control objectives. Industrial employers, backed by the United Party, were crying out for more semi skilled African workers; at this stage, whites satisfied the demand for skilled posts. The DBE was concerned to align African schooling with the labor market. Four years in school "was seen as a basis for semi-skilled labour requiring minimal numeracy, literacy and work discipline, and it was schooling at this level that the state sought to encourage."[17] In addition, the government saw the need to defuse urban social tension by, on the one hand, drawing as many youths as possible off the streets and, on the other hand, going some way to satisfy the demands of African parents for educational facilities.[18] The Bantu Education system succeeded in delivering primary schooling, albeit of lower quality, on a scale the old missionary-based system had never achieved. In 1955 there were 5,801 schools for Africans nationally, accommodating 9.76 percent of the total African population. In 1960, after five years of Bantu Education, the figures had risen to 12.84 percent in 7,718 schools.[19] Significantly, the tiny proportion of students in secondary school actually declined from 3.5 percent in 1953 to 3.2 percent in 1960, reflecting the DBE's initial emphasis on primary education.[20] By the mid-1960s the government was able to boast that 80 percent of the seven to fourteen age group of African children were in school.[21]

Government strategy in the second phase, 1962–1971, centered on the bantustan system. While primary schooling in the urban areas was allowed to expand roughly in accordance with the demands of the labor market, urban African secondary schooling was deliberately stunted. New secondary and tertiary education was provided almost exclusively in the bantustans. This was intended to discourage urban settlement and force those who wanted to study further to go to rural schools.[22] It was part of a wider scheme to develop bantustan infrastructure and encourage home-grown educated bureaucratic elites. The government provided subsidies and active assistance to rural communities trying to establish schools. In the urban areas it prohibited the establishment of new high schools even if the funding was available. By 1964, of the 309 African secondary schools nationwide, 72 were located in designated urban areas. Of the 63 that catered for students up to matriculation level, a mere 13 were urban.[23]

In spite of the urban secondary school freeze, more and more Soweto youths had some experience of schooling during the 1960s. Many as old as sixteen or seventeen actually attended primary school. Moreover, the natural increase in numbers and rising educational expectations created by the expansion of primary schooling put intolerable pressure on the eight secondary schools in Soweto. These schools, despite mounting overcrowding and under-resourcing problems, continued to deliver a reasonable quality of education, and many township residents identified them as a possible route out of poverty.[24] Secondary schools drew in students from diverse neighborhoods and provided Soweto youths with an increasingly visible alternative to narrow, spatially defined, street-level identities.

Schooling was merely one of several areas in which local and central government policy seemed irreconcilable. The broad approach to urban African administration differed fundamentally between the United Party–run Johannesburg City Council (JCC) and the Nationalist government. This was not a new development, but the rift widened during the 1960s. Whereas the JCC, through its Johannesburg Non-European Affairs Department (JNEAD), attempted to improve urban conditions for Africans, the central Bantu Affairs Department neglected and even obstructed services to urban Africans.[25] According to William Carr, the Manager of the JNEAD from the early 1950s to 1969, "the Nat approach" toward African residents in the 1960s was to "make urban life insufferable."[26] As part of an attempt to discourage African urbanization, the development of social infrastructure for Africans in the urban areas was virtually frozen. From the mid-1960s, new housing developments, secondary schools, and health facilities were consigned almost entirely to the homelands.[27]

Historically there had been a long struggle between the local government and the central state over the financing of urban African services. Even before 1948, the central state had tried to place as much of the financial burden as possible on the shoulders of the municipalities. During the 1950s the Nationalists relinquished all responsibility, arguing that urban African communities should be self-financing. In the 1960s, the central government went one step further; it often deliberately prevented municipalities and private sources from subsidizing local Bantu revenue accounts. During the 1950s and 1960s the JNEAD was able to finance Soweto's housing, schooling, and other basic services only with the help of profits from municipal beer halls, JCC subsidies, and private sector assistance. In the second half of the 1960s the BAD attempted to limit JCC subsidies and often refused to approve private sector loans; it began to freeze investment even in those services the JNEAD had managed to provide.[28]

This strategic divergence was clearly illustrated in the management of township crime. By the 1950s, crime had become one of the major grievances of township residents in the Johannesburg area. The situation almost certainly deteriorated in the 1960s, and juvenile crime rose steadily in proportion to overall crime. While the social mobility of urban youth was still largely blocked, improved standards of living in Soweto generated both more to steal and higher material aspirations.[29] Articulating their grievances through the advisory boards, older residents made constant appeals to government to provide better policing. They also called for improved schooling and recreation facilities in the hope that these would address the crime problem indirectly. Residents received a sympathetic hearing from the local JNEAD on the issue of crime but, whereas the local government saw solutions in terms of improving urban social conditions, the BAD solution again hinged on the control of African mobility. From the late 1950s until the early 1970s, urban crime was a social problem that the central government felt could best be combated through the strict implementation of influx control. The government took little notice of advisory boards, residents' associations, and other township bodies that appealed for improved urban services, choosing instead to deal with crime unilaterally.

The apartheid answer to township crime involved three basic elements: spatial containment, controls on mobility, and the raid system. Essentially, it was a strategy based on maximizing white security rather than tackling crime head on. The strategy of containment was simple enough. It involved separating African residential areas from white suburbs. The levels of township crime were considered tolerable as long as crime did not spill over into the suburbs. With the townships isolated beyond buffer zones, the South African Police (SAP) could concentrate on providing security to the white residential areas. Central to the second strategy was the use of influx control to curb crime. This entailed the equation of illegal urban status with criminality. Those who had no fixed home, who were unemployed, or who did not have their passes in order were assumed by the SAP to make up the "criminal element." Senior police officials believed that if "vagrants," "idlers," "loafers," and "undesirables," most of whom were young men, were removed from Johannesburg the crime problem would decline significantly.[30] Perhaps more importantly, influx control was used to reduce the competition for urban employment. The Urban Labour Preference Policy (ULPP), it was hoped, would keep urban unemployment to a minimum as well as reduce pressure on urban resources.[31] Although the ULPP was aimed at reinforcing a range of apartheid control objectives, its role in combating crime, and particularly juvenile crime, should not be underestimated.[32] To the extent that the SAP dealt directly with crime, its members depended heavily on the raid system. There was no permanent police presence in Soweto. The area was regarded as too big to control effectively.[33] Police patrols, particularly at night, were few and far between, and the SAP were unlikely to appear at the scene of a crime.[34] Instead, police would periodically swoop on the townships in large numbers, indiscriminately arrest and screen hundreds of residents, and then withdraw.

The JNEAD maintained a municipal police force and recruited dozens of ordinary residents as reservists. Because of the limited jurisdiction of local government, however, neither municipal police, known as "black-jacks," nor reservists could carry firearms. The JNEAD also created new sports facilities and sponsored youth clubs. Ultimately, its resources were too meager to make a real difference.[35] Increasingly, older residents established their own local civil guards in a desperate attempt to reassert control over youths who were perceived to be running amok. Advisory board members often took the initiative in setting up civil guards during the late 1950s and 1960s. The South African Police Force was implacably opposed to civil guards; it rejected any attempt to usurp its own powers and saw the guard movement as a potential political threat. The JNEAD occasionally gave limited, provisional recognition to civil guards, usually only in some sort of partnership scheme with police. But the JNEAD was generally suspicious of civil guards, fearing that vigilantes might take the law into their own hands and even commit crimes themselves. Despite official rejection, civil guards sprouted throughout Soweto during the 1960s. Some lasted longer and were more effective than others. Sowetan residents had few alternatives. They had to risk breaking the law in order to protect their lives and property.[36]

Despite constant monitoring from the BAD and drastically limited resources, William Carr managed to run a fairly efficient administration during the 1960s. Richard Maponya, a prominent businessman and advisory board member in the 1960s, recalls that Carr was effective and sympathetic compared to the West Rand Administration Board (WRAB) in the 1970s (which will be discussed in chapter 7). Under JNEAD control, refuse and litter were cleared away quickly, sewage and electricity systems were maintained. There was some sense of an upgrading program in Soweto.[37]

The most impressive initiative of the JNEAD during the late 1950s and early 1960s was its Soweto housing program. During the 1940s the African population expanded rapidly on the Witwatersrand. In the absence of adequate housing, new urban arrivals and former subtenants established numerous informal squatter settlements throughout the area.[38] By the end of the 1940s about 50,000 African families were living in squatter settlements in and around Johannesburg.[39] In the mid-1950s the Johannesburg NEAD identified the provision of housing for urban Africans as a top priority. William Carr, along with many city councillors, most notably Patrick Lewis, recognized that mass housing was essential to defuse rising tensions. In 1956, the Anglo-American Corporation provided the JNEAD with a R6 million loan, a crucial supplement to government housing loans, making possible the Soweto "housing boom" over the following ten years.[40] The face of Soweto changed dramatically between the mid-1950s and the mid-1960s (Map 5.1). In the early 1950s

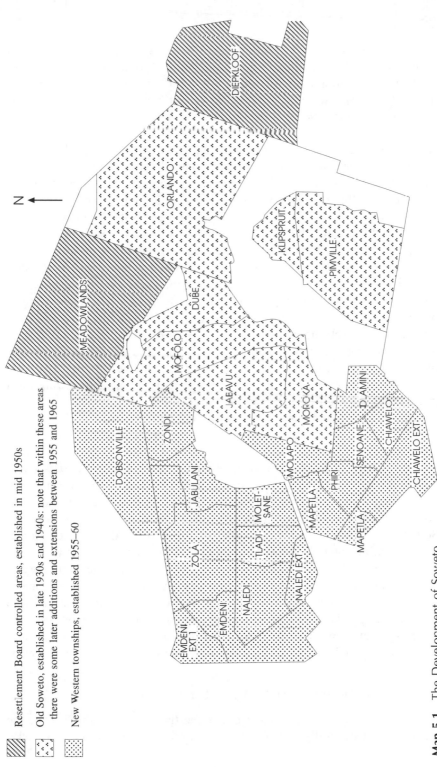

N

Resettlement Board controlled areas, established in mid 1950s

Old Soweto, established in late 1930s and 1940s: note that within these areas there were some later additions and extensions between 1955 and 1965

New Western townships, established 1955–60

Map 5.1 The Development of Soweto

DIEPKLOOF

ORLANDO

MEADOWLANDS

DUBE

KLIPSPRUIT

PIMVILLE

MOFOLO

JABAVU

MOROKA

D. AMINI

DOBSONVILLE

ZONDI

MOLAPO

CHIAWELO

SENOANE

PHIRI

CHIAWELO EXT.

ZOLA

JABULANI

TLADI

MOLET-SANE

MAPETLA

MAPETLA

EMDENI

NALEDI

NALEDI EXT

EMDENI EXT 1

the area consisted of Orlando, Mofolo, Jabavu, Moroka, Pimville/ Klipspruit, old Dube, and a largely undeveloped Meadowlands. Between 1955 and 1965 an average of roughly 4,400 houses were built each year in the JCC-administered section of Soweto.[41] New formal residential areas on the western rim of Soweto emerged within a very short space of time: Chiawelo, Dhlamini, Emdeni, Mapetla, Mofolo, Molapo, Moletsane, Naledi, Phiri, Senaoane, Tladi, Zola, and Zondi.[42] Unlike old Soweto, all of these new townships were ethnically zoned. The JNEAD, in order to secure BAD approval for the housing development in the mid–1950s, had accepted this compromise.[43] By 1966, Zola had become one of the biggest townships in Soweto with 5,596 houses; Naledi had over 4,000 houses, and Emdeni 2,300.[44] New extensions were also developed in older townships such as Jabavu and Dube. During the same period the Resettlement Board built 23,695 houses in Meadowlands and in freshly proclaimed Diepkloof to the east of Orlando. These two townships, designed to accommodate displaced former residents of the Western Areas, were financed and administered directly by the central government through the Resettlement Board.[45] By 1966 there were 87,500 formal houses in Soweto, at which point the BAD, in a bid to curtail the growth of African townships, placed tight restrictions on the funding available for housing; between 1966 and 1969 fewer than 2,000 houses were built in Soweto, and waiting lists for accommodation grew.[46]

Although the new housing developments provided upgraded living conditions for those who had arrived from the squatter camps or overcrowded (and overpriced) backyard shacks, Soweto was an inhospitable living environment. The new Sowetan townships were made up of low-cost box-like houses arranged in clinically geometric patterns. The sheer uniformity of the housing stripped residents of their individuality, and the absence of freehold rights discouraged them from investing in additions and improvements. Soweto's dirt roads turned to bogs after summer storms; dust swirled around in the cold, dry winters. Most households had no access to electricity and instead used coal fires, which caused a thick smog in the late evenings and early mornings. Soweto had no permanent cinemas or shopping malls and it was far from the center of Johannesburg. It was a drab commuter city that disgorged its workers into the industrial and commercial areas on weekday mornings. But, to most of the youth who stayed behind, Soweto was a permanent home, and the landscape itself was central to their sense of identity.

THE SPECTRUM OF MALE YOUTH IDENTITY

Although several large gangs did make their mark in the 1960s, the decade is not generally remembered as an era of gangsterism in Soweto.

Most of the notorious gangs that strike an immediate chord of recognition with Soweto residents operated either in the 1950s or the early 1970s. Nevertheless, juvenile crime and small neighborhood gangs continued to proliferate during the 1960s. The apparent hiatus in the 1960s indicates the decline of coherent subcultural gang style and the relative absence of noteworthy powerful gangs, rather than a lull in gang formation per se. Unlike the 1950s, in which the *tsotsi* subculture was virtually hegemonic among male urban youth, the following decade was a period of rather scrambled and shifting urban youth identity. The introduction of mass primary schooling, the Western Areas removals, and the ongoing relocation of communities tended to complicate and unsettle patterns of identity.

Soweto youths had a very narrow range of role models. They lived in a parochial world of limited horizons and aspirations. For boys, gangsterism was romantic and alluring. Famous Johannesburg gangs from the past decade, such as the Americans of Sophiatown and the Msomis of Alexandra, as well as movie gangsters and bandits, were idolized by younger boys. Al Capone and the Mafia were admired.[47] These distant exotic figures were made more tangible through much admired "senior clevers," famous ex-gangsters of the 1950s, such as Peggy Bel Air, who had been a member of the Americans. Peggy was a well-known personality in Moroka, especially amongst relocated ex-Sophiatown residents, who made his fortune through the liquor trade.[48] Gangsterism and sports provided possible routes to fame and stardom outside of the drudgery of education. Most of the youths who stayed on into high school aspired to become *umapalani*, the learned and literate, essentially teachers and clerks.[49]

As in the 1940s and 1950s, male youths who grew up together congregated at corners to socialize and pass the time. These networks shaded from indistinguishable play-groups and non- or petty-criminal gangs to hardcore criminal gangs. At the core of these groups were non-schoolgoing, unemployed males, aged roughly fourteen to twenty, who had plenty of unsupervised free time on their hands. Neighborhood networks, however, did not exclude students or formally employed youths. Although school itself was a world cut off from non-students, students did participate significantly in street life. This mixing was not an entirely new development, though it became more common during the 1960s along with the rising proportion of younger teenagers who attended school. After hours, students or employed youths would often spend their time with local unemployed youths. Even well-known identifiable gangs, some of which were involved in serious criminal activities, had a smattering of schoolgoing members. Johannes Radebe, for instance, while still attending school, became a member of the Top Eleven gang of Central Western Jabavu. "I joined this group because I could see I was not going to survive if I didn't join them. I was fourteen years old when I joined them." In 1965, at the age of eighteen, he became the gang's leader. "I attended school as usual and after school I would take off my school clothes and wear my gang clothes to take up the leadership where I left off when I was at school."[50] It was extremely unusual, however, for a gang leader to attend school since leaders generally needed to be visible throughout the day.

The street networks or gangs would assemble around the nearest shops for companionship and entertainment. "That's where you'd have to go to touch base with people."[51] They would gamble, "chase girls," and smoke dagga. Soccer was a particularly important point of connection; if there was a nearby soccer field, that too would become a central gathering point.[52] These neighborhood networks developed a strong sense of parochial identity. As Murphy Morobe, who grew up in Orlando in the 1960s, comments: "One love of every youngster growing up in the township is to have your group of colleagues who you meet at the shops or the streetcorner. . . . Over time it graduates into . . . a bunch of youngsters who begin to look at themselves in terms of the territory in which they play around."[53]

Despite some overlap between school and street, there was a fairly clear correlation between early school-leaving and violent, antisocial gangsterism. Most of the hardcore gangsters had dropped out of school by Standard Two or earlier.[54] Without school absorbing their time and providing a counterbalancing set of influences and aspirations, with little chance of finding employment until at least the later teens, these dropouts were, in the words of Fanyana Mazibuko, who taught at Morris Isaacson High School (MIHS) during the 1960s, "sitting ducks for the gangs."[55] As in the 1940s and 1950s, gang life offered non-schoolgoers a sense of companionship and belonging. Money, and consequently crime, became increasingly necessary for items such as cigarettes, dagga, liquor, stylish clothing, and presents for girlfriends. Gang culture emphasized street wisdom and scorned formal employment and education.[56] It had an aura of freedom, independence, and excitement that encouraged boys to drop out of school, particularly those who had had a taste of gang life after hours. Gangs seemed attractive to many who labored under the school regime of discipline, drudgery, and corporal punishment.

The exploration and assertion of masculinity continued to be central to gang culture in the 1960s. Although many township girls participated indirectly in gangs as girlfriends, they were basically excluded from street culture.[57] According to many ex-residents of the ganglands, parents tended to be more strict about the movement of girls and drew them more effectively into domestic duties.[58] T. W. Kambule, the headmaster of Orlando High School during the 1960s and 1970s, suggests that boys became increasingly difficult to control as they matured physically around fifteen or sixteen years of age, particularly in the numerous female-headed households.[59] Whatever the merits of this argument, it would be incorrect to imply that girls did not participate in associative structures outside of the home. Rather, they were attracted to different kinds of structures. For instance, girls generally completed more years of schooling than boys. Although their numbers thinned in Forms Four and Five, the 1960 census figures for Johannesburg suggest that fewer girls than boys dropped out during the higher primary and early high school stages. One table provides an age and gender breakdown for African educational levels. In the fifteen to twenty-four age category, which records a total of 57,000 males and 54,000 females, over 17,000 males had no schooling at all, compared to only 7,000 females. Perhaps even more significantly, just over 19,000 males compared to almost 28,000 females had a Standard Five or higher qualification.[60] Fanyana Mazibuko argues that this was partly explained by the powerful counterattraction of gangs for boys. Outside of the school, the church and Christian youth clubs represented alternative points of social contact for girls. According to the 1960 census figures on African religious affiliation in Johannesburg, 16,500 males in the fifteen to twenty-four age category had "no religion" or no religious affiliation compared to only 4,500 women. The 1970 census data do not supply a Johannesburg breakdown, but nationwide "urban" figures suggest at least continuity in the relative apathy of young males towards religion.[61] Wayfarers, Sunbeams, and Girl Guides, according to one ex-Girl Guide from Moroka, had a real presence in the township, unlike the male equivalents such as the Boy Scouts.[62]

Two popular male subcultural styles could be identified in Soweto during the 1960s and, indeed, into the 1970s: "clevers" and "ivies." Gangsters were invariably "clevers" but non-gangsters often aspired to the same style. As I showed in chapter 3, the term "clever" can be traced back into the 1930s, predating even *tsotsi*, which emerged in the early 1940s. "Clevers" were streetwise city-slickers. They asserted an urbanness that defined insiders and outsiders according to dress, language, and style codes. The antithesis to "clever" was *moegoe*, a country bumpkin. The *tsotsi* style was initially a sub-"clever" style in the 1940s but eventually became almost synonymous with "clever" by the 1950s. The term *tsotsi* gradually developed a much clearer criminal connotation through time. Noncriminal youths who aspired to "cleverness" would have to acquire money either through formal or informal employment or belong to wealthier families. "Ivies" were clearly noncriminal and shied away from violence; they tended to be employed or better-off youths. They probably acquired their name from the exclusive American "Ivy League" image, which was transmitted to urban Africans via films and style magazines. "Ivies" wore a different cut of clothes from "clevers." Whereas the "clevers," modeling themselves on American gangster and hustler imagery, wore their pants resting on their hips, the "ivies" wore their pants above the belly-button. The "ivy" style was clean-cut and dandyish, even prissy; it would emphasize, for instance, particular makes of aftershave and deodorant. "Ivies" were heavily influenced by elite American fashion and saw themselves as more classy than "clevers." "Clevers," with their particular brand of urban machismo, generally regarded "ivies" as "good boys" and "sissies."[63] "Clever" and "ivy" were loose style categories that included both school and non-school youth.

Another notable division in Soweto youth identity that emerged strongly during the 1960s was between the so-called *ndofaya* and *kalkoen*. This division first emerged in the 1940s. The *ndofaya* were youths of Sophiatown/ Western Areas origin. They had grown up speaking a *tsotsitaal* based on Afrikaans, probably because they came from mixed African/colored residential areas. They called youths of Soweto origin *kalkoene* (meaning "turkeys" in Afrikaans), taunting them that they "spoke like turkeys." The *kalkoen tsotsitaal* was Zulu based and evolved into *scamtho*, the dominant street language in Soweto in the 1990s.[64] The term of derision was eventually adopted positively by the youths of Soweto origin themselves. The two groups had subtly discrete styles, which each portrayed as the authentic urban youth fashion. Former JNEAD social worker Seadom Tloteng recalls, for instance, that the *ndofaya* liked jazz music while the *kalkoene* liked *mbaqanga*, a hybrid musical style made up of traditional African and jazz rhythms. Competition was heightened following the Western Areas removals as the *ndofaya* were often resettled in the heart of *kalkoen* country, particularly in parts of Moroka and Mofolo.[65] Males were central in asserting *ndofaya* and *kalkoen* identities (which were to some extent sub-"clever" identities). Nevertheless, unlike "cleverness," these categories could include girls.

Soweto youth culture, from as early as the 1940s, emphasized urbanness and underplayed ethnic diversity. (I exclude here the specifically migrant and largely insulated youth groups such as the *amalaita*.) This "melting pot" effect was reinforced by the existence of *tsotsitaal*, a hybrid language that, although regionally diverse itself, was intelligible throughout Soweto. However, during the implementation of ethnic zoning in the 1960s, ethnic identity became increasingly noticeable in urban youth culture. Through ethnic zoning, many neighborhoods, and by extension local gangs, became ethnically uniform. Gang competition was highly localized, ensuring that *interethnic* youth conflict remained fairly rare. Nevertheless, there were certain zone border areas where gang and ethnic conflict began to overlap. For example, on the border between Zola, which was a predominantly Zulu area, and Naledi, which was a Sotho area, youths on either side of the dividing road identified themselves ethnically during the 1960s.[66] There is no evidence to suggest that ethnic cultural imagery penetrated gang style. Although ethnic zoning must have had an impact on youth self identity, the assertion of urban sophistication remained a priority.

CONFLICT AND SOLIDARITY

A Soweto male teenager could think of himself all at once as, say, a Green Beret gang member, an Orlando High School student, a Sotho, a "clever," and a *kalkoen*. These were all possible identities that could be drawn on according to time and circumstance. Specific moments of conflict, threat, and competition sharpened these identities. Gang, neighborhood, and school were crucial loci of potential protection and support.

Although gangs within a neighborhood competed locally, they also felt a neighborhood solidarity. When a threat arose from outside the neighborhood, local gangs would generally come together in support. In the 1960s and early 1970s, according to an Orlando resident, Thebo Mohapi, Orlando youths fought regularly with those from Meadowlands over access to a dam on the border of the two areas. Although there were internal tensions among Orlando gangs, the "kids from Meadowlands" were identified clearly as the rivals. Catapults ("catties") and stones were used in these heated fights. *Ndofaya* and *kalkoen* identities were activated here to reinforce neighborhood unity. Meadowlands was heavily occupied by ex-Western Areas residents. "They would call us *kalkoen* and we would call them *ndofaya*."[67] Similarly, neighborhood solidarity was evoked in the border wars between Zola and Naledi youth. In this instance, ethnicity reinforced oppositional identities since the two townships were zoned as Zulu and Sotho respectively. There were routine stone-throwing fights across the dividing road in the 1960s.[68]

As in the 1950s, gangs felt a protectiveness toward their own neighborhoods. Residents, unless they were themselves members of rival street gangs, rarely felt threatened by a local gang. There was protection in familiarity. It was almost unheard of for a gangster to mug a person he knew. If a gangster killed or mugged a local he would be socially ostracized by that community. Danger lay precisely in anonymity; "outsiders" were victimized.[69] Gang members generally robbed and mugged on trains or in areas where they were not known as individuals. A similar observation can be made, more cautiously, with regard to sexual harassment. The relationship between gangster and "moll" was itself infused with compulsion, but local women were nevertheless provided with a certain protection from outside harassment.[70] The victims of gang rape were almost invariably outsiders.[71] Some gangs ran informal protection rackets in their areas. It was extremely unusual to find a gang that would organize collections, but shebeen owners would be expected to give local gangs free drinks, and residents and shop-owners rarely refused to "lend" money to gangsters who asked for a "loan."[72]

Neighborhood association may have obscured the divisions between *local* school and non-school youth. Nevertheless, throughout the 1960s and early 1970s tension mounted between schools and gangs. Schoolgoers were subjected to constant harassment and robbery from gangs, generally coming from other neighborhoods. This often led to outbursts of violent conflict. Gangsters, most of whom had received some schooling before dropping out, felt a mix of resentment and scorn toward schoolchildren. They felt resentment because they were excluded from the education system. Yet they adhered to the scornful anti-education, anti-work ethic of the gang culture, which, it could be argued, was reinforced by that very exclusion.[73]

Although students were engaged in a variety of networks outside of school, high schools were enclosed worlds with their own routines and way of life. They provided students with a range of potential social activities beyond the purely academic. Whatever other affiliations they may have had, high school students developed an intense sense of loyalty and solidarity towards their schools. According to two former students of Morris Isaacson High School (MIHS) in Soweto, there were no significant social barriers at their school during the 1960s. For instance, the working-class students and the small fringe of middle-class students socialized and worked together. There was also no discernible ethnic tension. Their identities were solidified by the fact that they wore uniforms and spoke English relatively fluently.[74]

School identity was highlighted most sharply during moments of tension and conflict with youth gangs. Soweto's secondary schools came into direct conflict with gang notions of territoriality. Because of their scarcity these schools drew in students from a wide range of neighborhoods and provoked territorial antagonism.[75] Schoolgoers were easy targets for gangsters. Female students were particularly vulnerable on their way to and from school; these moments provided gangsters with opportunities for sexual harassment, abduction, and rape. When fellow students came under threat from gangs, high schools were quick to unite in defence, often organizing anti-gang reprisals. MIHS and Orlando High School (OHS) had long traditions of effective resistance to gang harassment. Headmasters and teachers supported and even actively cooperated with students in their resistance to gangs. By the late 1960s both schools had become "no-go zones" for the gangs.

From as early as 1959, MIHS conducted a successful "war" against the Apaches of Orlando.[76] Fanyana Mazibuko recalls that when he joined Morris Isaacson as a teacher in 1966 there was a "spirit of unity and mutual support in the school". By the late 1960s every *tsotsi* in the Jabavu area knew that "he had to leave town" if he meddled with students from MIHS, and *tsotsis* never dared to enter school property.[77] Orlando High had a similar history with gangs. In the early 1960s the school suffered harassment from the Apaches, the Berlins, and, most persistently, the Black Swines. After a "serious incident," the headmaster, T. W. Kambule called out every male student from class and told them that a group of Black Swines from Jabavu was causing trouble. He ordered the students to "bring every one of those boys" to his office. "It was the most dramatic day the school had ever had," Kambule recalls. The Black Swines were dragged to Kambule's office where he personally beat them severely with a *sjambok*. From then on anyone who interfered with an OHS student had to "answer to the whole school." "Here at Orlando," Kambule used to say, "we are one gang."[78] Curtis Nkondo, an ex-OHS teacher, makes the same point. When schoolgirls were molested or abducted, "that resulted in the schoolboys becoming very angry and going into the location hunting for these *tsotsis*."[79]

GANG CULTURE IN THE 1960s

Johannesburg's gang culture of the 1960s revealed obvious continuities with that of the previous decade. Male teenagers gathered at street corners and developed strong street-level loyalties; they continued to explore their sexuality and compete over local women and resources; their participation in crime and violence was, as before, differential and shaded. But there were also significant departures from the 1950s. First, style shifted substantially and, perhaps more importantly, there was generally less of an emphasis on style. Second, beyond the older core townships of Soweto, and with at least two important exceptions, gangs tended to be smaller and less distinctive. Both of these developments were intimately related to the spatial reorganization of African residential areas in the Johannesburg/Soweto complex during the latter half of the 1950s.

Although the term *tsotsi* remained in use, the old *tsotsi* style of the 1950s evaporated by the very early 1960s. It was not until the end of the 1960s that a new wave, a new genre, of gang style emerged in Soweto.[80] For most of the decade the youth gangs lacked noteworthy style; they concentrated their energies on territorial protection, group leisure activities, and crime.[81]

This hiatus in gang style was almost certainly a result of the Western Areas/ Sophiatown removals. Sophiatown in particular had been the style generator of the *tsotsi* era. Although largely squalid, Sophiatown had a cosmopolitan atmosphere with two cinemas and easy access to restaurants and nightclubs. It was close to the center of the city and bordered on colored and Asian residential areas. Colored culture, most notably in the development of *tsotsitaal*, influenced Sophiatown street life heavily.[82] The famous Sophiatown gangs, such as the Americans, Berlins, and Vultures, were dispersed by the removals. Separated from their traditional territories and scattered to distant corners of Meadowlands, Moroka, and Diepkloof, they failed to regroup.[83] Territory had been vital for gang identification, and personal ties were difficult to maintain in the vast commuter city of Soweto, with its transport arteries running into Johannesburg and providing few links within the townships themselves.

The territory-bound *tsotsi* gangs of Johannesburg were less resilient than the "family mafias" of Cape Town's District Six, which were able to withstand geographical dispersal during the 1970s through their strong familial ties.[84] The youth culture of Soweto in the early 1960s had lost its access to the cosmopolitan melting pot of Sophiatown and, with it, its most important subcultural role models. In Alexandra, the other key style-generating freehold township, the Spoilers and Msomis, two supergangs that had dominated the area throughout the second half of the 1950s, were crushed in massive police clampdowns at around the same time that the Western Areas removals were being completed.

As far as the size and distinctiveness of gangs were concerned, it has to be stressed that there was relative continuity in old Soweto compared to the new western townships and Resettlement Board areas. Although style did appear to dissipate in the old-established townships of Orlando, Jabavu, Mofolo, Moroka, and Pimville, several large, powerful gangs survived into the 1960s. In the other areas only two or three noteworthy gangs (including, it must be conceded, one of the most prominent of the era) emerged before the late 1960s. Clearly, residential continuity is essential in the formation of distinctive gangs with large territories and membership. Whereas small, nameless street-corner gangs developed fairly quickly, the major gangs took time to emerge; prestige was built gradually through street tradition, through the crucial intersection of territorial and personal familiarity.

BIG GANGS IN OLD SOWETO

From around 1957–1958 to the mid-1960s the Mofolo/Jabavu area was dominated by two major youth gangs: the Black Swines and the Pirates.

Although their territories expanded and contracted through time, a basic north–south divide persisted with the Black Swines to the north and the Pirates to the south. A bitter gang war, punctuated by occasional truces, raged between 1958 and 1965. Several members on both sides were killed during these years.[85] Rivalry between the two gangs seemed to hinge on access to women, who were considered to be territory bound.[86] The Swines and Pirates were also involved in gang fights and criminal activity in neighboring townships throughout the late 1950s and early 1960s.

Of the two gangs, the Black Swines was the bigger and more powerful. It also appears to have entered popular memory more widely. In the early 1960s it had between forty and sixty members, most of whom were teenagers. They tended to be school dropouts with at best Standard Two or Three qualifications. They were often seen hanging around the Mphahlele Store or roaming the streets in large numbers. They frequented one particular shebeen in White City where they used to force customers to buy them drinks. The Black Swines were a rather ragged bunch that did not dress with any flash or style, although they apparently all wore a distinctive earring in one ear and similar khaki trousers. Their first leader, Scumba, was about twenty years old in 1960; he alone wore a black leather jacket, which made him immediately recognizable. Until his death in 1961 he was clearly a figure of great authority in the gang.[87]

The Swines, who made regular forays into Orlando, Moroka, and Dobsonville, had a Soweto-wide reputation for violence, mugging, and sexual harassment.[88] As I showed earlier in this chapter, the gang was involved in several flare-ups with high school students in the area. In February 1963 *The World* reported on a Black Swine "reign of terror" in Jabavu. The gang attacked and robbed a number of residents in their own homes. Young women were "forcibly taken from their homes after their parents had been assaulted."[89] The Swines and the Pirates gradually disintegrated around 1966 as older members moved out of gang life and a number of more senior gangsters were arrested and given long jail sentences.[90] By 1966, Fanyana Mazibuko observes, the Black Swines and the Pirates were a "dying species."[91] At least four other gangs operated in the Central Soweto area during the early to mid-1960s. In Central Western Jabavu, the Top Eleven, which later became known as the Ganda Eleven, competed with the Green Berets; in Moroka, the Quarters Gang competed with the Young Apudis in the early 1960s.[92] For a visual representation, see Map 5.2.

According to *The World*, Orlando, and particularly Orlando East, had been a major gang battlefield in the late 1950s. The newspaper claimed in 1959 that there were at least ten "child gangs" with huge memberships in Orlando East.[93] Two noteworthy gangs, the Apaches and the

Map 5.2 Soweto Ganglands, 1958–1967
Note: territorial boundaries are no more than rough estimates

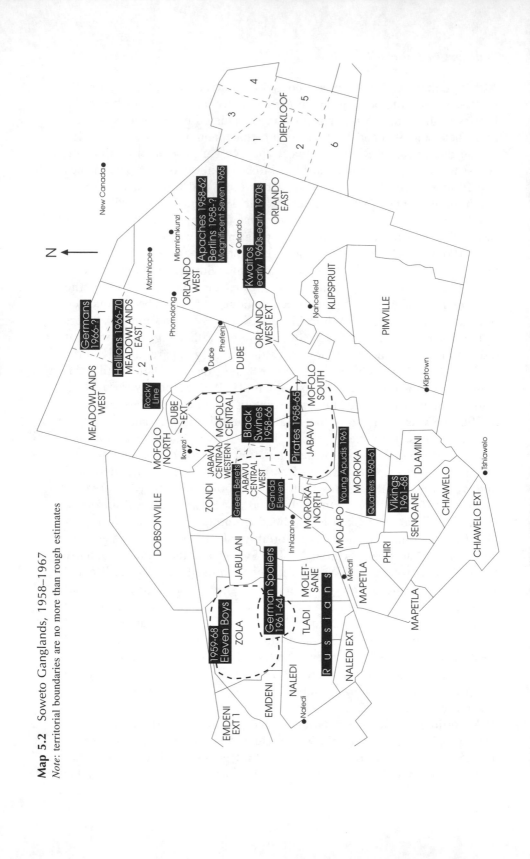

Berlins, survived from the late 1950s into the early 1960s. The Apaches and the Berlins fought a fierce territorial war in December 1958 in which four died.[94] Like the Black Swines, the gangs had a reputation for harassing schoolgirls, and both were targeted in school reprisals.[95] During the post-Sharpeville unrest of March 1960 the Apaches were amongst the gangs prominently involved in looting and spontaneous political intimidation.[96] In August 1962, after a series of gang killings, police arrested sixty-six Apaches in a massive swoop that, it would appear, broke the back of the gang since it never again received attention in the media or elsewhere.[97]

Around the time the Apaches went into decline, a new power, the Kwaitos, emerged in Orlando. I have found no conclusive explanation for the origin of the word "Kwaito." It is possible that it is a compound of two Afrikaans words: *kwaai*, meaning "angry" or "fierce," and *ou*, meaning "guy." It may also conceivably have been derived from the 1957 war film, *Bridge on the River Kwai*. There were about twenty core members of the gang, ranging in age between sixteen and the late twenties. They were armed with stones, "catties," and knives. Snuki Zikalala, who went to school in neighboring Diepkloof during the 1960s, recalls that the gang was particularly brutal. Its members continuously harassed schoolgirls, teachers, and elderly people and stole paypackets on Fridays. The Kwaitos were very protective over their particular home territory in Orlando; residents from that neighborhood never felt threatened by the gang. "It was something like an inheritance from that area . . . if a young person came from that area he used to idolise the MaKwaitos." Unlike most gangs, which, as peer group phenomena, tended to disappear when the founder members received long jail sentences or decided to go straight, the Kwaitos had a generational turnover of membership. There was ongoing recruitment and when older members left the gang, younger members moved into leadership positions.[98] This probably explains the longevity of the Kwaitos, which continued to be a force in Orlando well into the early 1970s.[99]

BIG GANGS IN NEW SOWETO

The contrast between old and new Soweto gang culture was most striking in Meadowlands and Diepkloof, the areas under Resettlement Board control. As dispersed communities from the old freehold areas resettled, there was a clear time lag in the emergence of prominent youth gangs. Although there were numerous small gangs and street-corner networks with as few as three or four members, virtually no distinctive gangs emerged in Meadowlands or Diepkloof until about 1966.[100] From the late 1960s, Meadowlands became something of a gang hotspot dominated by a powerful group called the Hong Kongs. Distinctive gangs also started to emerge in Diepkloof toward the end of the decade.

The pattern in the new western townships was rather different. Zola in particular quickly developed a reputation for crime. From as early as June 1959 it was reported that five different gangs, responsible for an "outbreak of assaults, robbery, housebreaking and rapes," were operating in Zola, although no specific names had yet come to the fore.[101] During 1961, three major gangs operating in the west and southwestern areas began to receive widespread attention: the Eleven Boys, the German Spoilers, and the Vikings.[102] Throughout the early 1960s there was continuous warfare between these three gangs in a wide arc stretching from Zola and Moletsane to Phiri, Dlamini, and even Pimville.[103] The Eleven Boys and the German Spoilers both came from Zola; the former gang had its heartland in Zone One while the latter was based in the south, taking in a part of northern Tladi. The Vikings came from Senaoane and Dlamini. The Eleven Boys were the largest and most feared of the gangs; although based in Zola, they seemed intent on dominating the whole western flank of Soweto in the early 1960s. According to local Senaoane residents, the Vikings developed as a defensive response "to fight off the menace" of the Eleven Boys. The two gangs battled for several weeks at the beginning of 1961 as the Eleven Boys tried to assert themselves in distant Senaoane.[104]

Meanwhile, in Zola itself, the Eleven Boys and the German Spoilers struggled for local supremacy. The war spanned several years and involved a number of deaths. It was during this period that Zola acquired several evocative nicknames, such as "Viet Nam," "Slagspaal" ("abattoir"), and "Kwa Mshay' Azafe" ("hit him until he dies").[105] On at least two occasions, in mid-1961 and in early 1963, Zola advisory boardmen in collaboration with the Juvenile Employment Section attempted to broker a peace between the war-weary youths. Brief truces were achieved and some gangsters found jobs, but there was no lasting peace.[106] Despite the energy-sapping internal war, both gangs were active in other areas of Soweto.[107] The Eleven Boys were also involved in ongoing clashes with the Black Swines in Mofolo/Jabavu.[108] After 1963 the gangs made very little news, suggesting a substantial decline in their power, probably as a result of an effective local civil guard initiative. Nevertheless, the Eleven Boys gang did not disappear entirely until its leader was killed by a rival gang in 1968.[109]

The Eleven Boys and German Spoilers were never to penetrate substantially southwards into Naledi, most of Tladi, and Moletsane, Mapetla, and Molapo because these were virtually homogeneous Sotho-speaking areas dominated by the powerful Sotho ethnic association, the Russians. The "Ama

Rashea," as they were also known, were older men who moved in large armed groups and had a long history of conducting fierce reprisals in response to *tsotsi* harassment.[110] This may explain why the Eleven Boys made forays into relatively distant townships such as Phiri and Senaoane rather than concentrating on neighboring areas. The German Spoilers did, surprisingly, manage to establish a foothold in the northern reaches of Tladi. Largely a defensive gang, the Spoilers were perhaps tolerated locally as long as they avoided criminal activity in Tladi itself. In this area the Russians treated the Eleven Boys as invaders and indirectly provided the Spoilers with protection.[111]

Little is known about the origins of the Eleven Boys. Although the gang achieved widespread fame only in the early 1960s, it is likely that it was founded in 1958 or 1959. There is some evidence that personal connections had already been established prior to resettlement in Zola. A resident of southwestern Soweto, who came into contact with the Eleven Boys as a teenager, suggests that the gang was started by a core group of boys who knew each other, initially from Evaton and then from the Moroka shelters, and later joined together for support when their families moved to formal housing in unfamiliar Zola.[112] At a trial of gang members in October 1962, one witness claimed that the gang started out as a soccer team based in Moroka before the youths moved to Zola.[113] This evidence, although based on two rather disparate sources, is reasonably convincing, first, because of the consistency of Moroka in both accounts and, second, because the name of the gang suggests soccer origins. In the early 1960s the gang consisted of between thirty and fifty unemployed youths ranging in age from fifteen to twenty. Like the Black Swines, they apparently wore an easily identifiable earring in one ear and walked in a distinctive manner. They were famous throughout the new western townships and beyond, for being skilled with knives and "never running away from a fight."[114]

The Vikings were famous in the southwestern areas of Soweto in the early 1960s. As I pointed out earlier, they apparently came together in 1960 or 1961, initially in response to Eleven Boys' aggression in their neighborhood. In May 1961 eight gang members, all eighteen-year-olds, with nicknames such as "Chopper," "Bible," and "Twins," stood trial for the murder of a Senaoane municipal policeman. The "blackjack" was allegedly killed by the youths with choppers after he had confronted them over a bicycle theft. The gang, described as being about fifty strong, met regularly on a field in Senaoane and was familiar to local residents. The gang was also apparently known as "King Vice" or "Vice Kings," probably a wordplay on "Vikings."[115] The Vikings reemerged in the news in June 1965, tangling with the Black Swines and Pirates at the Jabavu/Mofolo crossroads, and they apparently maintained a presence in the area until as late as 1968.[116]

While youth gangs and juvenile crime continued to be a major social issue in the 1960s, removals and relocations brought about significant shifts in male youth culture in the townships of Soweto. First, the destruction of Sophiatown/Western Areas left old central Soweto (particularly Orlando) as the center of urban sophistication and style. The Orlando, or *kalkoen*, tradition became dominant in the 1960s and 1970s. For example, Afrikaans gradually gave way to Zulu in the composition of *tsotsitaal*, and *mbaqanga* pushed the more American style of jazz to the margins. Second, gangs generally put less emphasis on style during the 1960s. As I argued earlier, this was almost certainly a consequence of Sophiatown's destruction and the scattering of famous role model gangs. Third, gang formation followed distinctly different patterns in old and new Soweto. While there was substantial continuity in old Soweto, it took a few years before big gangs became the norm in the new townships. This is explained by the disruption of established street networks.

Why, then, did prominent gangs emerge earlier in the "Wild West" than in the Resettlement Board townships? After all, both areas were settled more or less simultaneously. Broadly speaking, the communities of the new western townships were more homogeneous than those of Meadowlands and Diepkloof. From the mid-1950s to the early 1960s, families moved into Meadowlands and Diepkloof in "dribs and drabs," to use the term of a Diepkloof resident.[117] Communities did not move en masse. They came from Sophiatown, West Native Township, the "removed" parts of Alexandra, and other places with an assortment of ethnic and linguistic backgrounds. There were no obvious established social links; these had to be remolded almost from scratch.

In the new western neighborhoods, by contrast, communities were resettled in a more systematic fashion and appear to have retained many of their previous squatter contacts and social networks. Homogeneity may also have been reinforced by the ethnic zoning policy, which, although splitting some squatter communities, probably facilitated the formation of new community solidarities. Ethnic identity was more important for squatter communities, which were relatively recently urbanized, than for ex-Western Areas communities with their established urban traditions. Whereas ex-Western Areas groups relied heavily on networks forged in the city, ethnicity and common links to parts of the countryside remained a crucial source of identification for ex-squatters. The emergence of the Eleven Boys gang itself was important in triggering gang formation. It may have been a historical accident that the gang emerged in Zola so early in the new township's life, or the gang may indeed have had its origins in the Moroka shelters. One way or another, the assertive and territorially expansionist Eleven Boys encouraged a defensive concentration of power in other areas. In Meadowlands and Diepkloof there was little pressure to concentrate strength; street networks remained small, non-distinctive, and fractured because they were under no immediate territorial threat.

NOTES

1. South African Institute of Race Relations, *A Survey of Race Relations in South Africa (SRRSA)*, Johannesburg, 1969, p. 81.

2. D. Posel, *The Making of Apartheid 1948–1961: Conflict and Compromise*, Oxford, 1991, p. 249.

3. Jill Nattrass, *The South African Economy: Its Growth and Change*, Cape Town, 1981, p. 165. Nattrass does not supply a figure for 1960, but it is safe to assume that the numbers in manufacturing employment accelerated in the 1962–1970 period.

4. See Nattrass, *The South African Economy*, p. 189; and *SRRSA* 1968, p. 85.

5. I have deliberately flattened out some of the subtleties in National Party factional politics. Within the politics of ethnic self-determination, an important rift existed between the "visionaries" and the Verwoerdians, who emphasized practical political security. According to Lazar and Posel, the idealists called for total segregation with a gradual reversal of white dependence on African labor; they wanted to pump substantial resources into the homelands in the hope of making them viable political entities with complete political autonomy. The Verwoerdians were basically concerned to tighten up influx control with the ideological underpinning of ethnic self-determination. See John Lazar, "Conformity and Conflict: Afrikaner Nationalist Politics, 1948–1961," D. Phil. thesis, Oxford University, 1987; and Posel, *The Making of Apartheid*, pp. 241–243.

6. Posel, *The Making of Apartheid*, pp. 234–235.

7. During August 1961, for instance, it was announced that Johannesburg entry permits were being temporarily suspended because there was a "surplus" of African labor in the area (*SRRSA* 1961, pp. 128–129).

8. See J. Hyslop, "Social Conflicts over African Education in South Africa from the 1940s to 1976," Ph.D. thesis, University of the Witwatersrand, 1990, pp. 338–339.

9. P. J. Riekert, *Report of the Commission of Inquiry into Legislation Affecting the Utilisation of Manpower (Excluding the Legislation Administered by the Departments of Labour and Mines)*, Pretoria, 1979, RP 32/1979, p. 60.

10. Black Sash Collection, Historical Papers Library, University of the Witwatersrand, Johannesburg, AE 862, Johannesburg Advice Office: Annual Report 1964–1965; Report for November 1968 and Report for July 1969.

11. Interviews: Tloteng, Ngobese, Mtshali, Maseko, Simelane (a), Kheswa, Sirurufera, Zwane.

12. *SRRSA* 1969, p. 81.

13. See chapter 2 for a discussion of youth unemployment in the 1950s.

14. S. Bekker and R. Humphries, *From Control to Confusion: The Changing Role of Administration Boards in South Africa, 1971–1983*, Petermarizburg, 1985, pp. 7–8; interviews: Carr (a), McMurchie.

15. See, for example, Black Sash AE 862, Advice Office reports, December 1967, November 1968, July 1969, November 1969.

16. See *Post*, 14 January 1968, "Dead-End Jobs—Dead-End Kids," by Mike Ndlazi. In his feature on unemployment, Ndlazi reveals that 11,695 boys between sixteen and eighteen years old reported to the Johannesburg NEAD's juvenile employment section seeking employment during 1967. Only 2,189 could be placed in jobs. The total African male population between fourteen and eighteen years old was 23,400 in 1961, according to the Botha Commission (M. C. Botha, *Verslag van die interdepartementele Komitee insake ledige en nie-werkende Bantu in Stedeleike Gebiede* [Report of the Interdepartmental Committee into Idle and Unemployed Bantu in the Urban Areas], Pretoria, 1962). The total number of African male sixteen- to eighteen-year-olds was therefore unlikely to be more than 15,000. Even if the total population increased substantially over the next six years, the figure of 11,695 is astonishingly high. Official statistics were never completely reliable, but if we accept that numerous unemployed youths failed to register with the labor bureau, unemployment was likely to have been even more serious than reported in this age/gender bracket.

17. J. Hyslop, "State Education Policy and the Social Reproduction of the Urban African Working Class: The Case of the Southern Transvaal 1955–1976," *Journal of Southern African Studies*, 14, 3, April 1988, p. 451.

18. Hyslop, "State Education Policy," p. 450; see also J. Hyslop, "'A Destruction Coming in': Bantu Education as Response to Social Crisis," in P. Bonner, P. Delius, and D. Posel (eds.), *Apartheid's Genesis 1935–1962*, Johannesburg, 1993.

19. *Bantu Education Journal*, December 1974, p. 39.

20. *SRRSA* 1961, p. 230.

21. Hyslop, "State Education Policy," p. 454.

22. See Hyslop, "State Education Policy," pp. 454–455; and Hyslop, "Social Conflict," pp. 338–343.

23. *SRRSA* 1965, p. 248, and *SRRSA* 1966, pp. 236–237; see also Hyslop, "Social Conflict," p. 341.

24. For a detailed study of the key Soweto high schools during the 1960s, see Clive Glaser, "Youth Culture and Politics in Soweto, 1958–1976," Ph.D. thesis, Cambridge University, England, 1994, chapter 6.

25. Interviews: Carr (a) and (b). Carr made this point repeatedly.

26. Interview, Carr (b).

27. Posel, *The Making of Apartheid*, pp. 252–253. See also Kane-Berman, *Soweto: Black Revolt, White Reaction*, Johannesburg, 1978, pp. 78–79; and Hyslop, "Social Conflicts," pp. 338–340. Charles Simkins, *Four Essays on the Past, Present and Possible Future Distribution of the Black Population of South Africa*, Cape Town, 1983, p. 62, also points to a net decline in the number of Africans in the urban areas during the 1960s.

28. See Hyslop, "Social Conflict," p. 338, p. 340, and p. 345.

29. For a more detailed discussion on crime rates in Soweto in the 1960s see Glaser, "Youth Culture and Politics," pp. 158–162.

30. See *The Star*, 22 November 1960, "Rand Police Clamp Down on Vagrants"; *The Star*, 29 November 1960; and the *Rand Daily Mail* (*RDM*), 17 April 1967, editorial.

31. See Posel, *The Making of Apartheid*, for a fuller discussion of this issue.

32. See, for example, the argument in the Botha Commission report of 1962, par. 74, 82–83; and West Rand Administration Board Archive, Intermediary Archive Depot,

Johannesburg, (IAD WRAB) 401/44/20, extract from minutes of meeting of the United Municipal Executive of SA, 20/21 February 1962. See also the comments of Colonel H. D. Botha of the Newlands Police Station in the *Post*, 24 July 1966.

33. *The Star*, 13 July 1972, "Violence in Soweto."

34. See IAD WRAB N9 vol. 1, minutes of Jabavu AB meeting, 17 November 1962; IAD WRAB N9/4, letter from Dube Residents' Committee, UBC General Purposes and Housing Committee, UBC 95/1971. In 1972, a prominent Soweto businessman and councillor, Richard Maponya, complained that the SAP very rarely came to the scene of a crime in Soweto; see IAD WRAB N9 vol. 3, minutes of meeting of the Liaison Committee on Crime, 18 May 1972.

35. For a detailed discussion on local government initiatives, see Glaser, "Youth Culture and Politics," pp. 175–183.

36. For a more systematic account of civil guards, see Glaser, "Youth Culture and Politics," pp. 183–195.

37. Interview, Maponya.

38. See P. Bonner, "The Politics of the Black Squatter Movements on the Rand 1944–1952," *Radical History Review*, 46/47, 1990, pp. 89–115; A. Stadler, "Birds in the Cornfield: Squatter Movements in Johannesburg 1944–1947," in B. Bozzoli (ed.), *Labour, Townships and Protest*, Johannesburg, 1979; K. French, "James Mpanza and the Sofasonke Party in the Development of Local Politics in Soweto," M.A. thesis, University of the Witwatersrand, 1983.

39. Kane-Berman, *Soweto*, p. 58.

40. W. J. Carr, *Soweto: Its Creation, Life and Decline*, Johannesburg, 1990, p. 128; Kane-Berman, *Soweto*, pp. 58–59. The Anglo-American loan was, of course, not the only source of capital for housing projects. State housing loans, approved in the mid-1950s, provided the bulk of capital. However, the state financing, in itself, was insufficient for projected housing development. See R. B. Lewis, "A 'City' within a City— The Creation of Soweto," *South African Geographical Journal*, 48, December 1966, pp. 72–75, for a full breakdown of housing income and expenditure.

41. Kane-Berman, *Soweto*, p. 59.

42. See Johannesburg Non-European Affairs Department Annual Reports, 1958–1972, Municipal Reference Library, Johannesburg (MRL JNEAD), Annual Report, Manager NEAD, year ending 30 June 1966, Schedule B: "Houses per Location."

43. See G. G. Mashile and G. H. Pirie, "Aspects of Housing Allocation in Soweto," *South African Geographical Journal*, 59, 2, September 1977, particularly pp. 142–144. By 1973 the dominant ethnic group represented between 86 percent and 97 percent of the residents in each of the ethnically reserved areas.

44. MRL JNEAD, Annual Report, Manager NEAD, year ending 30 June 1966.

45. Lewis, "A 'City' within a City," pp. 58–59.

46. MRL JNEAD, Annual Report, Manager JNEAD, year ending 30 June 1966. There were 63,868 houses outside of the Resettlement Board areas.

47. Interviews: Mofokeng, Lebelo, Nkondo, Ngobese.

48. Interview, Seth Mazibuko (HWSFP).

49. Interviews: Seth Mazibuko (HWSFP), Makhabela (HWSFP).

50. Interview, Radebe.

51. Interview, Shubane.

52. Interviews: Shubane, Seathlolo, Morobe (HWSFP), Mohapi (HWSFP).

53. See also interview, Mike Siluma; he also talks of a territorial "ganging together."

54. Interviews: Kambule, F. Mazibuko, Msimanga, Motaung; see also interviews, Nkondo, Siluma, Duma, Tloteng.

55. Interview: F. Mazibuko; a point echoed by Nkondo, in an interview.

56. Interviews: Mokgotsi, "Sister Grace," F. Mazibuko, Motaung; see chapter 3 for a discussion on *tsotsi* attitudes to school and work.

57. See Clive Glaser, "Mark of Zorro: Sexuality and Gender Relations in the Tsotsi Youth Gang Subculture on the Witwatersrand," *African Studies*, 51, 1, 1992, which examines the construction of masculinity in the *tsotsi* subculture in the 1940s and 1950s.

58. Interviews: F. Mazibuko, Motaung, Msimanga, Modise, Khoza, and S. Mbuli.

59. Interview, Kambule.

60. Central Statistics Service, *Population Census*, 6 September 1960, vol. 7, "Educational levels, Africans, Johannesburg." Figures are rounded off. Unfortunately, there were no similar age breakdowns in the 1970 census figures. See also *SRRSA* 1961, p. 229. Kambule, in an interview, recalls that well over half of the students at Orlando High School were girls by the mid-1960s, a reversal of the situation in the 1950s.

61. Central Statistics Service, *Population Census*, 6 September 1960, Report on the Metropolitan Area of Johannesburg, vol. 2, 9, "Bantu: Religion by Age." Figures here are rounded off. For 1970 figures, see Central Statistics Service, *Population Census* 1970, Report No 02-05-03, "Religious Breakdown by Age (SA: urban)."

62. Interview, Mrs. Dlamini.

63. Interviews: Seth Mazibuko (HWSFP), Tshabalala (HWSFP), L. Nkosi. See also Helen Lunn, "Antecedents of the Music and Popular Culture of the African post-1976 Generation," M.A. thesis, University of the Witwatersrand, 1986, pp. 130–131 and pp. 162–163.

64. For some insights into *scamtho*, see K. D. Ntshangase, "Towards an Understanding of Urban Linguistic Varieties: The Case of Iscamtho in Soweto," paper presented to the Department of African Languages Seminar, University of the Witwatersrand, 6 May 1992.

65. Interviews: Mrs. Dlamini, Tloteng, Sirurufera.

66. Interview, Makhabela (HWSFP). Similarly, Linda Maseko recalls that, in the early 1970s, when distinctive gangs eventually emerged in Diepkloof, which was divided into ethnic zones, the gangs could be identified ethnically. The Biafras of Zone Six were "Sotho" and the Mongols of Zone Three were "Shangaan." These gangs will receive attention again in chapter 10.

67. Interview, Mohapi (HWSFP); see also interview, Whitey Khanyeza (HWSFP); this informant talks about the danger of crossing the territorial divide between Orlando East and Mzimhlophe.

68. Interview, Makhabela (HWSFP).

69. Interviews: Mofokeng, Siluma, Simelane, Dennis Nkosi, Tsidi Nkosi.

70. See discussion of this issue in Glaser, "Mark of Zorro."

71. Interviews: S. Khumalo, Gibi.

72. Interviews: S. Khumalo, Ndlovu, Nzimande.

73. Interviews: Kambule, Nkondo.

74. Interviews: Mxadana, Buthelezi; I have drawn also on general observations by Kambule, Mazibuko, Nkondo, and Msimanga.

75. See discussion on school–gang antagonism in chapter 7.

76. Interview, Thape.

77. Interviews: F. Mazibuko, Mxadana.

78. Interview, Kambule (b). The Black Swines were also involved in violent clashes with students from the Orlando Vocational Training Centre in 1958 and with students from a Moroka primary school in the early 1960s. See *The World*, 13 December 1958; interview, Mrs. Dlamini.

79. Interview, Nkondo. Musi High School in Pimville also experienced gang harassment in the early 1960s. There was apparently "constant trouble between boys in the street and school boys" during 1961. I have no further data on this point of conflict. See IAD WRAB 351/2, extract from Pimville AB meeting, 12 August 1961.

80. This will be the focus of chapter 6.

81. Interviews: Mattera (b), Moloi, Motjuwadi, Thwala, Magubane, Norris Nkosi, and Msimanga. See also *RDM*, 18 December 1967 and 20 December 1967, "The Bloodiest Place on Earth," and "The Big Gangs Have Lost Their Glamour," features on Soweto crime by Michael Cobden; *The World*, 12 May 1967, letter from Bert C. Selope of Diepkloof; Lunn, "Antecedents," pp. 124–125. In chapter 6, I stress that youth crime remained as serious a problem as ever in both new and old Soweto. The relative absence of style and famous gangs did not indicate a lull in crime. In fact, it could be argued that the very anonymity of the 1960s gangs made them more frightening to local residents.

82. See *The Star*, 22 February 1962, "A New Language Is Being Forged in the Townships," for some interesting insights on colored influences.

83. Interviews. Magubane, Mattera (b).

84. See Don Pinnock, *The Brotherhoods: Street Gangs and State Controls in Cape Town*, Cape Town, 1987, pp. 5–11.

85. *The World*, 23 July 1958, 25 June 1959, 18 June 1960, 22 June 1960, 9 July 1960, 10 June 1965; *The Star*, 16 June 1960; *RDM*, 17 June 1960; Jean McMurchie Collection, private papers, Johannesburg (JMC), 1960 press cuttings. See also interview with Thwala, who remembers ongoing war between the Pirates and Black Swines during the early 1960s.

86. Interview, Thwala.

87. Interviews: McMurchie, Kambule, Dlamini, Khumalo.

88. Interview, Makgene; *The World*, 15 April 1965 and 20 August 1967.

89. *The World*, 5 February 1963. See also *Golden City Post* (*GCP*), 26 November 1961, which reports on a Black Swine assault in West Native Township.

90. Interviews: F. Mazibuko, Thwala, Mbawu, and Ngwenya.

91. Interview, F. Mazibuko.

92. See interview, Radebe; *RDM*, 17 June 1960; and *The World*, 18 February 1961.

93. *The World*, 13 June 1959 and 1 August 1959.

94. *The World*, 13 December 1958.

95. *The World*, 27 September 1958; interviews: Thape, Kambule.

96. *The World*, 9 April 1960. See chapter 4 on gang involvement during the post-Sharpeville unrest.

97. *The World*, 19 August 1962. The newspaper reported "the quietest weekend in the township's history" following the arrests.

98. Interview, Zikalala. See also interview, Thape.

99. The Kwaitos receive further attention in chapter 6, focusing on the wave of gangsterism that started in the late 1960s. Some of the famous Sophiatown and Alexandra

gangs from the 1940s and 1950s, such as the Black Caps, Americans, Berlins, and Spoilers, also seem to have been cross-generational, with organized "youth wings." According to an ex-Diepkloof resident, Steve Lebelo (interview), another Orlando gang called the Germans also emerged in the late 1950s and remained prominent well into the following decade. This gang controlled a territory that became known as "Germany." During the mid-1960s, following the demise of the Apaches and Berlins and prior to the rise of new gangs in the late 1960s, only one other gang was noticed by the media, a group known as the Magnificent Seven. In August 1965, members of this gang were reported to be "on the rampage" in Orlando; they raided the homes of two businessmen after smashing down their doors with choppers. See *The World*, 24 August 1965.

100. Interviews: Mattera (b), Magubane, Lebelo, Kheswa, Mhlambi, Moloantwa. I have only one reference to a gang in either township prior to 1966: a group called the Rocky Line Gang was active in 1963. See *The World*, 7 May 1963. In 1963, two gangs made their mark more or less simultaneously in Meadowlands: the Germans of Zone One and the Hellions of neighboring Zone Two. A gang war, which police claimed was behind the killing of three local teenagers, broke out between the Germans and the Hellions in December 1966 over access to local girls. See the *Post*, 4 and 25 December 1966.

101. *The World*, 11 June 1959. See also interview, Nhlapho.

102. Both "Spoilers" and "Vikings" were names used by prominent gangs of the 1950s. Either the 1960s gangs drew on similar imagery for their names or they were deliberately evoking Johannesburg gang tradition itself. There was also a powerful 1960s colored gang in West Native Township known as the Vikings. The 1960 gangs had no apparent connections with the 1950s Spoilers or Vikings.

103. IAD WRAB 285/7, letter from the Juvenile Employment Officer to the Manager, NEAD, Johannesburg, 24 May 1961; *The World*, 18 March 1961; *RDM*, 9 June 1961; *The Star*, 5 July 1961.

104. *The World*, 18 March 1961

105. Lunn, "Antecedents," p. 124. There is one reference to a gang called the Young Italians, which also operated in Zola in the early 1960s, but it seems to have kept clear of the gang war. See *GCP*, May 1961.

106. Interview, Tloteng; *RDM*, 9 June 1961; *The Star*, 5 July 1961; *The World*, 24 October 1962 and 20 December 1962; IAD WRAB N9 (vol. 1), extracts from minutes of Southwestern Bantu Townships AB meeting, 17 January 1963.

107. In February 1963 the Eleven Boys were involved in skirmishes with taximen operating in Zola and Phiri, who had been robbed and harassed by the gang; in July 1963 the German Spoilers assaulted and robbed passengers on a Dube-bound train, killing three and injuring several others. See *The World*, 4 February and 29 July 1963.

108. *The World*, 17 April 1963; interviews, Sister Grace, Makgene.

109. Lunn, "Antecedents," p. 124; interview, Sister Grace.

110. There are dozens of references to Russian activity in the Naledi/Tladi area throughout the 1960s in *The World* and the *Post*. For an analysis and map of ethnic zoning in Soweto, see Mashile and Pirie, "Aspects of Housing Allocation in Soweto." For a detailed study of the Russians, see Phillip Bonner, "The Russians on the Reef, 1947–1957: Urbanisation, Gang Warfare and Ethnic Mobilisation," in P. Bonner, P. Delius, and D. Posel, *Apartheid's Genesis*, Johannesburg, 1987.

111. *The World*, 4 February 1963.

112. Interview, L. Nkosi.

113. *The World*, 24 October 1962.

114. *The World*, 20 December 1962; interviews: Tloteng, T. Nkosi, Sister Grace.

115. Criminal Cases of the Witwatersrand Legal Division (WLD), Central Archives Depot, Pretoria, 570/61, Mbele and seven others, 16 May 1961.

116. *The World*, 10 June 1963. In 1969 seventeen youths between sixteen and eigh teen years old stood trial for a series of robberies, assaults, and rapes committed in the Phiri area during 1968. According to witnesses, they were all members of the Vikings. The age of the accused suggests that this was either an entirely new gang that named itself after famous predecessors or, more probably, like the Kwaitos of Orlando, that persisted through generational turnover. See WLD 248/69, Leburu and sixteen others, 11 August 1969.

117. Interview, Lebelo.

6

THE TIME OF THE HAZELS: THE NEW WAVE OF BIG GANGS IN SOWETO, 1968–1976

Towards the end of the 1960s there was a striking resurgence of big gang culture in Soweto. During the mid 1960s it was possible to identify perhaps ten distinctive youth gangs in the Soweto area; by the early 1970s there were well over fifty.[1] (See gangland maps in chapter 5 and in this chapter [Map 6.1] for a comparative overview of the identifiable gangs in the two eras.) Moreover, gangs became more style conscious and more ambitious in establishing name and fame. At the epicenter of this new gang wave were the Hazels of Mzimhlophe, the most feared and the most admired of the Soweto gangs in the 1970s.

This chapter begins by looking at some of the socioeconomic developments in South Africa and Soweto during the late 1960s and early 1970s that help to contextualize the new gang wave. It then moves to a discussion of the general features of youth gangsterism during this phase, followed by a detailed description of the Hazels gang. The final section deals with older-generation responses to youth gangs.

ECONOMIC DOWNTURN AND "MULTINATIONALISM"

After achieving an average per annum GDP growth rate of almost 6 percent throughout the 1960s, the South African economy stuttered in the early 1970s. Average GDP growth for 1971–1973 tailed off to around 4 percent and then slumped to 2.2 percent in 1975 and 1.5 percent in 1976.[2] With an annual population growth of 3 percent and 200,000 new jobseekers entering

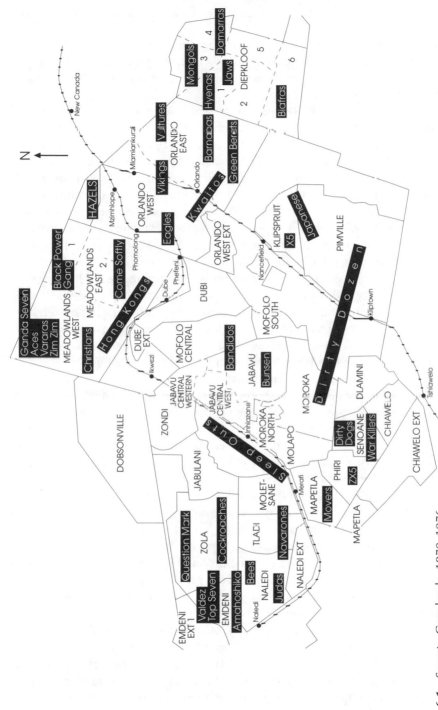

Map 6.1 Soweto Ganglands, 1970–1976

the job market each year, the country required a growth rate of between 4 and 6 percent to maintain existing levels of employment and per capita income; as Kane-Berman and others pointed out, a high growth rate was a necessity rather than a luxury.[3]

By the end of the 1960s the South African economy ran into structural difficulties. A critical skilled labor shortage constrained the capacity for economic growth. Whereas in the first half of the 1960s the white population, boosted by immigration, was able to satisfy the demand for essential semi-skilled, technical, clerical, and managerial posts, by the end of the decade the economy had grown too rapidly to rely exclusively on white skilled labor.[4] Simultaneously, the South African manufacturing sector found that, in order to remain viable, it required greater markets than the local economy could provide. Access to other African markets was severely restricted because of political hostility to apartheid. In order to compete on wider international markets, South African manufacturing required much higher levels of productivity and, therefore, a more skilled workforce.[5]

The logic of the apartheid economy, then, began to turn in on itself. The very elements that had made such high growth possible in the 1960s were exposed as the economy's greatest weaknesses by the end of the decade. A vast, cheap, unskilled labor force, subdued and controlled under repressive conditions, had nourished local industry and encouraged foreign investment. By the end of the decade, the shortage of skills impeded growth and productivity, while low wages restricted the potential local consumer market. Moreover, the apartheid system was becoming a political embarrassment, particularly in the context of a decolonized Africa, and South Africa faced increasing international hostility, which had obvious implications for foreign markets and investment.

Around 1973–1974, foreign as well as local investment in manufacturing went into decline. This was partly a result of a worldwide recession and partly a response to the wave of labor unrest centered on Durban in late 1972 and, even more significantly, between March and December 1973. Investors began to sense the vulnerability and instability of the South African economy.[6] It was only the high gold price that kept the economy relatively stable until 1974. When the gold price fell in 1975 the economy was plunged into deep recession.[7]

From 1968 to 1971 an unresolved factional struggle took place within the National Party between the hardline conservative *verkramptes* and the somewhat more forward-looking *verligtes*. Initially, Vorster himself wavered between the two factions. By late 1971, however, in a climate of post-boom economic uncertainty and deepening international isolation, Vorster moved closer to the *verligte* camp.[8] Government policy became more pragmatic; it accepted the economic need for a stable urban African working class and for the relaxation of the skills color bar. A new ideological formulation called "multinationalism" superseded the rigid Verwoerdian doctrine. "Multinationalism" continued to emphasize ethnic difference "but maintained that once the identities of the various black and white 'nations' of SA were securely established, they could mix and cooperate with each other as they did with other nations."[9]

By 1971 the government came under a great deal of pressure from the manufacturing sector to counteract the skilled labor shortage.[10] Despite heavy opposition from white trade unions, Vorster committed himself to allowing urban blacks into skilled and supervisory positions as well as to narrowing the wage gap between whites and blacks.[11] Logically, the government also accepted the need to improve education and training facilities for urban blacks. Crucially, it allowed the expansion of African secondary schooling in urban areas, a development that will receive more attention in chapter 7.

The creation of new skilled job opportunities, coupled with a general improvement in African wages following the nationwide strike wave of 1973, brought relative prosperity to many urban families.[12] Rising unemployment, however, brought new hardships to other families, which had to stretch already overextended incomes even further to support more people. Widening wealth disparities exacerbated the township crime problem. While the pickings in the ghetto became richer, more people were thrown into poverty. Though unemployment also affected older working class people during the economic downturn, the urban youth were the hardest hit by redundancies. The middle income bracket and the pool of young urban unemployed grew simultaneously; this conspicuous proximity of poverty and relative wealth encouraged crime as a social option. According to local newspapers and their readers, the "juvenile crime problem" in Soweto deepened throughout the late 1960s and early 1970s. Although official statistics showed that a major escalation in general crime occurred only around 1973–1974, public concern seemed to peak during 1972.[13] Gangs were perceived by many to be the cause of crime but, if crime and the formation of big gangs were indeed linked, it was crime that seemed to precipitate gang formation rather than the reverse. As more young men became involved in the criminal underworld, greater criminal competition forced them to organize more effectively or risk being squeezed out and victimized as individual operators.

Although the Vorster government accepted the presence of a permanently urban African population, it sought to sharpen the distinction between urban insiders and outsiders. While Section 10 rights (to permanent urban residential status) were entrenched and even extended in certain categories, those who did not qualify for urban status were hounded with even greater intensity.[14] The conflation of unemployment with urban illegality and the intensified persecution of urban "outsiders" marginalized the unemployed urban youth more than ever before. Unregistered youths, unable (or unwilling) to find jobs, moved increasingly into the urban underworld.[15]

Though more flexible than Verwoerdian apartheid on the issue of black urban settlement, Vorster's "multinationalism" continued to emphasize homeland development at the expense of urban development. The regime insisted that Soweto was large enough, and it restricted investment in black urban housing to a minimum.[16] Despite a growing demand, the rate of house building in Soweto declined even from the stagnant levels of the late 1960s.[17] No new townships were proclaimed in the Soweto complex. By the end of 1977 the official housing shortage in the area stood at 18,817 units. In reality the shortage was much greater because deserted wives, divorced women, and unmarried mothers were removed from the housing waiting lists.[18] Furthermore, thousands of residents deemed "illegal" were in need of accommodation but could not even consider applying for housing.

Overcrowding problems mounted in African townships during the 1970s. The Association of Chambers of Commerce of South Africa (Assocom) estimated that during the five years up to 1975 the African urban population grew by roughly 50 percent, whereas the number of available houses increased by only 15 percent. In Soweto the average number of people per house, almost all box-shaped with four or fewer rooms, had risen from thirteen in 1970 to seventeen in 1975.[19] By the mid-1970s, Soweto consisted of roughly 100,000 units for a supposed population of about 700,000; in fact, there were probably between one-and-a-quarter and one-and-a-half million inhabitants. Of these houses, 14 percent had electricity and only 3 percent were equipped with hot running water.[20] Domestic squalor and overcrowding encouraged youths to escape the home environment; to seek space, recreation and companionship in the streets. As the new western neighborhoods, built between 1955 and 1965, became more established, more of the bigger, distinctive territorial youth gangs took root.

THE NEW WAVE

As in the 1950s and 1960s, the new gangs were fiercely territorial; numerous wars erupted as they competed for women and attempted to assert control over local facilities and criminal hunting grounds. Each gang tended to have a core membership of between fifteen and thirty youths. The more influential gangs, however, had dozens of "hangers-on" and seemed able to mobilize over a hundred followers in times of conflict and crisis. Their criminal activities were concentrated on transport routes and in the Johannesburg city center. Far more than in the 1960s, gangs indulged in conspicuous consumption. They stole less in order to survive than to look good and acquire social status.[21] As I argued in chapter 5, the "clevers" of the 1960s were also style conscious but in a less overt way; they tended to emphasize language and social behavior and certain subtle, internally comprehended clothing variations. It was only around the turn of the decade that flash and display became fashionable again. The early 1970s, then, saw a shift not only in the range and intensity of gang conflict but also in the degree of concern with youth subcultural style.

In the older parts of Soweto there was substantial continuity from the 1960s. In particular, the Kwaitos of Orlando and the Dirty Dozen of Moroka/ Pimville, both dominant gangs during the later 1960s, remained powerful throughout the first half of the 1970s. Both gangs were important role models and style generators for the new wave, which arrived first in old Soweto.

Big, distinctive gangs were a new phenomenon in the resettlement areas of Diepkloof and Meadowlands. By the turn of the decade, neighborhoods had established themselves; there had been no significant new resettlement for several years. The youth were able to develop a greater sense of personal and territorial familiarity. Both Diepkloof and Meadowlands border on Orlando; local youths began to organize themselves into more assertive gangs both through example and out of defensive necessity. In Diepkloof it was the Biafras of Zone Six who first made their presence felt. They were soon followed by the Hyenas and Jaws of Zone One, the Damarras of Zone Four, and the Mongols of Zone Three. These were style-conscious, powerful gangs that competed furiously in Diepkloof throughout the first half of the 1970s.[22] Meadowlands was dominated by two major gangs: the Hong Kongs and the Black Power Gang. The Hong Kongs were influential throughout Meadowlands while the Black Powers, known more for their criminal activity than their style, were prominent in Zones One and Two.[23]

In the "Wild West" there had been a big-gang precedent during the early 1960s with the Eleven Boys and the German Spoilers of Zola. During the early 1970s, however, the phenomenon was far more widespread, with substantial gangs emerging in virtually every township on the new western rim of Soweto. As in Diepkloof and Meadowlands, this development was linked to the solidification of neighborhoods that followed a few years after the housing boom ended in the mid-1960s. The most prominent gangs in western Soweto were probably the Judas of Naledi, the ZX5 of Phiri, the Cockroaches of Zola, and the Sleep Outs, who dominated the open veld bounded by Jabulani, Moletsane, Jabavu and, Molapo.[24]

The rise of the Hazels in 1970–19771 precipitated a number of defensive responses throughout Soweto. The Kwaitos and the Dirty Dozen were prominent gangs that pre-dated the Hazels but, although these other gangs also perhaps triggered substantial neighborhood gang coalescence, it was the Hazels that were responsible for the dramatic acceleration of the process in the early 1970s. Pre-Hazel gangs such as the Dirty Dozen, the Kwaitos, and the Bandidos of Mofolo were forced to mobilize on a larger scale to defend themselves against the Hazels. Not only did the Hazels threaten the neighborhoods in their immediate territorial hinterland but they also caused defensive responses along the railway lines that fed out of Soweto. Based near the intersection of the Kliptown and Naledi lines, the Hazels were able to dominate the criminal activity on both major rail routes through Soweto. New defensive gangs, most notably the Judas of Naledi, emerged along the rail routes to challenge the Hazels on the trains.

Many of the famous gangs of the era, even the Hazels themselves, initially emerged as defensive networks. The Bandidos, for instance, were apparently formed by a group of Jabavu "clevers" who were persistently waylaid by local gangs and bullies while on their way to see movies in Fordsburg. Oupa Ndala, an ex-member of the gang, recalls: "Every time they used to wait for us and beat us up for our money. One day after we all lost our money to those guys we decided to protect ourselves. . . . In the first place we started fighting by stones and later as we grew up we used knives." By 1970 the gang had a core membership of about thirty and its influence had spread into parts of Mofolo.[25]

The Japanese of Pimville/Klipspruit started out as a school-based defensive network responding to gang harassment. By 1972 most of its membership had dropped out of school, and the network evolved into a fully fledged, style-conscious gang. The Japanese were involved in relatively little criminal activity but were increasingly locked into gang wars between 1972 and 1974 through a cycle of killing and retaliation.[26]

The ZX5 was another classic case. Spokes Ndlovu, an ex-member of the gang, claims that his gang started out as a defensive response to the Sleep Outs. He was one of a group of Phiri teenagers who worked for a newspaper company in the city. On paydays the Sleep Outs intercepted the working youths at Merafe Station and relieved them of their wages. The working youths were often beaten and stabbed as well. Eventually they decided to form a gang of their own. There were about fifteen members and they were basically concerned with defending themselves. Some of them continued to work initially, but gradually they became absorbed in full-time gang activity. The first leader of the ZX5 was killed by the Sleep Outs at Merafe Station, and the ZX5 then had to put up with the indignity of the Sleep Outs and the Movers of Mapetla occupying the Phiri Hall during music shows or movies. The ZX5, initially too small and disorganized to intervene, had to stand aside as two outside gangs fought for supremacy in their own community hall. Some of the local youths were hurt in the cross-fighting. "Because of that we organised into a big gang that grew in membership." By 1972–1973 the gang had established territorial supremacy in Phiri.[27]

Settled neighborhoods, widening inequality of wealth, and defensive responses to a few new powerful gangs probably accounted for the reemergence of big gangs in Soweto. These factors do not, however, explain the centrality of style in the new wave of gangs. It could be argued that the proliferation of big gangs naturally heightened gang competitiveness, which, apart from actual physical conflict, was expressed through style and conspicuous consumption. In order to assert status, gangs had to dress better, drive flashier cars, and generally spend more. The Hazels themselves seem to have been important in generating style. They quickly became famous throughout Soweto, and to many male ghetto teenagers they became heroes and role models. Their criminal methods and their style of dressing were admired and emulated by other gangs.[28] The Dirty Dozen were also expensive dressers and big spenders and may also have been role models for Soweto youth.

It is also possible that the expansion of secondary schooling and the growth of the African middle class in the early 1970s had an indirect impact on gang style. The reemergence of style seems to coincide with the rise of visible affluence in Soweto. As schooling became more accessible to urban youth, along with improved future employment opportunities, gangs, and "clevers" more generally, may have been challenged to assert a more obvious tycoon image. In many cases these displays may have been part of an attempt to deny their own marginality and blocked mobility but, as I suggested earlier, youth gangs simultaneously held middle-class values in contempt and aspired to middle-class levels of comfort and consumption. They were eager to display their wealth, power, and success and mock what they considered to be the undignified and submissive options of "respectability" and regular employment.

It would be incorrect to see the 1970s gang wave as a reversion to 1950s gang style. Gang culture and the sociospatial context in which it occurred had changed inexorably since the 1950s. Sophiatown, before its destruction, had guided and inspired township gang culture on the Rand. Although the old parts of Soweto had already become well established by the 1950s, it was Sophiatown and the other Western Areas townships that provided Soweto with a bridge to Johannesburg and to the world beyond. Sophiatown, though squalid in many ways, was close to the city; it had nightclubs and cinemas and a cosmopolitan atmosphere. During the 1940s and 1950s, much of the style generated in Sophiatown trickled through to Soweto.

By the 1970s the rivalry between the two "clever" styles, the *ndofaya* of Sophiatown origin and the *kalkoen* of Orlando, became less significant. The *ndofaya*, who used a more Afrikaans-based *tsotsitaal,* who preferred American jazz in a fairly pure form, and looked down upon their Orlando-bred counterparts as somewhat unsophisticated and "hickish," began to disappear from Soweto. The more Africanized *kalkoen* culture, on the other hand, flour-ished. The Orlando "clevers" spoke a more Zulu-based *tsotsitaal* and lis-tened to *mbaqanga*, a blend of traditional African music and jazz.[29] *Mbaqanga* was, according to David Coplan, multiethnic, blending "various local Afri-can musical traditions in the urban areas over the past several decades" in an attempt "to find musical 'common denominators' among the heteroge-neous urban audience."[30] *Mbaqanga* was promoted and developed by the state's new Bantu Radio, partly to encourage a traditional ethnic conscious-ness among its listenership. Apartheid ideologues saw jazz as too western-ized and multiracial; it contradicted their vision of cultural separateness. Nevertheless, Coplan argues that *mbaqanga* "has been developed by Afri-cans out of their own cultural resources, and the size and enthusiasm of its mass audience are too great to be dismissed as self-deception."[31]

By the 1970s the apartheid spatial isolation of Soweto was complete. The cosmopolitan influences of Sophiatown were removed. Although pockets of *ndofaya* style survived in the relocated areas of Soweto, this style was gradu-ally superseded by the Orlando tradition. Without the presence of Sophiatown, the *ndofaya* tradition was kept alive nostalgically by an older generation of ex-Sophiatown "clevers." The differences between the two "clever" tradi-tions should not be exaggerated; they tended to cross-fertilize each other in the 1950s, and layers of the old Sophiatown influences continued to be dis-cernible into the 1960s and 1970s. Nevertheless, Afrikaans gradually re-ceded in *tsotsitaal* throughout Soweto, and *mbaqanga*, encouraged by in-creasingly common portable radios, became the dominant music taste of Soweto youth. Jazz suffered a body blow with the destruction of Sophiatown. The Sophiatown dance halls and other accessible inner-city multiracial jazz venues, which had been the lifeblood of local jazz, were closed down as the grip of apartheid tightened. The moneyed white middle-class market was no longer available to African musicians, who became increasingly dependent on radio performances to survive. Needless to say, this involved tailoring their skills to the demands of Bantu Radio producers.[32] Johannesburg's Af-ricans were effectively sealed off in the bleak landscape of Soweto with its endless rows of drab, uniform, low-cost housing. Soweto in the 1970s still had no "downtown" and no shopping malls; it had one established night-club, one permanent cinema, one hotel, and a few scattered discotheques. Community halls were left as the only significant concert and film venues. The small, generally illegal, domestic shebeens and private parties were the focus of nightlife in Soweto.

The youth gangs of the late 1960s and 1970s, even those epitomizing contemporary high style, were less spectacular and less glamorous than the Sophiatown gangs of the 1950s. Clothes styles were more casual, though this probably had less to do with changing context than with new movie role models. The more casual style, it should be stressed, was probably no less expensive. The formal jackets of the 1950s gave way to lumberjackets; tight-fitting *tsotsi* trousers were superseded by looser fits; stetsons gave way to floppy sports hats called "sporties"; upmarket, usually Italian, leather shoes were replaced by state-of-the-art sneakers. The youth gang members also spent a lot of money dressing their girlfriends elegantly so as to emphasize their own status.

The way a gang walked and talked added to its distinctive image. An ex-Diepkloof resident remembers, for instance, that the Biafras and Hyenas "had a particular way of walking: limping, limping, limping."[33] All "clevers" were dexterous with the street argot but some gangs cultivated their own distinctive dialects. The ZX5, for example, spoke an esoteric brand of *tsotsitaal*, intelligible only to themselves, which they called "the rings."[34]

Gang style in the late 1960s and 1970s, like postwar "clever" culture generally, was heavily influenced by B-grade Hollywood action movies and Westerns. As Oupa Ndala observes of the Bandidos, "Movies provided the theory for us. And then we would put the theory into practice."[35] Clint Eastwood and Bruce Lee were apparently the most popular screen idols of this period. Cinemas were much less accessible after the Western Areas removals. Youths in the northeastern parts of Soweto had relatively easy access to Fordsburg's Rio, Majestic, and Starlight cinemas. But, especially in the western reaches of Soweto, they depended on shows in local township halls, which often became focal points of territorial conflict.[36]

Gang names reveal the popular movies of the late 1960s and 1970s. The Dirty Dozen took its name from the action thriller starring Charles Bronson, while the Navarones and Eagles were derived from Allistair McLean screen adaptations (*The Guns of Navarone* and *Where Eagles Dare*). "Bandidos" and "Valdez" were titles of 1960s Westerns; "Jaws" came directly from Spielberg's gory shark thriller. Some names were less directly derivative. The Mongols, for instance, almost certainly got their name from a movie about Genghis Khan, and the Judas may well have been inspired by the antihero of Hollywood's numerous biblical epics. The Japanese probably identified with the enemy in Hollywood movies about the Second World War, most notably *Bridge over the River Kwai*.[37]

It was essential for gang names to evoke violent, warlike contemporary images that offended the middle class and respectable working class. The Biafras took their name from the Nigerian civil war, which received widespread coverage in the local newspapers, *The World* and the *Post*.[38] They adopted as a symbol a war that, because Africans were killing one another in the postindependence era and because the carnage was on a large scale, appalled the average adult Sowetan. The Black Power Gang probably took its name from the American Black Power movement, which received substantial attention in local newspapers. The militancy of the American movement, its sanctioning of violent methods, and the general horror it evoked among the white middle class no doubt met with the approval of Meadowlands' street youth. It is unlikely that the gangsters had any knowledge of, let alone contact with, the emergent *local* Black Power movement, which, at the beginning of the 1970s, was very much confined to student and intellectual circles.

One other influence on gang naming was soccer. The Eleven Boys gang of the previous era was an obvious example. In the 1970s, the Damarras of Diepkloof took their name from a professional Namibian footballer, known as "the Damarra," who played for the Orlando Pirates.[39] Many gangs started out as informal soccer teams before rivalries gradually spilled over into more violent territorial struggles.[40]

The big-time Sophiatown gangsters, although often crudely romanticized by some ex-residents and writers, were more socially acceptable than the 1970s gangsters. The Americans of Sophiatown, in particular, are often remembered almost as heroes who stole only from whites, as benign leaders of what Coplan calls "shebeen society."[41] They were known as individuals, along with their families, and accepted as part of the community. Whether this applied to any of the other Sophiatown gangs is unclear; nevertheless, as the ultimate role models for 1950s youth gang culture, the example of the Americans must have carried some weight. Their 1970s equivalent, the Hazels, were feared and isolated. They were hated by all but a stratum of young males. Although they generally did not victimize local Mzimhlophe residents, the Hazels were never admired by adults, even in their home neighborhoods. In contrast to Sophiatown, Soweto was huge, sprawling, and impersonal. Although networks and solidarities were eventually established, the sense of community tended to be much narrower; most of the gangsters encountered were anonymous, unfamiliar, and dangerous. In addition, Soweto residents, unlike those of Sophiatown, were largely dependent on trains to reach their places of work. The criminal activity of the Hazels and other gangs on the trains was therefore particularly iniquitous. Of course, the experience of *tsotsi* train crime was all too familiar to the Orlando, Mofolo, Jabavu, and Pimville commuters during the 1950s. But the image of the Sophiatown gangs was not tainted in this crucial respect. It was the old Soweto tradition of gangsterism, rather than the Sophiatown tradition, that survived and then flourished in the 1970s.

Gang warfare continued to be fueled by competition over women and scarce facilities, such as parks and community halls. The masculine dignity of the gangsters depended on their ability to defend their territory and "property." Ndoza, recalling his life as a member of the Damarras, comments:

> Sometimes you will find that we were fighting for the babies. You will find that perhaps there is a girl that Mandla [a friend in the Damarras] is "jolling" [going out] with and the other guy from the other gang also wants that girl, you would find that there wouldn't be any understanding there because of that. The money business? . . . Ah, no. We were only fighting for women, the babies. Or you would find that perhaps a young boy is sent to the shops and then he is grabbed and robbed. He's gonna come back and ask for help from us just to protect him, you see. Yes, we were fighting for real things. Like maybe I sent a boy to [another zone] to buy dagga, then he comes back and the dagga has been taken. There I must also go and report to my guys: "Hey, a boy has been attacked, let's go out this way for them." And when we arrive there, it's gonna be a big fight, you see.[42]

Any territorial incursion—an assault on a gang member or even a neighborhood acquaintance, a sexual advance towards a local woman—constituted an attack on a gang's dignity that demanded immediate retaliation. The all-out war between the Dirty Dozen and the Bandidos was sparked by the killing of a Dirty Dozen member in about 1971. Shortly afterwards, a prominent Bandido was thrown out of a moving train and killed. After that, Oupa Ndala remarks, there was no way out of gang life: "neutrality became impossible."[43]

Gang wars could involve literally hundreds of youths as gangs mobilized neighborhood boys beyond their core membership during times of heightened conflict. For instance, in July 1971, the *Post* reported on a massive conflict between the Vultures of Orlando East and the Hyenas of Diepkloof. "Teenage gang warfare swept Diepkloof's Zone One for two days at the weekend. About 400 crazed members of the Vultures and Hyenas, two growing gangs, battled with bottles, bricks and knives on Friday and Saturday." Police detained forty-nine youths, eighteen of whom were under eighteen years old.[44]

Individuals who were uninhibited about killing, who were the most violent and daring among their peers, became gang leaders. Nothing evoked respect more than a track record of violence. The leader of the Bandidos, Teaser, was a good example. Aside from being fast and acrobatic, Teaser was a left-hander, which gave him a certain advantage in fights. "He used to stab and kill," Ndala recalls. "He was not afraid." If anyone in the gang revealed any squeamishness about violence, Teaser would accuse him of being a *bangaat*, a "chicken." "We were frightened by dead people; death never used to affect him."[45] The leader of the Hong Kongs, Kong Colombia, is remembered as a "psychopathic killer" who "used to kill for the sake of it."[46]

The rise in gang competitiveness and the conspicuous consumption that accompanied it led gangs increasingly into serious crime beyond the gang subculture itself. Trains, train stations, taxi ranks, and bus stations were the key target areas for muggings. Migrant workers, who developed a particular loathing for the gangs, were often victimized near their hostels. Some of the more powerful gangs, especially the Hazels, Dirty Dozen, and Damarras, also operated extensively in the city center. Some gangs ran informal protection rackets in their own areas. "Sometimes," recalls Oupa Ndala, the Bandidos "used to escort people going to work and protect them after work against other *tsotsis* and they would reward us every Friday."[47] Similarly, in Diepkloof some workers were offered a safe passage to and from their homes in exchange for a small fee. "People used to get paid on Fridays and a certain portion of their wages went to the gangs."[48] Gangs, then, could make a living both from mugging and from protecting local residents from other criminals.

The Dirty Dozen and the Bandidos, the two big gangs that fought for supremacy in Central Soweto during the late 1960s and early 1970s, might be seen as the initiators of the new gang wave. They continued, or revived, the tradition of central Soweto gang war, which had raged between the Black Swines and the Pirates until around 1965. Unlike their predecessors, however, they were more obviously style conscious and appear to have ushered in the youth gang era that was later epitomized by the Hazels. The Hazels, therefore, did not emerge in a void. They did, however, raise the stakes and the style, and they made youth gangsterism a major issue in Soweto again.

THE HAZELS

There is an abundance of historical reference to the Hazels gang: not only did they feature regularly in the local *World* and *Post* newspapers, but they retain a place in the popular memory of Soweto, particularly in Mzimhlophe (Photo 6.1). A key source of information on the Hazels comes from outsiders: ordinary residents of Mzimhlophe and members of other gangs. There is also a record of a trial of gang members in 1972. It is possible to construct a fairly intimate picture of the gang because two of the original members, Manfred ("Bra Forker") and Clifford Mashiloane, after surviving gang wars and stretches in prison, were willing to talk about their experiences.[49] Although there are certain minor contradictions in their testimonies, particularly on chronology, their stories are largely consistent and provide textured insights into gang life.

Photo 6.1   Hazels waylay a worker for his pay packet at Mzimhlophe Bridge. Hazel members, who claimed they had decided to go straight, told their story to *Drum* and staged this mock mugging for the magazine's photographer. In the *Drum* feature a sequence of three pictures is displayed under the captions: "1. Au and Satch at Mzimhlophe bridge wait for a victim"; "2. They move in . . . the pay packet goes"; "3. And that's what happens if you try to make a fight of it. This scene was recreated for DRUM by former Hazels, who have promised to keep good from now." Note the distinctive "sportie" hat of the 1970s Soweto gangsters. (From *Drum*, 8 April 1972. © Bailey's African History Archives. Reprinted with permission.)

Manfred attended primary school in Mzimhlophe but was forced to drop out when his father died. "We were nine children in the house and my mother was not working. She worked part-time jobs." Clifford's father was also absent during his teenage years. His father, who moved to Mzimhlophe in 1951 and worked as a "witch doctor," apparently became involved with the ANC and went to prison for politically related offenses in the late 1960s. Around this time, Clifford left school, and he worked for the *Beeld* newspaper for a while.

In 1970 a group of about five "clevers" from Mzimhlophe, including Manfred, Clifford, and a friend called Killer, came together to form a gang.[50] They were in their late teens and early twenties. Initially they were simply "very clean," well-dressed adolescents going out together and having a good time. They used to visit girlfriends and frequent shebeens and private parties in other parts of Orlando. Early on, they ran into territorial trouble. "Guys from Orlando used to be jealous of us. . . . When we go there to visit our girls they used to harass us." It was then that they decided to form a gang to protect themselves. "We told ourselves that since we were not staying in that territory we had to kill to survive."[51] Clifford tells the story of how the gang got its name:

> There was a certain lady by the name of Hazel. She was very beautiful. She was so beautiful everybody loved her. In my group there were five of us involved with her. It happened that at one time we organized a picnic. At that time we were not yet called the Hazels. On that day we found other groups from Orlando, Mofolo, Naledi, and other places. She had a boyfriend in each group. We had to fight in order to get her. We had a fight over her. The winner was going to be the one to get her. We decided to go away; some of us did not have partners so we were very sad. Like me. I had thought I was going to be with her. It was when we came back from the picnic that we called ourselves the Hazels.

Many years later Hazel apparently married Killer and they moved to Diepkloof. But neither Clifford nor Manfred is still in contact with Hazel.[52]

Following several successful fights in Orlando, the membership of the Hazels grew rapidly in Mzimhlophe. As new members joined and their fame spread it became necessary to keep up appearances and display their success. From very early on they turned to crime to finance their lifestyle: expensive clothes for themselves and their girlfriends, big cars, abundant drink, parties, movies, and nightclubs. By April 1971 *The World* identified the Hazels as the "most dreaded" of the "new gangs" in Soweto.[53] They were feared and talked about throughout Soweto, as much a part of daily life as passes or soccer.[54]

The Hazels drift in and out of Mbulelo Mzamane's autobiographical novel, *Children of Soweto*, almost incidentally. Though the gang is peripheral to the story, it is clear that the Hazels were a powerful presence in the life of Sowetans in the early and mid 1970s. School-going youths, like Mzamane himself, were particularly wary of them.

[My friend] and Violet began to drift apart the moment she left school. I was not at all sorry to see them break up because, among other things, she had taken up with the Hazels, a knife-happy gang of merciless thugs who reigned over our township with an iron hand. They terrorized school kids by taking all the money we had brought to school for lunch or waylaying us when we were sent to the shops by our parents. The Hazels had bluntly told him that if he carried on with Violet, they'd cut him to pieces. I convinced him, though he was adamant at first, to drop the affair. I'm not sorry that I did, for there are moments in the townships when it is folly to play brave.[55]

In 1971 there were about thirty core members ranging in age from seventeen to twenty-five. There was no formal hierarchy in the gang; leadership seemed to shift according to status and prestige. "It all depended," according to Manfred, who became known as Bra Forker, "on who had the heart of a lion and was never afraid to penetrate the enemy with a knife." Forker and Jokes, a youth admired for his fighting skill and ruthlessness, were generally regarded as the leaders. Forker claims that his own prestige was based on his success at rooting out and beating up "sell-outs," people passing on information to "enemy groups." As founder members, Clifford, whose nicknames were "Bagaza," which means "bullet," or "38," no doubt referring to the caliber of bullet, and Killer were also leadership figures. Other core members included Cairo, Sjambok, MaFashion, Sweetboy, Star, Fats, Staff, Javas, and Sash.[56]

Like all the youth gangs of the time, the Hazels were extremely territory conscious. Many gang members apparently lodged at the house of a Mzimhlophe woman with whom they shared their spoils.[57] They felt a loyalty to their neighborhood and rarely robbed or assaulted established Mzimhlophe residents. In fact they offered the locals tacit protection from outside gangs. "If they knew you personally," Whitey Khanyeza recalls, "you were generally all right."[58] Mzimhlophe women, however, were automatically assumed to be available to the gang; they had little option but to accept overtures from Hazel members. According to Mofokeng, "if they wanted a woman they'd simply take her." Once women accepted this inevitability they were lavished with presents and protected from outside gangsters. Beyond Mzimhlophe the Hazels raided schools, shebeens, and parties and brazenly abducted and raped women.[59] As Lunn observes, women, more than men, feared the Hazels. Women were terrified of them.[60] Young men from Mzimhlophe were also expected to be loyal to the Hazels. Although many considered it an honor to be a member of the gang, many others were pressurized into joining for protection. It was dangerous for a youth from the area not to be identified as friendly and supportive.[61] While the core membership of the gang remained around thirty, they were, according to Forker, able to count on over a hundred followers when necessary.[62]

Although some of the Hazels attended nearby high schools themselves before they became gangsters, they were consistently hostile toward the new Orlando North Secondary School in Mzimlhlophe. The school was probably seen as a challenge to their authority amongst local youths. In 1972, T. W. Kambule of Orlando High School claimed that his school was experiencing an overcrowding problem partly because so many students refused to go to the new school for fear of Hazel harassment. Orlando High itself never suffered from the Hazels, possibly because the school, in Orlando East, was too far away to threaten the gang's territorial domination.[63]

The Hazels, one Mzimhlophe resident recalls, "dressed like gentlemen."[64] They were immediately recognizable by their clean-shaven heads, or "cheese-kops," and dressing style. Their most distinctive items of clothing were Barracuda lumberjackets, often worn inside-out to display the checkered interior pattern, and "sportie" hats. Their sporties generally had the letters "HZ" imprinted on them. Another distinctive item was a blue military-style jacket, unusual at the time in that it was blue rather than khaki. Mayfair slacks or light polyester trousers known as "Star Press" were favored. They always chose expensive labels, such as Evance and Saxon, and frequented the American Showroom, an upmarket clothes shop in the Johannesburg city center.[65] It was common for Hazel "molls" to wear red. Mzimhlophe women who wore red, in particular red berets, were immediately identified as "belonging" to the Hazels.[66]

The Hazels were often seen at shebeens, concerts, parties,. and cinemas showing off their girlfriends and spending money extravagantly. On Friday afternoons the gang would sometimes hire up to ten cars to use for weekend excursions.[67]

The Hazels were a terror on the Soweto trains. They specialized in extortion and armed robbery of passengers. During 1971 and 1972 the local newspapers reported several incidents of assault and armed robbery by Hazels on city-bound trains. It seems clear, however, that the gang fleeced passengers almost routinely. Only a small proportion of Hazel crime was reported by victims, who feared gang intimidation, did not trust the police, and felt a sense of sheer resignation. It was common for several gang members to board a train as it pulled out of a station; once the coach doors locked automatically they drew their long knives, or *swaarde*, and made their "collection" from the trapped passengers. Those who resisted were dealt with brutally; they were beaten, stabbed, and even thrown out of moving trains. The Hazels never made any attempt to hide their identity; on the contrary, they usually announced their presence clearly, enjoying the terror their name evoked.[68]

Although their notoriety was established on the trains, the Hazels also operated in the Johannesburg city center and around major railway stations. At these points they encountered much stiffer gang competition, most notably from the Dirty Dozen, who prided themselves on their power in the city center.[69] Like most major gangs of the time, the Hazels had an organized branch in jail. They were particularly powerful in Leeuwkop maximum security prison, a section of which they continued to dominate even after the gang had disbanded on the streets. Life in jail was particularly harsh for unaffiliated individuals; inmates who belonged to gangs quickly cohered around their street identities for protection.[70] Unlike many of the Cape Flats gangs, however, the Hazels' power was not based in the jails. They were rooted firmly in the streets and on the trains.

The Hazels were territorial over particular train coaches. They would always occupy the last coach, 9430, known as "Dumani," and they traveled at particular times. The name "Dumani" probably derived from the Zulu word *duma*, meaning "fame" or "notoriety," combined with the suffix *ni*, which can be used to mean "possessor of." According to Mashiloane, other gangs knew that they would risk a gang war with the Hazels if they traveled in any coach, let alone 9430, at those specific times. "Dumani was the main coach where the bosses met. . . . We would go in last. Everyone would then make his girlfriend comfortable first and then we would stand on our feet and drink liquor. The others knew that if they came in they would have to fight." Few would be foolish enough to do so. "The Hazels were an absolute terror," Murphy Morobe recalls, "I would never be seen dead or alive on the 2:10 train on Saturday from Park Station."[71]

The Hazels fought numerous gang wars, both on the trains and in the streets, and became skilled and experienced fighters. "Bagaza" Mashiloane describes knife fighting on the trains graphically:

The important thing was to be fast, you could not afford to sleep. Even when you heard a person's steps from behind, you were supposed to move. Your knife was to be ready at all times. You had to be alert and fast. If you were not fast they could stab you. And sometimes you had to do some staffriding [moving on the outside of the coach, along the sides or the roof]. . . . You had to make sure you were strong enough to fight. In a knife fight, when you are facing someone like this, you must make sure

that you don't look anywhere else, you must make sure that you look him
in the eye. He is also looking at you and he may be faster. If you were not
sure of your speed you took off your lumber and wrapped it around your
hand so that you could use it to block; you held the knife in one hand and
used the other hand to block. Sometimes you could also use your sportie,
which anyway might be obstructing your view; it was also used as a block.
He can rather tear your hat or your lumber.[72]

On the streets a fighter would use a dustbin cover as a shield while wielding
a knife, a broken bottle, or even a brick in his free hand.[73] A Mzimhlophe
resident recalls that the Hazels used a successful strategy of outflanking
their opponents. Their forces would split, even when they were not necessarily expecting a fight. They learned to be vigilant. Half of the group, for
instance, would separate off and drink at a shebeen across the road. When
attacked, one group would hold off the enemy while the other came up
behind.[74]

The Hazels fought gang wars primarily for fame and recognition. According to outside observers they were fighting "for sweet," fighting "for
fun."[75] To the Hazels, however, prestige was everything; a Hazel had to hold
his ground at all costs. Making money was a secondary concern, a means to
an end.

The Hazels were not unchallenged in Orlando. Although they were comfortably in control of Mzimhlophe itself, the gang members had very little
freedom of movement in the rest of Orlando, which was largely dominated
by the Kwaitos and the Vikings. Both gangs were established before the
Hazels; it is likely that the Hazels actually arose in response to Kwaito and
Viking harassment in wider Orlando. Although well known in their own
right, neither gang achieved the same kind of notoriety as the Hazels during
the 1970s.

The Kwaitos dated back to the mid-1960s. It is difficult to construct a
clear picture of the gang's territorial limits, not least because the boundaries probably shifted through time, but the gang seemed to dominate
the southern swath of Orlando stretching from Phefeni Station in the
southwest to parts of southern Orlando East. They had their clubhouse in
Orlando East. The Kwaitos clashed several times with the Hazels in the
early 1970s and were regarded by some as the most serious rivals to the
Hazels throughout Soweto. Like the Hazels, they were fiercely territorial
and offered a certain protection to their own neighborhoods. They had a
core membership of perhaps twenty but could also count on a much
greater following through a combination of neighborhood loyalty and
intimidation. They do not appear to have made a significant impact on
the trains or in the central city; their criminal activity primarily targeted

commuters in the vicinity of Phefeni Station. Like many of the gangs of this era, they had a reputation for brutality and for assaulting and harassing schoolgirls in Orlando. The Kwaitos were known to be avid supporters of the Orlando Pirates Football Club and frequently beat up soccer spectators who did not demonstrate appropriate respect for their team. It was not a particularly stylish or style conscious gang. This, at least partially, accounted for its limited impact and fame during the 1970s.[76]

The Vikings of Orlando should not be confused with the 1960s Vikings of Senaoane/Dlamini. It is possible that the Orlando group got its name from its 1960s predecessor; more probably the same movie inspired both names. The Orlando Vikings emerged towards the end of the 1960s with their territorial heartland in central Orlando, south of Mlamlankuzi Station. They stood out prominently amongst the rag-tag gangs of central Orlando. The Vikings were quick to confront outsiders entering their territory and clashed with the Hazels in the early 1970s both in Orlando and in the city center, where the Hazels carried out most of their mugging operations. The Vikings had a younger sub-gang known as the Junior Vikings; the seniors tended to be in their early twenties while the juniors were generally in their middle teens. The seniors could often be seen driving around at high speed in a huge black Pontiac. The gang, however, did not have a particular reputation for style.[77]

With the Kwaitos and Vikings commanding territories to the south and east of Mzimhlophe, it was initially easier for the Hazels to make territorial incursions westwards into neighboring Meadowlands. Initially they apparently "ruled over" parts of Meadowlands in addition to Mzimhlophe.[78] But they were soon to run into stiff opposition from the two powerful gangs that began to dominate Meadowlands from the early 1970s, the Hong Kongs and the Black Power gang.[79]

The power of the Hazels was based less on territorial supremacy than on their strategic control of the train routes into Johannesburg. But even on the trains they were not without opposition. During 1971 there was bitter and constant rivalry, almost exclusively on the trains, between the Hazels and the Judas gang of Naledi. Naledi, positioned at the western edge of Soweto, was highly dependent on trains and suffered the Hazel menace more keenly than most other townships. The Judas gang initially emerged to protect Naledi youths traveling to and from the city. The Judas gang members were regularly seen on the trains wielding pangas. As they became more stylish and assertive under the leadership of a youth called Makhanda, they developed a reputation for mugging commuters.[80] According to Bra Forker, the Judas took a tremendous pounding in a bloody coach battle towards the end of 1971 and never posed a serious threat to the Hazels after that.[81] Aside from the Judas, the Hazels regularly encountered two other western Soweto gangs on the trains: the Bees, also of Naledi, and the Amaphela (or "Cockroaches") of Zola.[82]

Between about 1973 and 1975 the Hazels had constant train battles with the Bandidos, who boarded the train either at the Inhlazane or the Ikwezi Station and probably competed with the Hazels for both prestige and criminal trade.[83] The Hazels also often came across the Dirty Dozen on the trains throughout the first half of the 1970s, though they seemed to compete over the city center more than the rail routes.[84]

Migrant workers at the Mzimhlophe Hostel were regularly robbed and victimized by the Hazels during the early 1970s. One local resident recalls how she once had to plead with a group of Hazels to prevent them beating a migrant to death at her doorstep.[85] Migrants occasionally organized retaliatory raids against the gang. In chapter 7 I show how the Hazels became enmeshed in the conflict between Zulu migrants and youths during the political upheaval in 1976.

A number of gang members were arrested and put on trial during 1972 and 1973. Sixteen were detained towards the end of 1971 following a gang raid on a Naledi-bound train. Most of them were acquitted. About twenty of the gang were rounded up in 1972 following the huge Hazel–Judas battle in which at least one Judas member was killed. The ensuing court case dragged on for two years and most of the accused were eventually released due to insufficient evidence, but several, including Bra Forker, eventually received jail sentences ranging from one to three years.[86]

Clifford was one of the twenty arrested in 1972, and he spent some time in jail before being released on bail. His father was able to visit him in prison during his detention, not to comfort Clifford but rather to discipline him. Clifford's father apparently had some sort of an agreement with the wardens. Presumably the father had himself been released from prison by then. The middle-aged man was obviously enraged by his son's involvement with the Hazels.

> My father went looking for me at the police station. He then found me. Everybody knew, even the other gangsters, that every night he would come and beat me up. . . . Every day before I went to bed I had to get a hiding. . . . The rest would start laughing and say, your father is coming. It was true; at night you heard the keys and he would beat me up. He did not just beat me a little and leave it for tomorrow. He would go on until he was all full of sweat and tired. It was only when he was wet with sweat [that] he would be satisfied.

Clifford spent the next few years in and out of prison for lesser offenses. He also spent three months in hospital recovering from a serious knife wound inflicted on him by another gangster when he left the Dumani coach one day to go to the toilet. By the mid-1970s Clifford became increasingly war-weary. After yet another battle on the train, he decided it was time to "resign" from the Hazels. "I threw the knives away. I decided that I am old enough and I want to go forward." He tried to leave the country and start life afresh but his plans fell through and he was "left behind." Clifford resumed his involvement with the Hazels, and during 1976 he found himself in the thick of the conflict between Zulu migrants and Mzimhlophe youths.

In the months leading up to Bra Forker's initial arrest in 1972 and, it seems, in the months that followed while the trial dragged on, the Hazel veteran was constantly on the run. "Cops used to want me all over the place. But still I was a leader of the Hazels. I never used to sleep in Mzimhlophe. Cops hunted me for robbery in Fordsburg and Park Station. Railway police also knew me and hunted me." It was only in 1974 that he was jailed for his part in the Judas gang killing. His three-year sentence was extended after he committed a further crime in prison, and he was released only in 1980. "When I came back the [gang] was squashed." Forker was employed briefly but soon got involved in criminal activity again. In 1982 he was shot and crippled while attempting to rob a jewelry shop. He went back to Leeuwkop Prison, where he linked up with a convict remnant of the old Hazels gang. He was released in 1988 but remains wheelchair bound and largely dependent on his employed younger brother for survival.

The gang's strength began to wane around 1974 as continual arrests and trials, as well as deaths and injuries, began to take their toll.[87] Nevertheless, the Hazels remained a significant force in Soweto until at least 1976–1977 when a combination of jailings, student anti-crime measures, and the advancing age of members brought about the gang's final demise.[88]

"LET US NOT BE BULLIED BY OUR CHILDREN"

The 1970s gangs, along with generally spiraling juvenile crime, wore down the patience of older, employed township residents. A typical response came from this Meadowlands householder in August 1972:

It is surprising that the teenager "Black Power" gang should terrorise residents so openly and yet the police and residents don't come together to smash the gang. What really beats me is that residents know the youngsters responsible for the gang but seem to do nothing about it. Instead, they are stopping their kids from going to the shops and in certain cases agree to pay protection fees to these youngsters. . . . Unless something is done the Black Power will turn into another terror like the "Hazels" and I believe we are all sick and tired of this kind of thuggery. All in all there is nothing in Black Power. They are just a bunch of dagga-smoking small boys who must be disciplined.[89]

From 1972, with the introduction of the West Rand Administration Board, the traditionally inept official policing deteriorated even further throughout Soweto.[90] In 1973, new community policing efforts were initiated, and these, during the following year, coalesced under the banner of the Makgotla movement.

Like distinctive gangs, coordinated home guards emerged along with more established neighborhoods. Organized guards, which involved the active participation of numerous householders, generally required a substantial degree of community cohesion. This was the case in Sophiatown and the Western Areas during the 1940s and 1950s. The civic guards in these areas were given added coherence and credibility through strong links with the ANC.[91] By the 1960s the old-established communities of the Western Areas had been resettled and the ANC had been banned.

With some exceptions, civil guards in the 1960s, like youth gangs of the time, tended to be scattered and sporadic. It took time for neighborhood networks to mature in the resettled areas. In the absence of the ANC and PAC, residents were forced to look to the ineffectual advisory boards for leadership. In the first half of the 1960s, the most persistent civic guards were located in the older parts of Soweto, particularly Orlando, Moroka, and Mofolo. Orlando had a civic guard tradition stretching back to the 1950s. In new Soweto only Zola and Chiawelo could raise successful civic guards during the 1960s.

In the early 1970s a number of independent and isolated community guards did exist. They were referred to as *izibonda* (the Zulu word for "council of elders") or *amadoda omuzi* ("fathers of the homes") or simply "street committees." In Zola, for instance, the "fathers" continued a tradition from the 1960s of meeting every month to organize neighborhood watches and apparently had some success in curbing juvenile crime.[92] Similar structures, enjoying sporadic success, operated in parts of Pimville and Diepkloof.[93] There was a cluster of *izibonda*, generally based in Orlando and Diepkloof, that had institutional links to the Urban Bantu Council (UBC) and the Sofasonke Party. But these groups were chiefly concerned with housing allocation and the mediation of domestic disputes.[94] Peter Lengene, the influential Rockville councillor and former "mayor," was an important voice within the UBC on the crime issue. He railed against the ineffectiveness of the SAP and gave moral support to home guard initiatives.[95]

The Makgotla came into being when two strong and like-minded home guards, one in Naledi and one in Meadowlands, joined forces. What made the Makgotla distinctive from previous Sowetan civil guards was first, its high degree of cross-township coordination and, second, its overt appeal to "traditional" African values. In the latter respect it may have drawn inspiration from James Mpanza's controversial "parents' court," which operated clandestinely in the late 1960s until Mpanza's death in September 1970.

The Meadowlands guard was established in Zone One under the leadership of a powerful local figure, Mrs. Sinah Madipere Makume, usually known simply as "Madipere." A series of street committees were set up by household heads to protect property and discipline youths. The Black Power Gang, Madipere recalls, acted as a major catalyst for the setting up of the street committees. "They were killing people. There were gangsters, the Black Powers. . . . So I went to buy me a *sjambok* and a whistle and I started it."[96] Apart from the neighborhood watch, which involved organized responses to whistled distress signals, Madipere ran a court along the lines of Mpanza's parents' court, which had lost prominence by the end of the 1960s. Youths who had allegedly committed crimes were dragged before the court, given a summary trial, and publicly flogged, usually with the consent of their parents.[97] A Meadowlands resident recalls that the street committees enforced a seven o'clock curfew for girls, aimed at protecting them from gang harassment.[98]

At around the same time as the Meadowlands street committees were being set up, a similar initiative was taken in Naledi under the leadership of a UBC councillor, Siegfried Manthata. Along with Letsatsi Radebe, his neighbor, he set up a home guard and a residents' court; he called this structure a *lekgotla*, the Sotho word for a meeting of elders. Manthata used his base within the UBC to argue his case for the *lekgotla*. Like Madipere's group, the Naledi *lekgotla* served both as a residents' patrol and as a court. Wayward youths were tried and lashed with a *sjambok* for various misdemeanors.[99]

It was a testimony to the splintered diversity and parochiality of Soweto society that Madipere and Manthata, although running very similar operations, had little idea of each other's activities during 1973. It was only once both groups started to receive media attention and mounting criticism in early 1974 that they thought of joining forces. Manthata supported Madipere in the UBC and in the newspapers and she, in turn, wrote to him to suggest a link-up. At a meeting in Naledi in March or April, they announced the formation of a movement called "Makgotla." The name, which is the plural form of *lekgotla*, was chosen to emphasize community unity. As Letsatsi Radebe explains: "People who . . . have come together and unite to solve a problem, that's a single word that is being used. . . . Now, when I say *lekgotla*, I mean anything where people come together. . . . But now by using the

term *makgotla* we want to differentiate from all these other small group-
ings."[100] The new organization's first task was to set up as many new branch
committees as possible. A committee was to consist of five permanent members: a chairman, a secretary, and three others. Every Sunday the committee
would meet to solve problems. During the week, committee members would
act as judges in trials.[101]

The Makgotla grew rapidly. In May two new branches were established, in Moletsane and Tladi.[102] By the middle of June branches had
been established in Chiawelo, Dlamini, Orlando West Extension,
Diepkloof, Mzimhlophe, Dobsonville, Klipspruit, Central Western Jabavu,
and Molapo. On June 16, Manthata addressed a joint organizational rally
in the Naledi square that attracted nearly 300 residents.[103] By mid-July
further branches had been established in Orlando East and Senaoane.[104]
Towards the end of 1974 a new branch was set up in Phiri under the
leadership of an influential UBC councillor, Bob Cindi. The local *lekgotla*,
he commented, was a response to soaring crime and the activities of the
ZX5 gang in particular.[105]

The Makgotla argued that it had to take the law into its own hands because of the ineffectiveness of the South African Police and the inappropri-
ateness of the Western judicial system. Makgotla members were scornful of
the judicial system, which let juvenile delinquents off with warnings and
often acquitted known criminals for lack of evidence. They called for a
system which disciplined juvenile criminals effectively. As *World* reporter
S. L. Sidzumo explained: "Trial by magistrate may be the right thing, they
say. But it can easily result in acquittal because the witnesses fail to turn up.
And even if it results in a conviction, jail affords the dangerous tsotsi no
deterrent. He regards it as free board and lodging until he can resume his
dirty work."[106]

At the core of Makgotla ideology was the belief that urban life had brought
about the moral degeneration of Africans. "Ever since they settled permanently in the urban areas," the organization stated in a memorandum to the
Viljoen Commission, "their pattern of living has contributed heavily to the
factors of destruction of some social norm cherished, upheld and respected
by the community."[107] In the city, a Makgotla sympathizer lamented, youths
were "aggressively assertive" and no longer respected their parents.[108] Whenever a new crime wave, real or imagined, swept Soweto, the breakdown of
parental authority was always a popular explanation. It was in this context
that the Makgotla's appeal to traditional values struck a chord with many
older residents. The Makgotla was a conservative backlash; a response to a
perceived moral crisis over the waywardness of youth. The solution to urban decline, it insisted, lay in reasserting traditional values and age hierarchies.[109] Sinah Madipere made the point bluntly at a Makgotla meeting in

Jabavu in July 1974: "Let us not be bullied by our children. They must know what is right and wrong."[110]

Flogging was central to Makgotla's disciplinary strategy. According to Radebe, sentences usually ranged from six to ten lashes with a *sjambok*. Girls were lashed until about the age of sixteen but young men could be lashed well into their twenties if it was deemed necessary.[111] Flogging was endorsed by many of the older residents. Parents were often present at the courts, and they usually gave their consent to the sentence.[112]

The Makgotla was very concerned, both in cases of juvenile discipline and in domestic dispute resolution, to involve parents and extended families. This was an extension of the Makgotla's emphasis on traditional family structures, its vision of an ordered society based on close-knit, cooperative patriarchal families. A contravention of discipline or a domestic dispute was not an individual problem but an issue that had to be discussed and dealt with by the whole family.[113]

The Makgotla had both a policing and a judicial function. Organized patrols stood by to respond to calls for help. They also walked the streets, searched youths at random, and confiscated weapons. Numerous sympathetic parents fed the Makgotla with localized information. Known or suspected criminals were dragged to the court, tried, flogged, and, thereafter, often handed over to the police. The courts also summoned witnesses, usually with the threat of coercion. Like the 1960s civil guards, the Makgotla tried to use its links with the UBC to evict, or threaten to evict, households that were "known" to harbor criminals. This was a weapon that the Makgotla tried to develop, though apparently with little success.[114]

Although the leadership of the Makgotla was primarily Sotho speaking, the organization attempted to develop a pan-ethnic image by drawing on cross-ethnic traditional themes of eldership and the patriarchal family. Manthata and Madipere constantly emphasized a set of common "Black" traditional values.[115] Nevertheless, the Makgotla could never entirely shake off its Sotho image. The organization was strongest in Sotho areas, most notably in the predominantly Sotho arc of townships including Naledi, Tladi, Moletsane, and Molapo. The Makgotla was also conspicuously absent from the predominantly Zulu townships of Emdeni, Zola, Jabulani, and Zondi.

Another issue that damaged the Makgotla's pan-ethnic credibility was its close association with the Basotho migrant gang network, the Russians. Radebe admits that he was on good terms with the Russian leadership in Naledi; they saw eye-to-eye on many issues, particularly on how to deal with unruly and criminal youths. The Russians, who themselves ran protection rackets and frequently broke the law, would often act as reinforcements to support the Makgotla in its struggle against youth gangsterism.[116] The

Makgotla and the Russians had an alliance of convenience. The Russians had a long history of violent conflict with *tsotsis*, and they felt comfortable with the traditionalism of the Makgotla. The Makgotla, for its part, needed the muscle of the Russians.

Although it is clear that many older Sowetans approved of the Makgotla's methods and recognized its effectiveness in containing crime, it is difficult to assess overall community support for the Makgotla.[117] The Makgotla succeeded in drawing regular audiences of two to five hundred residents to its meetings, particularly during 1974.[118] Its ability to win a UBC council seat on an explicit Makgotla ticket, as it did in 1974, also suggests a relatively large stratum of support. But the organization clearly had most of its appeal in Sotho-speaking areas, while many people felt ambivalent toward the Makgotla, accepting the need to combat crime but disapproving of corporal punishment or traditionalism.[119] Most of the men who made up the patrols were ordinary working-class householders. Like the leaders, they seemed to be established urban residents who, in the context of an urban juvenile crime blight, drew nostalgically on traditional imagery of generational authority and harmony.

The Makgotla courts and patrols rarely challenged the big gangs directly. The Makgotla patrols were far more effective in deterring street crime than in actually rooting out "criminal elements." There appeared to be a mutual stand-off between gangs and street patrols. Each group seemed to fear the other. The patrols were generally made up of middle-aged householders doing voluntary service; they had many other commitments and responsibilities. They did not constitute a permanent vigilante squad. They were prepared to walk the streets in large groups, disarm youths, and intervene in crime on the spot. They often beat criminals who were caught red-handed before handing them over to police. The average father on patrol, however, probably felt it was too dangerous to seek out and confront gangs like the Hazels or the Dirty Dozen head on. Gangs had the advantage of having continuous, battle-hardened memberships. Gang members had few responsibilities; they were streetwise and familiar with violent clashes. The gangs, nevertheless, were also wary of the large squads of stick- and *sjambok*-wielding fathers. For the most part, it appears, the gangs kept their distance. They tended to see other gangs as their most serious rivals rather than the "fathers' gang." Gangsters rarely moved in groups big enough to feel safe confronting Makgotla patrols, and the patrols were unlikely to intervene in gang warfare, which did not seriously threaten the lives and property of ordinary residents.

While the Makgotla had some localized success in reducing crime between 1974 and 1976, it had only a limited impact on the gang subculture. Only in Meadowlands and to a lesser extent in Diepkloof and Phiri did it contribute to breaking gangs. With unarmed and untrained part-time manpower and without official recognition from the South African Police, the Makgotla could never realistically hope to defeat the big gangs. A far more powerful challenge came not from older residents but from a less expected quarter: politicized students. As I show in chapter 7, gang culture was buffeted, and then overwhelmed, by the 1976 student uprising. Under moral and physical pressure from the students both to get involved politically and to give up their parasitic criminality, the gangs of Soweto were forced into retreat.

NOTES

1. It is clear that the early 1970s are recalled in the popular memory as an era of gang resurgence. Numerous Sowetans remembered the gangs of the early 1970s and felt that the 1960s were relatively gang-free.

2. South African Institute of Race Relations, *A Survey of Race Relations in South Africa* (*SRRSA*), Johannesburg, 1972, p. 215; *SRRSA* 1973, p. 182; *SRRSA* 1974, p. 220; Jill Nattrass, *The South African Economy: Its Growth and Change*, Cape Town, 1981, p. 25; J. Saul and S. Gelb, *The Crisis in South Africa*, New York, 1981, p. 23.

3. J. Kane-Berman, *Soweto: Black Revolt, White Reaction*, Johannesburg, 1978, pp. 49 and 51; see also R. W. Johnson, *How Long Will South Africa Survive?* London, 1977, p. 84 and p. 187; and Saul and Gelb, *Crisis*, p 23.

4. See Saul and Gelb, *Crisis*, p. 18; Jonathan Hyslop, "Schools, Unemployment and Youth: Origins and Significance of Student and Youth Movements, 1976–1987," *Perspectives in Education*, 10, 2, 1988–1989, p. 61; J. Hyslop, "State Education Policy and the Social Reproduction of the Urban African Working Class: The Case of the Southern Transvaal 1955–1976," *Journal of Southern African Studies*, 14, 3, April 1988, pp. 464–466.

5. Tom Lodge, *Black Politics in South Africa since 1945,* Johannesburg, 1983, p. 326; see also Saul and Gelb, *Crisis*, p. 18 and p. 28.

6. Saul and Gelb, *Crisis*, p. 23; Johnson, *How Long Will South Africa Survive?* p. 87.

7. The sudden increase in the gold price in 1974, following South Africa's deliberate restriction of the gold supply, was responsible for high growth in that year; the subsequent fall in 1975, following large-scale selling of gold reserves by the United States, precipitated the recession. Lodge, *Black Politics*, p. 326; Johnson, *How Long Will South Africa Survive?* p. 87. See Wilmot James, *Our Precious Metal: African Labour in South Africa's Gold Industry, 1970–1990*, Cape Town, 1992, pp. 17–20, for more detail on the economic impact of the gold price fluctuations.

8. Hyslop, "State Education Policy," p. 464; Merle Lipton, *Capitalism and Apartheid: South Africa 1910–1984*, Aldershot, England, 1985, pp. 49–50. It could be argued that "liberalisation" was an expression of political confidence on the part of the Nationalists rather than defensiveness, i.e., the government could afford to liberalize because of years of economic growth and political stability. Clearly, though, Vorster was far more sensitive to international opinion than his predecessor.

9. Lipton, *Capitalism and Apartheid*, p. 50.

10. See Hyslop, "State Education Policy," p. 466 and p. 471.

11. See Lipton, *Capitalism and Apartheid*, p. 59 and p. 65. The term "blacks" here includes all official population categories other than "white," i.e., coloreds, Indians, and Africans.

12. See Lipton, *Capitalism and Apartheid*, pp. 65–66.

13. See *The World* throughout 1969–1972; the references are too numerous to cite individually. See also, for example, *The Star*, 28 January 1972, 5 February 1972; 8, 11, and 14 July 1972 (editorial); 5 and 7 October 1972 (editorial); the *Rand Daily Mail* (*RDM*), 4 January 1972 and 5 October 1972; West Rand Administration Board Archive, Intermediary Archive Depot, Johannesburg (IAD WRAB) N9 (vol. 3), notes of meeting of Liaison Committee with officials of the South African Police, 23 March 1972. See my discussion on crime in chapter 5. According to official statistics, quoted in *The World*, 11 April 1975, crime rose by 20 percent between mid-1973 and mid-1974. See also report on crime in *SRRSA* 1974, p. 88. Kane-Berman, *Soweto*, pp. 54–55, points out that market research in 1975 revealed crime to be the most serious single problem for Sowetan residents.

14. See Lipton, *Capitalism and Apartheid*, pp. 68–69; P. J. Riekert, *Report of the Commission of Inquiry into Legislation Affecting the Utilisation of Manpower (Excluding the Legislation Administered by the Department of Labour and Mines)*, Pretoria, 1974, RP 32/1979, p. 60; Black Sash Collection, Historical Papers Library, University of the Witwatersrand, Johannesburg, AE 862, Advice Office Reports, 1970–1976.

15. See Black Sash AE 862, monthly and annual Advice Office reports, 1970–1976.

16. Riekert Report, RP 32/1979, p. 108. Central government support for African housing in "white areas" was meager. Between 1972 and 1976 the Department of Community Development spent only R34.6 million on African housing, compared to R256 million on white housing. Interestingly, Community Development allocated substantial funds to colored and "Asian" housing during this period: R250 million and R69.6 million respectively. See also expenditure table on p. 110 of the report.

17. Kane-Berman, *Soweto*, p. 59. Between 1973 and 1976 an average of 746 new units were built per annum, compared to 772 between 1965 and 1969 and 4,413 during the 1955–65 housing boom.

18. Kane-Berman, *Soweto*, p. 59; Riekert Report, RP 32/1979, p. 112.

19. The Association of Commerce of South Africa evidence to the Cillie Commission, quoted in Kane-Berman, *Soweto*, pp. 50–51.

20. Johnson, *How Long Will South Africa Survive?* p. 189; see also Kane-Berman, *Soweto*, p. 53. Charles Simkins shows that the apartheid state managed to contain African urban immigration in the 1970s, although without quite the same success as in the 1960s. Natural increase and single migrants accounted for most of the urban African population increase. See Charles Simkins, *Four Essays on the Past, Present and Possible Future Distribution of the Black Population of South Africa*, Cape Town, 1983, particularly essay two and tables on pp. 61, 63, 71, and 72. I have found no convincing explanation for the relative success of influx control in the 1960s compared with the 1970s. It is possible that the striking successes of the 1960s were partly fictitious, that figures were gerrymandered to fulfill bureaucratic objectives, and that the 1970s figures were simply more realistic. It is also probable that pressures on rural resources accelerated during the 1970s and encouraged urban migration. The population of the home-

lands grew rapidly during the 1960s as a result of tightened influx control and "black spot" removals.

21. See, for example, interviews: Mofokeng, Ndala, Nzimande, Tsidi Nkosi. See also *RDM*, 5 February 1992, "Hold onto Your Hats in Gay, Soulless Soweto," by Woody Manqupu.

22. Interviews: Maseko (a), Duma, Lebelo, Ndoza (HWSFP).

23. Interviews: Moloantwa, Zodwa, L. Nkosi. On the Black Power Gang, see also *The World*, 8 and 11 August 1972, 21 23 February 1973, 19 March and 22 August 1974.

24. Interviews: Ndlovu, Mtshali, "Johannes."

25. Interviews: Ndala, Tsidi Nkosi, Mokgotsi. See also *The World*, 28 April and 25 May 1971. Note the position of the Hazels' territory in the 1968–1976 gangland map.

26. Interviews: Gibi, Mabhena, Moosie, Thotela.

27. Interview, Ndlovu.

28. Interview, Mofokeng.

29. Interviews: Tloteng, Mrs. Dlamini, Sirurufera. See chapter 5 for a discussion of *ndofaya* and *kalkoen* identity in the 1960s.

30. David Coplan, *In Township Tonight! South African Black City Music and Theatre*, London, 1985, p. 161. See also, for a more general discussion, pp. 161 188.

31. Coplan, *In Township Tonight!* pp. 181–188. See also Helen Lunn, "Antecedents of the Music and Popular Culture of the African post-1976 Generation," M.A. thesis, University of the Witwatersrand, 1986, pp. 110–111.

32. Coplan, *In Township Tonight!* pp. 161–165.

33. Interview, Duma.

34. Interview, Ndlovu.

35. Interview, Ndala.

36. Interviews: Nzimande, Ndlovu.

37. It is conceivable that the Kwaitos derived their name from this movie, although the more likely explanation is that it comes from the Afrikaans *kwaai ouens* ("angry/ fierce guys").

38. Interview, Maseko (a).

39. Interview, Lebelo.

40. This is apparently particularly true of three gangs that emerged in Emdeni during the early 1970s: the Amahoshiko, Valdez, and Top Seven (interview, Thotela).

41. See Coplan, *In Township Tonight!* p. 163. The level of social acceptance that the Americans enjoyed in Sophiatown was actually extremely unusual. Coplan underestimates the generational tension in Sophiatown. He also underplays the persistent sexual harassment and coercion by the gangs and the extent to which even the Americans were admired far more by men than by women.

42. Interview, Ndoza (HWSFP).

43. Interviews: Ndala, Mokgotsi. See also *The World*, 25 May 1971.

44. *Post*, 18 July 1971.

45. Interview, Ndala.

46. Interviews: Zodwa, Moloantwa.

47. Interview, Ndala.

48. Interviews: Nzimande, Ndoza. See also *The World*, 11 August 1972, letter from "Matabese," on Black Power Gang protection fees in Meadowlands.

49. Forker spoke to Meverett Koetz in June 1992. Unfortunately, it was a once-off interview. Mashiloane was interviewed by the History Workshop Soweto Film Project (HWSFP) in 1992.

50. According to Forker, a founding member who was widely regarded as the most important leadership figure in the Hazels, there were initially four members. Clifford Mashiloane, another founding member, claims there were five. Interviews: "Bra Forker" and Mashiloane (HWSFP).

51. Interview, Bra Forker.

52. Interviews: Bra Forker, Mashiloane (HWSFP), Chris Hlatswayo. There appears to be consensus on the origins of the name "Hazels." (Interestingly, a woman from Soweto by the name of Hazel Futa was crowned as the first Miss Africa South in April 1969. Given the emphasis on Hazel's beauty, the relatively uncommon name, and the timing of the gang's infatuation, it is not inconceivable that this is the same person. See *The World*, 18 April 1969.)

53. *The World*, 28 April 1971.

54. Interviews, "Gladys," Mampiki, Maseko, Mofokeng, Lebelo, Tloteng, Kambule, Morobe (HWSFP). All refer to the Soweto-wide fame of the gang.

55. Mbulelo Mzamane, *Children of Soweto*, Harlow, England, 1982, p. 81. The Hazels are also mentioned on pp. 77, 82, 112, 113, and 153.

56. Interviews: Mofokeng, Mashiloane (HWSFP), Bra Forker, Chris Hlatswayo, Gladys, Mampiki, Modise. See also Criminal Cases of the Witwatersrand Legal Division (WLD), Central Archives Depot, Pretoria, 474/72, State vs Paul Maroka and fifteen others.

57. Interview, Gladys.

58. Interviews: Khanyeza (HWSFP), Mashiloane (HWSFP), Mampiki, Gladys, Modise.

59. Interviews: Mofokeng, Khanyeza (HWSFP), Bra Forker, Mampiki, Modise.

60. Lunn, "Antecedents," pp. 181–182. See also Mzamane, *Children of Soweto*, p. 113.

61. Interviews: Gladys, Modise.

62. Interview, Bra Forker.

63. *The World* 2 February 1972; Interview, Kambule (b).

64. Interview, Gladys.

65. This is a composite picture drawn from interviews: Bra Forker, Mashiloane (HWSFP), Mofokeng, Lebelo, Chris Hlatswayo.

66. Interview, Modise.

67. Interview, Mashiloane (HWSFP).

68. Interviews: Mashiloane (HWSFP), Khanyeza (HWSFP), Morobe (HWSFP), L. Nkosi, Mampiki, Maseko, Msimanga, Motaung; *The World*, 8 January 1971, 20 October 1971, 7 January 1972, 21 March 1972, 11 October 1972; *Post*, 31 October 1971; WLD 474/72, State vs Maroka and fifteen others.

69. Interviews: Mashiloane (HWSFP), Bra Forker.

70. Interviews: Bra Forker, Mashiloane (HWSFP).

71. Interviews: Mashiloane (HWSFP), Morobe (HWSFP).

72. Interview, Mashiloane (HWSFP).

73. Interview, Bra Forker.

74. Interview, Gladys.

75. Interviews: Gladys, Mampiki.

76. This is a composite picture drawn from interviews: Zikalala, D. Nkosi, Sirurufera, Ndala, Nzimande, Seth Mazibuko (HWSFP). See also *The World*, 9 and 22 November 1972.

77. Interviews: Mofokeng, Bra Forker, Thotela, Mashiloane (HWSFP), Seth Mazibuko (HWSFP), Morobe (HWSFP).

78. Interview, Chris Hlatswayo.

79. Interview, Zodwa.

80. *The World*, 13 December 1972; interview, Masoka.

81. Interviews: Mofokeng, Mampiki, Bra Forker. See also WLD 474/72, State vs Paul Maroka and fifteen others; during the trial the Hazel defendants alleged that a key prosecution witness was a member of the Judas gang and therefore unreliable.

82. Interviews: Mashiloane (HWSFP), Mbuli, Mofokeng.

83. Interview, Ndala.

84. Interviews: Bra Forker, Mashiloane (HWSFP).

85. Interview, Gladys. See also *The World*, 24 October 1973, reporting on the alleged attack by a group of Xhosa migrants on a member of the Hazels; it is likely that this was a reprisal against harassment.

86. Interviews: Mashiloane (HWSFP), Bra Forker; *The World*, 20 October 1971, 14 February 1972, 21 March 1972, 11 October 1972, 1 May 1973, 29 June 1973, 7 November 1973; WLD 474/72, State vs Maroka and fifteen others. Interestingly, there was remarkable uniformity in the ages of the Hazels brought to trial throughout this period. Their ages ranged between eighteen and twenty-three, with only two over twenty-one.

87. Interviews: Gladys, Mampiki, Bra Forker.

88. Interview, Mashiloane (HWSFP). For student anti-crime initiatives, see interview, Seathlolo.

89. *The World*, 11 August 1972, letter from "Matabese" of Meadowlands.

90. See chapter 7 for more detail on the West Rand Administration Board.

91. See David Goodhew, "The People's Police-Force: Communal Policing Initiatives in the Western Areas of Johannesburg, circa 1930–1962," *Journal of Southern African Studies*, 19, 3, September 1993.

92. Interviews: Tsidi Nkosi, Xhaba.

93. Interviews: Gibi, Simelane, Nzimande.

94. Interviews: Sibiya, Makgene, Kheswa, Tsidi Nkosi, Xhaba.

95. *The World*, 13 February 1973, 2 January 1974, 5 June 1975.

96. Interview, Letsatsi Radebe and Sinah Madipere Senakoane (Jeremy Seekings, Johannesburg, 7 May 1991). Madipere's surname changed after her remarriage. Interviews: Thotela, Zodwa. See also *The World*, 19 March 1974, in which the newspaper singles out the Black Power Gang as the main target of the new anti-crime initiative; and 5 March 1974, in which a Killarney resident looks to neighboring Meadowlands for an example of effective crime control.

97. Interview, Radebe and Madipere (Seekings). Interview, Thotela. See also *The World*, 4, 6, and 8 March 1974.

98. Interview, Zodwa.

99. Interview, Radebe and Madipere (Seekings).

100. Interview, Radebe and Madipere (Seekings).

101. Interview, Radebe and Madipere (Seekings).

102. *The World*, 27 May 1974. See also interviews with Mawela and Ngobese, who testify to effective Makgotla activity in Tladi and Moletsane.

103. *The World*, 17 June 1974. See also G. Viljoen, *Report of the Commission of Enquiry into the Penal System of the Republic of South Africa*, Pretoria, 1976 (Viljoen Report), RP 78/1976, p. 38. Viljoen observed that the Makgotla had many affiliated branches spread throughout Soweto.

104. *The World*, 15 July 1974.

105. *The World*, 15 November 1974 and 23 January 1975.

106. *The World*, 6 June 1974. See also Viljoen Report, 78/1976, p. 40, par. 3.2.19; and *The World*, 20 May and 29 August 1974.

107. Viljoen Report, 78/1976, p. 39, par. 3.2.15.

108. *The World*, 5 July 1974, letter from Z. R. Benghu.

109. See, for example, the Makgotla memorandum handed to the chief magistrate of Johannesburg, in *The World*, 29 August 1974. See also Viljoen Report, 78/1976, p. 39, par. 3.2.9.

110. *The World*, 8 July 1974.

111. Interview, Radebe and Madipere (Seekings).

112. See, for example, *The World*, 6 and 12 March 1974 (letter from Vincent Bojang of Meadowlands), 20 May 1974, and 20 August 1974. For other Makgotla flogging incidents that received media attention, see *The World*, 9 July 1974, 22 August 1975, 11 February 1976, and 26 February 1976.

113. Interview, Radebe and Madipere (Seekings). See also Makgotla memorandum in the Viljoen Report, 78/1976, p. 40, par. 3.2.15.

114. Makgotla memorandum in the Viljoen Report, 78/1976, p. 40, par. 3.2.15. See also *The World*, 17 June 1974, 19 May 1975, and 26 April 1976, "Makgotla to Evict Families of Criminals."

115. Interviews: Maponya, Radebe and Madipere (Seekings); Makgotla memorandum to the Johannesburg Chief Magistrate in *The World*, 29 August 1974; Makgotla memorandum in the Viljoen Report, 78/1976, p. 39, par. 3.2.9.

116. Interview, Radebe and Madipere (Seekings).

117. Interview, Thotela; see *The World*, 5 March 1974, letter from Ramarulu of Killarney, and 12 March 1974, letter from Vincent Bojang of Meadowlands.

118. See, for instance, *The World*, 19 May, 17 June, 21 June, and 5 July 1974.

119. See Viljoen Report, 78/1976, p. 40, par. 3.2.16 to 3.3.23.

"1976 STOPPED ALL OUR FUN": SOWETO GANGS AND THE RISE OF STUDENT POLITICS, 1970–1976

The gangs were almost entirely unaware of the political culture gathering momentum in Soweto's high schools during the early 1970s. They did notice, however, that more youths from their neighborhoods were going to high school than ever before and that students were becoming far more confident in defending themselves against gang harassment. Like most parents and political commentators, the street youths were surprised by the student protests of June 1976. But once Soweto erupted into violence and the uprising broadened beyond educational issues, the gangs found they could identify with the antiestablishment anger of the students. In this respect, there were striking similarities to the political foment of 1959–1960, although by 1976 the high school students were far more numerous and assertive. As in 1960, many gang members participated in the rebellion, albeit in a sporadic, disorganized, and often opportunistic fashion.

In this chapter, I begin by focusing on the tensions which arose between street gangs and increasingly politicized high school students during the 1970s and argue that the two groups developed a heightened sense of oppositional identity. Then I show that, despite the eagerness of the South African Student Movement (SASM) and other Black Consciousness groups to "conscientize" and embrace street gangs during the mid 1970s, the organizations made little concrete progress in this respect. Finally, I examine the role of gangs during the 1976–1977 uprising itself and argue that no formal links between gangs and political organizations were established. Moreover, in order to enhance its credibility with the wider Soweto community, the

Soweto Students Representative Council (SSRC) actively curbed gang involvement in political campaigns and even took upon itself the responsibility of combating gang crime during 1976–1977.

SCHOOLS AND POLITICAL CONSCIOUSNESS

The conditions that had encouraged a relatively acquiescent urban African population during the 1960s altered significantly during the early 1970s. The economic boom was over and the newly introduced administration board system proved extremely unpopular: jobs were scarcer, housing projects ground to a virtual halt, and local services went into decline.[1] The new administration boards, designed to centralize the running of urban African affairs in the hands of the Department of Bantu Administration and Development, operated according to a strict self-financing principle. Basic services in Soweto simultaneously deteriorated and became more expensive under the West Rand Administration Board (WRAB), which, unlike the Johannesburg Non-European Affairs Department, received no subsidy from the Johannesburg City Council. The WRAB employed dozens of new, well-paid white bureaucrats, which increased the portion of the budget allocated to salaries and left even less for services. WRAB officials also developed a reputation for arrogance and authoritarianism.

Despite these hardships, the adults of Soweto remained politically docile during the early 1970s. There was widespread fear of the Security Police and informers were believed to be everywhere. Workers seemed concerned primarily to keep their jobs and stay out of trouble. Even the 1973 Natal strike wave had little impact in Soweto.[2] The adults of the 1970s had experienced the political clampdown of the early 1960s, the banning of the ANC and PAC, and the Rivonia trial. Politically demoralized, they held out little hope for substantial changes to the status quo. The teenagers of the 1970s were a fresh generation filled with dissatisfaction and unfamiliar with the bitterness of defeat. As school-based youths began to search for political expression they found most parents, even if often sympathetic to their ideals, unresponsive and fearful.[3]

The secondary school constituency grew rapidly in Soweto from about 1972. Once the government acknowledged the need to widen the urban African skills base, the Department of Bantu Education (DBE) made additional funding available and the ten-year freeze in local secondary school construction came to an end. The number of secondary schools in Soweto doubled between 1972 and 1976 while enrollment almost tripled during this period from 12.600 to over 34,000.[4] By 1976, roughly one-fifth of the 170,000 schoolchildren in Soweto were in secondary school. Though government expenditure on education rose rapidly, it could not keep pace with the expansion in numbers. Secondary schooling became much more accessible to the average Sowetan household but the quality of schooling suffered. To make matters worse, the recession of 1975 forced the government to cut back on Bantu Education spending at precisely the moment of greatest expansion and rising expectations.[5] Within a very short space of time, high school students emerged as a significant force in Soweto. Not only did their numbers increase almost exponentially, but their frustrations began to mount, both with the education system itself and with life under apartheid generally.

The process of politicization in Soweto's high schools began, albeit in subtle forms, towards the end of the 1960s, especially at Morris Isaacson High School and Orlando High School. Despite limited resources, these two schools had maintained a "culture of learning" throughout the 1960s. Their headmasters, Lekgau Mathabatha and T. W. Kambule, were broadminded and offered protection to teachers who raised socially relevant issues in the classroom. Both headmasters were respected figures in Soweto, and the DBE realized that their dismissal would seriously damage the credibility of Bantu Education. Debating societies and Christian youth groups, which flourished in most Sowetan secondary schools, provided another small opening for political ideas. Though initially politically innocuous, both groups encouraged intellectual curiosity and allowed a layer of intellectually confident student leadership to emerge. Perhaps the most important development was the establishment of a student organization called the African Student Movement (ASM) in 1968. The ASM was a largely apolitical organization concerned with improving educational conditions in Soweto (which is probably why it was initially tolerated by the state). It organized extra tuition for students and criticized incompetent teachers and excessive corporal punishment. It also tried to develop student representative structures in the school system, establishing footholds in several Sowetan secondary schools. The ASM not only improved student representation in individual schools, but established crucial links between Sowetan schools.

The ASM, the debating societies, and the Christian groups became radicalized quite suddenly once they linked up to the Black Consciousness movement. From 1968 until about 1971 the South African Black Consciousness movement was confined almost exclusively to Steve Biko's South African Students' Organisation (SASO), which drew its support from university-based intellectuals. In the Transvaal it established an important stronghold at the University of the North at Turfloop near Pietersburg, one of the new rural campuses designed to cultivate home-grown bantustan elites. From 1971, SASO recognized the need to reach beyond black campuses. It helped set up the Black People's Convention (BPC), an organization of primarily urban-based older professionals. More importantly, SASO was searching for ways of extending its influence into high schools, and its opportunity arose when the ASM sent out feelers towards the Black Consciousness movement. The ASM soon had representatives at SASO conferences and even received some financial assistance from the university body. In 1972 the ASM changed its name to the South African Students' Movement (SASM) in line with SASO's more inclusive interpretation of black identity. From then on it adopted an explicitly political agenda and transformed school debating societies into dynamic political forums. Through its Black Theology wing, SASO also influenced and encouraged the school-based Student Christian Movement (SCM).[6]

Black Consciousness was reinforced in the schools by a number of politically conscious Turfloop students (many of them expelled before finishing their studies) who took up jobs as teachers in Soweto's high schools. The most prominent of these teachers was Ongopotse Tiro, who taught at Morris Isaacson in 1972 and early 1973.[7] The DBE forced some of these teachers out of their Soweto jobs, but they were often able to make a major impact even in the few weeks or months of their stay. Besides, the state could not keep track of all the Turfloop graduates who had been influenced by Black Consciousness ideology. These ex-Turfloop teachers encouraged political debate and spoke regularly at SASM functions.

Political ideas seeped through from Morris Isaacson and Orlando High to Naledi, Sekano Ntoana, and Orlando West high schools before spreading to other secondary schools in Soweto. Links were made through debating societies, SASM, SCM, and other Christian youth groups. In the mid-1970s, Black Consciousness ideology spread rapidly in many of the new post-1972 schools such as Lomula High, Diepkloof Junior Secondary, Phefeni Junior Secondary, Orlando North Secondary, and Dr. Vilakazi Secondary. Almost from their inception the new schools were exposed to an atmosphere of mounting political assertiveness, unlike the older schools, which had experienced many years of political vacuum. By the mid-1970s most secondary schools in Soweto had politically active cores of between thirty and a hundred students, concentrated heavily in the more senior classes. Sympathy and support extended well beyond the politicized core.[8]

SCHOOL AND STREET: 1972 TO EARLY 1976

In the 1960s, schools were relatively marginal and posed little serious threat to gang prestige. It was possible to take school seriously and simultaneously associate with a neighborhood gang. But in the 1970s, school and gang identities polarized. This is not to suggest that male youth identity suddenly split neatly between schoolgoers and gang members. Rather, school and gang sharpened as two opposite poles in a continuum of possible identities. At one end were committed and increasingly politicized high school students whose aspirations were based on education and professional achievement. At the other end were members of large and distinctive gangs, such as the Hazels and the Dirty Dozen, who understood social prestige in terms of territory, physical prowess, street wisdom, and style. Probably the majority of Sowetan male youths floated between these two poles. Identities were still often blurred and ambiguous, and they shifted through time. There were a few gang members who attended school, and there were probably many schoolgoers who admired gangs and even aspired to gang membership. These students, however, were unlikely to complete their schooling; polarization made this sort of overlapping identity increasingly unlikely. Girls and young women, it seems, were more attracted to the school environment, although their identities may have been complicated by their emotional or familial association with individual gang members. Most of the ambiguity existed amongst the vast number of non-schoolgoing male youths who did not clearly associate with gangs. Many were employed and many aspired to return to school while simultaneously mixing at the neighborhood level with both gang members and students. The gang member and the committed senior student, each with his own style and value system, acted as the most important alternative role models for the large floating majority of youths.

If anything, school identification became stronger during the process of politicization. Politics provided students with a new sense of common purpose; high school students were no longer united purely by their educational aspirations but also by liberatory camaraderie. This was clearly the case at Morris Isaacson, Orlando High, Naledi, and Sekano Ntoana by 1972–1973. Young activists emerged as powerful new role models. There was growing participation in school-based political and cultural activities that continued well after class hours. Within the world of the high school it became increasingly fashionable to be politically active and knowledgeable.[9] While non-schoolgoers did not necessarily join hardened gangs, and even by early 1976 only an active minority of high school students were intensely involved in politics, the worlds of the high school and the gang drew further apart.[10] Tension between street gangs and school students regularly spilled over into violent confrontation during the early 1970s. The gangs saw schools as challenging their territorial prestige, particularly the secondary schools, which, unlike the junior and primary schools with their narrow neighborhood intake, drew together students from a fairly wide geographical area. Not only did secondary schools muddy neighborhood identities, but they often competed directly for membership and loyalty. In addition, more teenage girls were exposed to gang harassment as the availability of secondary schooling drew them out of their neighborhoods in increasing numbers. It was the harassment of schoolgirls, more than any other issue, that triggered violent clashes between school students and gangs.

As I noted in chapter 5, urban primary schooling expanded significantly during the 1960s; this was eventually followed by secondary school growth in the early 1970s. As a result, many gang members of the late 1960s and 1970s had attended school until late primary or even early secondary levels before becoming seriously involved in gang life. Some dropped out of school because they could not cope with the work or because of financial difficulties. For many, however, gang life seemed more attractive than school. Most students had neighborhood friends who were involved in gangs—they often played soccer together after hours—and there was an ever-present temptation to abandon the discipline and drudgery of school. This was so in the case of Oupa Ndala, who became a member of the Bandidos gang after spending some time at Morris Isaacson: "I had a lot of friends who never attended school and at the end of the day I ended up joining them because the life they led was interesting." This generation of gangsters, unlike that of the 1950s, was widely exposed to at least primary schooling. Possibly to compensate for their feelings of failure or exclusion, this generation scorned education and emphasized the freedom of street life. "It was fun," says Ndala, "We enjoyed staying in the township during the day; it was our choice, not to say there was no employment." The Bandidos, like the Hazels and the Dirty Dozen, were particularly hostile to schoolgoing or employed youths. They developed a reputation for robbing and assaulting students and teachers. Ndala describes a typical day for the Bandidos: "As loafers we hang around the shops and smoke dagga; when it's break time for the school students we would open our knives and take whichever girls we wanted. They were afraid of us because they knew we would stab them even if we would not kill them."[11]

Gang harassment of school students mounted steadily from the late 1960s and peaked during the phase of secondary school expansion between 1973 and 1976. Two Sowetan headmasters observed in October 1972 that students were staying away from certain schools for fear of gang intimidation.[12] In 1973 it was reported that several school students died at the hands of gangsters annually and "the toll of brutally assaulted pupils" was "on the increase."[13] Harassment solidified school identification as students came together to defend themselves and organize reprisals against troublesome gangs.

As in the 1960s, gangsters encountered powerful opposition from Morris Isaacson and Orlando High students. Mary Mxadana, a former teacher, was impressed by the unity with which Morris Isaacson students "disciplined" criminal elements during the 1970s. "If you wore a school uniform you were really protected."[14] In February 1976, Morris Isaacson students made headlines when they beat up a youth who had allegedly been molesting students. Students resisted attempts by the police to intervene and proceed with official charges. They claimed that the police were ineffective and that students had their "own courts" to deal with the youth.[15] Orlando High also retained its reputation for forceful reprisals against gangsters who molested schoolgirls. This school had relatively little trouble from gangs in the 1970s.[16] Naledi High and Sekano Ntoana developed a similar reputation in the 1970s. At Naledi the students had a real sense of "self-identity and solidarity." If any student suffered at the hands of gangsters, the student body would organize self-defense units to "punish" the culprits.[17] At Sekano Ntoana, former student Jake Msimanga recalls, the gangsters "really lacked the guts to pounce on you. There would be no school for two or three days until they were apprehended. So they knew what it meant. . . . People had no faith in the police. People would go out, even teachers would go out together with the students, to hunt the thugs, apprehend the thugs, bring them back into the schoolyard and thrash these guys."[18]

Gangsters were killed or assaulted in a number of school offensives during the 1970s. In August 1973, sixteen Pimville school students appeared in court following the death of an X5 gang member in a school reprisal during 1972. The students argued in their defense that the Kliptown police had failed to act against the gang, which had been making life in the area "unbearable."[19] In April 1974 a Zola youth, who had apparently been involved in constant gang harassment, was stoned to death by a group of students from the recently built Jabulani Junior Secondary School.[20] The best-publicized incident occurred in November 1974 when students from the Phiri Higher Primary School clashed with members of the ZX5 gang. Two gangsters were killed and five injured. Two teachers and seven students were later committed for trial. The accused were said to have cornered the gangsters in a house after an intensive search. The accused were eventually given suspended sentences after the headmaster of Phiri Higher Primary submitted evidence in mitigation, much as in the Pimville X5 case, that students had been subjected to ongoing harassment and were frustrated by the failure of the police to act effectively.[21] A witness to the Phiri incident emphasizes the brutality of the students. It was rumored that when the brother of the ZX5 leader was killed "his intestines were taken out of his stomach."[22] Spokes Ndlovu, who was a member of the gang, recalls that students were in the process of hacking the leader's leg off with a hacksaw when the police intervened.[23] In early 1976, Diepkloof Junior Secondary School organized reprisals against the Damarras. "After the Damarras butchered one of our boys," a former student recalls, "we went to their homes; we rounded them up and quite a lot of them were severely beaten up. . . . We were wild."[24] In another well-publicized case in May 1976, two young men who were molesting a school teacher on her way to work were beaten to death by students in Orlando North. *The World* reported the following:

> The children stormed out of the school and attacked the men when they heard [the teacher] screaming for help. The two would-be robbers fled when they saw the hundreds of children pouring out of Orlando North Secondary School. But one of them was caught and stoned near the school. The other was beaten to death by a group of children who chased him more than a mile through the streets before cornering him in a yard. . . . An onlooker said later that he had never imagined that school children could be so vicious.[25]

These incidents illustrate the intensity of the anger that school students felt toward intimidatory gangs and the unity with which they responded to harassment.

BLACK CONSCIOUSNESS AND THE NON-SCHOOL YOUTH

Beyond the schools the Black Consciousness movement had little impact on young Sowetans. Non-school youth had low levels of literacy and no institutional access to the ideas of the movement. Those involved in neighborhood gangs were absorbed in immediate parochial rivalries. Although they felt anger over blocked mobility, pass controls, and racial discrimination, they had no interest in politics, no sense of social or community responsibility. Apart from very localized loyalties, they chose their victims indiscriminately; they targeted the most vulnerable rather than the most prosperous or privileged.[26]

From as early as 1972, SASO recognized the need to penetrate and "conscientize" the urban youth constituency beyond the schools. A resolution to this effect was carried unanimously at the 1972 General Students' Council:

> That this Congress noting: 1. The large number of black youth who have been condemned by the system to be virtual outcasts; 2. that this group has been ignored by most black organisations; 3. that the youth of any

community are its most important members; 4. that there is an urgent need for this section of the black community to be given the attention it deserves; Therefore resolves: (i) That the BPC devise youth programmes directed at: (a) instilling a sense of belonging in this group to the rest of the community, (b) re-orientating their basic values towards Black Consciousness and Black Solidarity, (c) develop their potential so as to make them useful members of the Black Community; (ii) That the National Executive in conjunction with regions and branches and other black organisations conduct leadership seminars for this section of the Black Community.

A further resolution noted the general need to establish youth clubs that would cater to those both in and out of school.[27]

SASM, meanwhile, came independently to the conclusion that it was important to make contact with non-school youth. Between January and June 1973, SASM, in collaboration with SASO, set up first the Transvaal Youth Organisation (TRAYO) and then the National Youth Organisation (NAYO) primarily to organize among the non-school youth constituency.[28] Khehla Mthembu, an ASM and SASM leader during the early 1970s, explains why SASM felt its constituency to be too limited:

> I come from a very tough area called Zola. Just to give you a perfect example: I think I am the only university graduate in my area. All my friends were just what you can call ordinary boys in the street. . . . So we felt a bit distanced [at] the Deep Soweto branch [of SASM] because this was not only me, all of us in Deep Soweto felt that we cannot be seen as just a student body out there. We want to have something that would include the other people in the community . . . to have an organization that includes all the youth and everybody ... that was the birth of [TRAYO and] NAYO. . . . These were formed after SASM, these were the projects of SASM. SASM said, we are the student movement but we feel we are incomplete, we need the so-called *tsotsis*, the so-called thugs, we need to involve them.... We wanted an organization to relate to the youth irrespective of whether they were students or not.[29]

Between 1973 and 1976, there was ongoing discussion within the Black Consciousness movement over the need to draw in the unemployed street youth. SASO's Commission on Community Development, for instance, addressed the issue of "social drop-outs": "Voluntary group workers and professional social workers and other relevant and interested parties should join in the recruitment of the so-called 'Outcasts,' towards redirecting their thinking towards Black Consciousness."[30] In July 1973 the Black Consciousness–

affiliated People's Experimental Theatre stressed the importance of "redirecting the energy of so-called juvenile delinquents into something positive."[31] From about 1974 the movement began an internal debate over the use of violence in the resistance struggle. There was growing support for more aggressive methods.[32] At a SASO "Formation School" in September 1974, Rubin Hare, SASO's vice-president, argued that Black Consciousness had to infiltrate the "tsotsi element" in the cities and turn their criminal energy toward whites. The writer of a later organizational report on the Formation School argued that the movement should recruit members who are prepared to fight. "Whilst we are intellectualising, the *tsotsis* are far more brilliant than us. If any infiltration is to be done, we must infiltrate the tsotsis."[33] Amos Masondo, who was a SASM national organizer until his arrest in September 1975, recalls that by 1975 the Black Consciousness leadership knew that it "had to go down to the masses and grassroots conscientizing. The high school students were not grassroots; the grassroots were those who weren't conscientized, organized to prepare for the next stage, to fight."[34]

In practice, TRAYO and NAYO seem to have concentrated on coordinating the activities of a number of youth clubs and associations, most of which were church affiliated and already operational.[35] The clubs may have drawn in non-school youth, but there is little evidence to suggest that the organizations engaged substantially with the gang constituency. The Cillie Commission and Security Police memoranda point only to the *intentions* of the BCM organizations; none of their evidence suggests effective influence or recruitment within the gang constituency.

Khotso Seathlolo, who became president of the SSRC for a brief period, argues that many early school-leavers were politicized "outside of the schoolyard" through youth clubs and the church but it is unlikely that he is referring to hardcore dropouts who had very few years of schooling and little interest in church organizations.[36] Fanyana Mazibuko does recall some gang members becoming politicized during the early to mid 1970s. Ongopotse Tiro, a SASO activist who taught temporarily at Morris Isaacson, used to make an effort to engage with street youths who molested school students. Occasionally, according to Mazibuko, a few gang members even came to Black Consciousness meetings in Soweto. They were always distinctive not only because of their clothes but because of their emotional and spontaneously "unsophisticated" approach to political issues.[37] It is probable that some individual gang members were "converted" through neighborhood or familial contacts. Black Consciousness activists at schools recognized that gang youths were social victims. During anti-gang reprisals, the activists were uncomfortable with mere beatings; they always attempted to talk to the apprehended youths, to convince them that what they were doing was wrong, to redirect their energies positively.[38]

Despite the rhetoric to the contrary, the Black Consciousness movement made no systematic attempt to draw the street youth into political organizations. SASO and SASM had a highly intellectual political tradition that was inaccessible to youths outside of school or university.[39] Moreover, the Black Consciousness philosophy was "best articulated in English." The gang constituency spoke *tsotsitaal* and was largely inarticulate in English. Few activists seemed able or willing to engage with gangsters in their own language.[40] The movement, it appears, disapproved of *tsotsitaal* both because of its criminal connotations and because of its substantial Afrikaans component.[41] The movement was also out of touch with the interests of the street youth; it concentrated on issues that affected students directly, such as student representation, corporal punishment, and Afrikaans-medium teaching.[42] A former member of the Damarras of Diepkloof emphasizes the remoteness of Black Consciousness politics from his own world during 1976:

> I did not know why they were fighting. Some were saying it was because of the Afrikaans language. Aah, but I was no more at school so I never involved myself in those things. All I wanted for myself was just money, that's all. I would just go and do housebreaking and gain something. Then I wouldn't give anyone any trouble. All what the school kids were doing had nothing to do with me.[43]

STUDENTS, GANGS, AND THE 1976 UPRISING

Simmering discontent with Bantu Education boiled over in 1976 when the DBE formally introduced Afrikaans-medium teaching in key subjects at the junior secondary level. The DBE went ahead with the dual-medium plan in spite of heavy criticism from parent, teacher, and student bodies. Junior secondary schools were already struggling to deal with the fallout of a double intake in 1976 following the official scrapping of the final year of primary schooling, Standard Six. In May a series of protests and a class boycott were organized at Orlando West Junior Secondary School, and these quickly spread to several other Sowetan junior secondaries. In late May, SASM organized solidarity boycotts at all its affiliated schools. An affiliation drive was launched in an attempt to unite student opposition to Afrikaans. On 13 June, SASM called a meeting attended by representatives from most secondary and higher primary schools in Soweto. An Action Committee was mandated to organize a massive protest march on 16 June.

The march, according to those who participated, was peaceful and well-coordinated. The Action Committee only lost control of events once the police, feeling cornered and threatened, panicked and opened fire on the advancing crowd of singing children. The police violence changed the mood of the demonstration entirely. In the evening, anger overflowed and riots, looting, and arson broke out spontaneously.[44] Over the following two weeks of unrest and repression, the Action Committee transformed itself into a more permanent structure, the Soweto Students' Representative Council. The council, which was elected by and answerable to a body made up of two representatives from virtually every secondary and higher primary school in Soweto, attempted to coordinate and direct student—and wider—political activity in Soweto.

The participants in the initial demonstration on 16 June were exclusively uniformed students. Hirson estimates that there were 15,000 students ranging in age from ten to twenty.[45] After the shootings the picture became more blurred. That evening, students were central actors in a vengeful rampage against WRAB property and anything identified as a symbol of "the system." It is clear that street youth joined in at this point.[46] According to the report of the Cillie Commission, established to investigate the causes of the upheaval, "tsotsis, skollies and vagrants in general showed a tendency towards crime and violence. Where they constituted a large proportion of a rioting group, their contempt for justice and the law and their urge to commit crime and demonstrate their power probably carried the others along to further and worse riots and violence."[47] The commission tended to emphasize the role of *tsotsis*, possibly to delegitimize the political motivations for the uprising. But Sowetan residents themselves generally support this impression. One observer, for instance, suggests that gang members, familiar with streetfighting and violence, were often regarded as leaders during attacks on government property.[48]

In the days and months that followed, looting and robbery became an increasingly prominent feature of the unrest. Criminal activity was dominated by the gang youth but it was by no means exclusive to them. There was a carnival atmosphere in Soweto as government authority in the area broke down. Residents helped themselves to large quantities of liquor that flowed from the shattered beerhalls.[49] "Liquor was free," recalls a Meadowlands resident, "so they got gloriously drunk." A Zola resident claims that, as a twenty-year-old, he "started drinking on June 16; I drank everything I laid my hands on."[50] Goods trucks and delivery vans entering Soweto from Johannesburg were hijacked continuously; this became almost a sport for local youths, which they dubbed *sibamba ama* targets or "catching" targets. Occasionally students joined in but this was primarily the sport of the gangs. The vans were stopped, the

Photo 7.1 A car is overturned and burned by youths outside Kwa Thema Stadium during the 1976 rebellion, which spread beyond Soweto to several other townships on the Witwatersrand. It became difficult to distinguish between students and gang members. (From *The Star*, 1976. Courtesy of Bailey's African History Archives. Reprinted with permission.)

drivers ejected, and the goods distributed freely to participants and passers-by.[51] Attacks on beerhalls and WRAB offices were primarily politically motivated but the *tsotsis* were never far behind, stealing money, liquor, furniture, and anything else of value.[52] A former Orlando West student relates a typical scene: "Down the road a beerhall was destroyed and the youths found a safe which they struggled for hours to open. There was jubilation once they opened it and everyone was grabbing money, helping themselves to money. Kids were running past my house clutching notes."[53] In the second major wave of unrest in August, the pattern repeated itself. *The World* reported that there were clear instances of *tsotsi* criminal activity when thousands of students poured into the streets to attack beerhalls. "Eyewitnesses said the situation got out of hand when tsotsis joined the students." In one incident, "a dry-cleaner's van was hijacked by a mob of tsotsis who looted it and took clothing. They later overturned the van. It was then set alight."[54]

Political and criminal activity became difficult to separate, as did the gang element from the students (Photo 7.1). The usual spatial separation broke down once the students began the boycott. Although students initially wore uniforms to demonstrate solidarity and unity, they came to realize that they were making themselves easy targets for the security forces and switched to the anonymity of other clothes.[55] Certainly the Cillie Commission found the task of categorizing the youth elements bewildering:

> Black people of all age groups and of both sexes took part in the rioting. However, young people were particularly prominent. The following are included under the term young people as used here: Pre-schoolgoing children, schoolchildren, youths who had already left school and were working or were unemployed, and tsotsis. It is not always possible to distinguish between these classes. To begin with, Black children do not go to school until they are seven, and very often are even older before they start going to school. In the second place, it is not uncommon to find children of twenty years and older at school. In exceptional cases, this could also happen at higher primary schools. Witnesses' observations are consequently not always accurate or reliable. It is also possible to be mistaken about post-school youths; the tsotsi does not always wear the clothing that is considered characteristic of his kind.[56]

Cillie notes that both males and females participated in the riots, without attaching any significance to the detail. It may, in fact, have been a useful clue in distinguishing student from gang elements. Several interviewees observe that girls participated widely in student politics during the 1970s (even if only very rarely in leadership positions). This was not altogether surprising given the greater numbers of girls at school and their relative confidence within school, as opposed to street, culture. School was the most important collective environment for teenage girls. It is unlikely that non-schoolgoing girls participated in the rising in significant numbers. Evidence in this regard is, however, extremely thin and impressionistic. The participation of female youth in the 1976 uprising remains a subject for further inquiry.

Did youth gangs play a purely criminal role in the uprising? The general consensus among residents is that gangsters simply took advantage of the upheaval. The police were stretched to contain the political opposition and the gangs were protected by large, volatile crowds. Moreover, in an atmosphere of racial polarization, robbery of white-owned or "collaborationist" property lost any criminal stigma in Soweto; it was seen almost as a positive act of symbolic revenge.[57] Gangs, according to a Pimville resident, "continued with their criminal activities in the name of the struggle."[58] The Cillie Report supports this view: "Some witnesses said that the scholars [school students] created a situation which was then exploited by the tsotsis. There is no doubt that, with their criminal tendencies, tsotsis welcomed the opportunities for violence, theft and looting that the situation offered them."[59]

The attitudes of the youth gangs during the uprising were, however, more complex than this picture suggests. Brooks and Brickhill are correct to point out the uneven response of the gangs: "Countless tsotsis, like many unemployed youth (and how is one to draw a clear line between them?) were drawn to the side of the students."[60] In many instances the gangs displayed clear sympathies with the students. They could identify with immediate, confrontational political action. Gang participation in attacks on government and white-owned property was not always merely opportunistic. Many gangsters were expressing an antiestablishment rage and, for once, felt themselves in common cause with the wider youth constituency. Gangs also carried out numerous acts of spontaneous political sympathy in which they stood to gain little, such as confronting boycott breakers or other individuals perceived to be undermining black unity. There can be little doubt that they contributed to the effectiveness of stayaways by waylaying and intimidating workers who ignored the stayaway calls. Some gangs did apparently become more selective in their criminality by, for instance, concentrating on "white" targets or uncooperative local shop-owners. In the wake of the June and August shootings, students and street youth could identify with each other most easily through their common hatred of the police. Students, following Malcolm X's dictum, were now prepared to defend themselves "by any means necessary," something the gangs had always taken for granted. Gang members joined with relish in the stoning and petrol bombing of security force vehicles.[61]

The political links between students and gangs, it must be stressed, were informal and spontaneous. Gangs were never mobilized by the SSRC, nor were alliances negotiated. In fact, as I show below, the official SSRC position was extremely antagonistic toward gangs. Nevertheless, a number of individual gang participants, particularly those few who attended school or had close familial ties with students, did convert to politics during the uprising.[62] According to Snuki Zikalala, who was centrally involved in ANC recruitment in Botswana at the time, many of the exiles who fled from Soweto to the ANC camps during 1976–1977 were "raw street youth." They were politically unsophisticated but very willing military recruits. They often became very effective soldiers because "they were not scared of death" and were prepared to take on dangerous assignments. They were, however, difficult to discipline because they were not interested in political education and were generally unable to shake off their addictions to dagga and alcohol.[63] For many unemployed Sowetan youths who had wavered on the fringes of gang life, politics became "more cool" than gangsterism. These youths looked increasingly to the SSRC for role models and leadership rather than to the big-time gangs.[64]

THE 1976–1977 SOWETO
STUDENTS' REPRESENTATIVE COUNCIL

For more than a year after the 16 June upheaval, the SSRC was the most effective political force in Soweto.[65] The 1976 uprising marked an important turning point in the generational balance of power in Soweto, as in other urban centers. Parents, although often alarmed at the power invested in inexperienced youths with few responsibilities, generally accepted the student leadership because, as one older resident puts it, "they opened our eyes." Parents knew that they had to support their children to win back their respect, particularly after so many youths had been killed in police shootings.[66]

For the average gang member, though, the SSRC held little authority. The council, as its name suggests, was most effective within the school student constituency. It established a remarkably successful system of representation and communication within Soweto high schools. There were regular secret SSRC meetings during 1976–1977, attended usually by about a hundred students from a wide spread of schools.[67] The council was largely dependent on the school to mobilize students and disseminate information. In the early chaotic days of spontaneous boycotts following 16 June, the SSRC explicitly called for a return to school because it felt unable to regroup and organize outside of school networks.[68] The SSRC recognized the importance of winning over the support of a wider community and of broadening its focus beyond educational issues. The SSRC had no ready channels of communication with older residents, trade unions, migrants, or non-student youth.[69] Although it did make some attempts to negotiate and consult with non-student sections of the community, the council ultimately depended on taking political initiatives and hoping that Sowetans would accept its leadership through a mixture of moral persuasion and threats.

The initial strong approval that parents gave to the SSRC began to diminish during the series of stayaway calls between August and November 1976. The SSRC distributed pamphlets to parents and workers asking for their support but failed to explain adequately what they stood to gain from risking their jobs.[70] The pamphlets, moreover, were sometimes threatening. A pamphlet calling for a stayaway in September, for instance, concluded: "N.B. Your sons and daughters and all Black leaders shall be on the watch-out for sell-outs and traitors of the Black struggle! UNITED WE STAND."[71] In December, student–parent relations came under further strain as the SSRC called for a boycott of white-owned shops and, in respect for the dead, a somber, ascetic Christmas season. The SSRC's tone became distinctly intimidatory. Soweto residents who ignored the buy-at-home campaign "would regret it if found carrying goods bought in Johannesburg," a spokesman of the SSRC warned.[72] This caused much dissatisfaction among hardpressed workers since white-owned shops in Johannesburg sold goods more cheaply than the small Soweto stores. Workers often felt that students disregarded worker interests; that they were inadequately consulted. Many older residents began to resent being treated as mere equals by unmarried youths. The students, they argued, were too young and had too few responsibilities to wield such authority.[73] Workers also complained of coercion. During stayaways, bands of youths often waylaid workers on their way to work and motorists were stopped at makeshift roadblocks.[74] Shoppers were searched and often had their goods confiscated. The SSRC made genuine attempts to stop the intimidation of workers by students and blamed the coercive excesses on the "criminal element," over whom the council had no control. The council officially dissociated itself from coercive activity.[75] Nevertheless, the confusion between students and *tsotsis* damaged the image of the SSRC in the eyes of most Sowetans.

The residents most antagonistic toward the SSRC, especially during August and September 1976, were the migrant workers who lived in Soweto's hostels. In the early days of the uprising, the students made no effort to communicate with the hostel residents. They were entirely ignored as a constituency. The students had preconceptions of them as apolitical, unsophisticated outsiders. The migrants were enraged by the August stayaway calls. They were the most vulnerable workers, who stood the most to lose if fired; they felt unconsulted and neglected. Moreover, their more traditional attitudes made the youth leadership and the apparent disrespect for elders all the more unpalatable. The involvement of *tsotsis* in looting and the coercion of workers infuriated migrants, who had a long history of victimization at the hands of youth gangs. Migrants drew no distinction between *tsotsis* and students and reacted violently and randomly against Soweto youth during August. (It seems clear that they received backing from the police, who were eager to cultivate potential black allies and sow division among Sowetan residents.) Youths defended themselves with stones and petrol bombs in a series of bloody clashes with the migrants.[76] During these attacks, students and gangs found themselves on the same side warding off migrant incursions. Mzimhlophe, for instance, was home to both a large migrant hostel and the Hazels gang. The Hazels saw the migrant attacks as a direct challenge to their own territorial dominance. Clifford Mashiloane recalls these times:

> In 1976 we heard the Zulus were coming. Before that, people used to tease and insult them. . . . Some would even mug them and take their money away. When they came back to retaliate, they would go into the area where they were attacked or insulted. . . . They would attack anyone they saw. You were attacked for just standing at your gate. In 1976 they decided to retaliate in large numbers. . . . The lower end of Mzimhlophe was Hazel territory. Only two Hazels lived on the other side of Mzimhlophe. We told ourselves that we were not going anywhere, we were going to fight. So we resisted. . . . The police were helping them by shooting us with tear gas. We then decided they were not going to work. We prevented them from going to work by closing them off at Mzimhlophe and Phomolong stations.

According to Mashiloane, the clashes in Mzimhlophe built up towards a huge climactic battle. "It was about two o'clock in the day when they came down. They came in big trucks which off-loaded them inside the location, some next to my house there. We approached from the area next to my house. We fought with them and that is where we killed many of them. When the police intervened it was all over."[77]

After a number of disastrous confrontations, the students made a concerted effort in late 1976 to approach hostel leaders and discuss the clashes. Their efforts at reconciliation proved remarkably successful. It was important for the SSRC to stress its opposition to *tsotsi* crime and coercion. Migrant hostility was largely neutralized; some migrants even came round to supporting the students' stand against apartheid.[78]

Relations between the SSRC and non-student residents improved during the first half of 1977. Stayaways ceased, and the council took up issues that affected the wider community. The SSRC's successful campaign against rent increases and its onslaught against the Urban Bantu Council system were both extremely popular.[79] The anti-liquor campaign was more controversial, but it was widely supported by wives who resented the squandering of limited household income at shebeens and beerhalls.[80] The SSRC's apparent ability to curb crime also enhanced its credibility and authority in Soweto.

The relationship between the SSRC and the non-student youth was a complex one. Despite the Black Consciousness movement's initial enthusiasm for the idea of mobilizing and recruiting youth gangs, the SSRC made very little real progress in this regard. Certainly some attempts were made. Tsietsi Mashinini, the first leader of the SSRC, was apparently "streetwise" and acquainted with many gang members in his area. He addressed several open-air meetings in the early days of the uprising and tried to win gangs over in a disciplined way.[81] There is little evidence to suggest that he had any striking success. Mashinini fled into exile at a very early stage in the uprising, and this probably nullified much of the contact that had been achieved. The rapid turnover of SSRC leadership as a result of state repression (there were four SSRC presidents in the space of sixteen months) probably hampered the council's ability to build personal contacts and trust with gang leaders. Khotso Seathlolo, who succeeded Mashinini as the SSRC president, claims that, via neighborhood networks, the council was able to disseminate information and instructions to youth beyond the schools: "almost every street had someone who was at school." School students felt a responsibility to keep other neighborhood youths informed.[82] Nevertheless, communication with gangs worked at best on an ad hoc basis; ties were never formalized and activities were never coordinated. The political participation of gangs throughout 1976–1977 was sporadic and unorganized.

As the uprising progressed, the SSRC found itself increasingly forced to dissociate itself from gang activity. In fact, it was not long before it was declaring open hostility towards gangs. Like the PAC during 1959–1960, the Black Consciousness movement argued that an alliance with the street youth was essential. The gangs, as I have shown, were recognized as having great revolutionary potential. Once the 1976 uprising was underway, however, the SSRC realized the political dangers of such an alliance. First, the gang constituency proved to be uncontrollable; almost by definition the gangs rejected external discipline. The language and codes of the gangs were too distant from those of the politicized students. Moreover, too many of the students' political demands seemed to be centered around educational issues that were of no concern to the street youth. The gangs could identify easily with the anti-apartheid anger of the students but their methods and intellectual paradigms were worlds apart. Second, and perhaps more importantly, the SSRC began to find any association with the gangs politically embarrassing and divisive. The SSRC recognized the importance of forging township unity and consensus. Reconciliation with the migrants, for instance, would have been unthinkable without a clear declaration of hostility towards *tsotsis*. In order to retain sympathy with workers and parents, the SSRC had to curb coercive excesses; this involved discouraging gang participation in political activity and even at times apparently using *tsotsis* as scapegoats for its own internal breaches in political discipline. Third, the SSRC began to recognize the importance of crime as a popular grievance. By actively combating crime the SSRC could demonstrate its authority and community responsibility.

The SSRC formed special squads to prevent gang excesses during political campaigns and to curb gang crime generally. "We didn't want our people being harassed," Seathlolo explains. The student squads disarmed "out-of-control" youths and monitored gang involvement during campaigns.[83] Equally important, the students cracked down on gang crime, in many ways taking over the patrol functions of the Makgotla. They were, however, more effective in "disciplining" the gangs. The SSRC was able to mobilize on a larger scale than the Makgotla and the student activists could operate virtually full-time, particularly during the long months of the school boycott. With fewer responsibilities and greater muscle, students, unlike middle-aged fathers, were prepared to engage in violent confrontation. Gangs throughout Soweto were thrown into retreat.[84] Former Bandido Oupa Ndala comments: "1976 stopped all our fun. These school kids started terrorizing us as gangs. They started burning our houses. When the students turned against us I started realizing that gangsterism was a bad thing. 1976 gave the students the power to do anything they wanted to do. Students used to hunt us and, if they do not get you, they burn your family house."[85] On one occasion, after receiving complaints that train passengers were being molested by criminal youths, two hundred students patrolled a Soweto station to protect commuters.[86] Residents recall that there was a noticeable lull in crime and gang activity during the 1976–1977 uprising. Students managed to achieve what the police and Makgotla could not. The Christmas of 1976 proved to be the most peaceful festive season in Soweto for many years.[87]

As the township revolt of 1976–1977 unfolded, the Black Consciousness movement gradually came to understand that it had more in common with ordinary working-class residents than it did with the gang subculture. Although Black Consciousness was primarily a political movement of black youth, cultural rifts within the youth constituency proved to be too wide to enable the movement to forge a common black youth identity. Like the ANC of the 1950s, the Black Consciousness movement, although sympathetic to the plight of the street youth, was too concerned with the creation of a broader township consensus to risk taking on board the volatile and feared gang constituency. Like the ANC, the Black Consciousness movement could only contemplate recruiting youths involved with gangs once the youths had undergone a process of "rehabilitation." Few politicians were able to accept or understand the cultural logic of the gangs.

The decline in gang activity was largely a result of student crackdowns. However, as I have suggested, the political and community consciousness of the gangs was partially raised during the uprising. Some individual gang members did embrace the "struggle" while many more became at least more scrupulous in their choice of victims. Gangsterism lost much of its subcultural appeal. As bold, assertive activist role models multiplied, the prestige of political involvement rose in the streets. Gang life was gradually eclipsed by a rising alternative youth subculture.

NOTES

1. The best overview of socioeconomic conditions in Soweto in the years leading up to the Soweto uprising is in J. Kane-Berman, *Soweto: Black Revolt, White Reaction*, Johannesburg, 1978.

2. See Tom Lodge, *Black Politics in South Africa since 1945*, Johannesburg, 1983, p. 334.

3. Interviews: Morobe (HWSFP), Makhabela (HWSFP), Seth Mazibuko (HWSFP), Mohapi (HWSFP), Seathlolo, Nkondo, Duma.

4. A. Brooks and J. Brickhill, *Whirlwind before the Storm*, London, 1980, pp. 42–43.

5. J. Hyslop, "Schools, Unemployment and Youth: Origins and Significance of Student and Youth Movements, 1976–1987," *Perspectives in Education*, 10, 2, 1988–1989, p. 64.

6. For more detail on politicization in Soweto schools from the late 1960s until 1976, see N. Diseko, "The Origins and Development of the South African Students Movement (SASM)," *Journal of Southern African Studies*, 18, 1, March 1991; and Clive Glaser, "'We Must Infiltrate the Tsotsis': School Politics and Youth Gangs in Soweto, 1968–1976," *Journal of Southern African Studies,* 24, 2, June 1998.

7. After continual police harassment, Tiro eventually fled to Botswana in 1973 where he became involved in exile politics. He was killed by a parcel bomb in 1974.

8. Interviews: Masondo (Gerhart), Msimanga, Motaung, Siluma, Duma, Seathlolo, Morobe (HWSFP).

9. Interviews: F. Mazibuko, Mxadana, Seathlolo, Shubane, Ndlovu, Ndala, Mabhena.

10. Interviews: F. Mazibuko, Msimanga, Zikalala, Mofokeng, C. Hlatswayo, Khoza, Ngobese, Duma, Motaung.

11. Interviews: Ndala, T. Nkosi, Mabhena, F. Mazibuko, Lebelo, Ndoza (HWSFP).

12. G. M. Simelala, headmaster of Madibane High in Diepkloof, and T. W. Kambule of Orlando High, in *The World*, 4 October 1972; Kambule observed earlier that year in *The World*, 2 February 1972, that many students refused to go to Orlando North Secondary School, the first of the new Soweto secondary schools, for fear of the Hazels.

13. *Rand Daily Mail* (*RDM*), 30 April 1973.

14. Interview, Mxadana. See also interviews: Mofokeng, Tsotetsie, Moosie.

15. *The World*, 13 February 1976.

16. Interviews: Kambule, Nkondo.

17. Interviews: Seathlolo, Siluma, Motaung.

18. Interview, Msimanga. See also interview, Mabhena.

19. Criminal Cases of the Witwatersrand Legal Division (WLD), Central Archives Depot, Pretoria, 174/73, State vs Bennett Dieta and fifteen others; *The World*, 23 August, 27 September 1972, and 18 April 1974.

20. *The World*, 9 April 1974.

21. *The World*, 13 November 1974, 15 May 1975, and 24 September 1975.

22. Interview, Johannes.

23. Interview, Ndlovu.

24. Interview, Duma.

25. *The World*, 13 May 1976; *Weekend World*, 16 May 1976.

26. Interviews: Zikalala, Siluma, Mawela, C. Hlatswayo, Gibi, Simelane (a).

27. SASO/BCM Collection, University of South Africa Archive, Pretoria (UNISA SASO), Acc 153, Minutes of the proceedings of the Third General Students' Council of the SASO, St Peter's Seminary, Hammanskraal, 2–9 July 1972, resolutions 19/72 and 24/72. The Cillie Commission (RP 55/1980) noted that "Saso decided as long ago as 1972 to infiltrate the tsotsi community so that they could propagate their objectives there and use the tsotsis in their struggle against the authorities." This strategy, Cillie argued, "was nothing out of the ordinary. Some overseas organisations that were bent on causing revolt, disorder and chaos had seen fit to draw on people such as the tsotsis because they had experience of crime and violence, which are related to revolt and chaos." (RP 55/ 1980, pp. 416–417, par. 2.2.4, and p. 140, par. 4.3.9.) It seems likely that, on this issue as many others, the commission drew heavily on the evidence in the Security Police memoranda now located in the UNISA SASO collection. The memoranda were probably compiled specifically for the Cillie Commission. Although he was not explicit, Cillie was probably referring to the Black Panthers, given the attention that the earlier Schlebusch Report (RP 33/ 1974) gave to the organization. See P. M. Cillie, *Report of the Commission of Inquiry into the Riots at Soweto and Elsewhere from the 16th of June 1976 to the 28th of February 1977*, Pretoria, 1980; A. L. Schlebusch, *Fourth Interim Report of the Committee of Inquiry into Certain Organizations*, Pretoria, 1974.

28. UNISA SASO Acc 153, Security Police memorandum on Youth Organisations, pp. 1–3; interviews: Seathlolo, Masondo (Gerhart), Mthembu (Gerhart). See also Diseko, "Origins and Development of SASM," pp. 58–59.

29. Interview, Mthembu (Gerhart); see also interview, Seathlolo.

30. UNISA SASO Acc 153, "Commission Report: Community Development," undated (probably presented during the Fourth GSC, 14–22 July 1973).

31. UNISA SASO Acc 153, Report of the People's Experimental Theatre to the Fourth GSC, St Peter's Seminary, Hammanskraal, 14–22 July 1973.

32. Interview, Seathlolo.

33. UNISA SASO Acc 153, Security Police memoranda, "South African Students' Organisation" and "Memorandum on Attempts By Black Organisations to Recruit Tsotsis, School Students and Teachers." Hare claims to have made contact with colored gangs in western Johannesburg, such as the Spaldings, Fast Guns, and Vultures, in an attempt to influence them.

34. Interview, Masondo (Gerhart).

35. Interview, Masondo (Gerhart).

36. Interview, Seathlolo. The term "pushout" is favored over "dropout" by many observers of the 1976 uprising because "pushout" implies that students were forced to leave school for reasons beyond their control. "Pushout," however, underplays the often voluntary dimension of school-leaving.

37. Interview, F. Mazibuko.

38. Interviews: Motaung, Mofokeng, F. Mazibuko.

39. Interviews: Mthembu (Gerhart), Motaung, Msimanga, Mofokeng, Siluma.

40. Interview, Msimanga.

41. See UNISA SASO Acc 118, SASO memorandum, "Commission on the Damaging Effects Of Afrikaans as a Medium of Instruction," undated. One point made in the memorandum is that Afrikaans "encourages thuggery, i.e. tsotsitaal." The observation itself is tautologous and absurd. Nevertheless, it reveals the writer's association of *tsotsitaal* with criminality as well as his distaste for the Afrikaans content in the street language.

42. Interviews: Siluma, Msimanga.

43. Interview, Ndoza (HWSFP).

44. Interviews: Morobe (HWSFP), Mofokeng, Nkondo, Seth Mazibuko (HWSFP), Masoka.

45. B. Hirson, *Year of Fire, Year of Ash: The Soweto Revolt: Roots of a Revolution?* London, 1979, p. 181.

46. South African Institute of Race Relations, *A Survey of Race Relations in South Africa*, Johannesburg (*SRRSA*), 1976, pp. 24–25; *The Star*, 17 June 1976; Hirson, *Year of Fire, Year of Ash*, p. 194; interviews: Gibi, Masoka, Tsotetsie, Mofokeng, Zikalala, Mkhonza (HWSFP), Seth Mazibuko (HWSFP). "Doctors at Baragwanath hospital," according to *The Star*, 17 June 1976, "have gained the distinct impression that amongst the casualties are a number of known tsotsis." Unfortunately, no information exists on the social profile of those arrested. Police records seemed to include age and gender but little else. Police simply stated that 99 percent of the arrested "offenders" during police crackdowns in the months that followed were "students and young drop-outs." See Kane-Berman, *Soweto*, p. 142.

47. Cillie Report, RP 55/1980, p. 479.

48. Interview, Zikalala. See also Cillie Report, RP 55/1980, pp. 480, par. 8.3.3. The commission points out here that "the misdeeds of the violent sometimes became feats worthy of emulation in the eyes of young people."

49. Interviews: Zodwa, Masoka, G. Dlamini, J. Khanyeza (HWSFP).

50. Interviews: G. Khumalo, Masoka.

51. Interviews: Lebelo, Maseko, C. Mbuli, Zodwa.

52. Interviews: Duma, Maseko, Zodwa, Mhlambi, Simelane (b), Lebelo. See also M. Mzamane, *Children of Soweto*, Harlow, England, 1982, p. 112, in which the Hazels participate in a beerhall attack. Though it is not clear whether this account is fictional or drawn from Mzamane's own experience, the scene was designed to capture the atmosphere of the uprising. That the Hazels feature in his narrative confirms their prominence in Sowetan consciousness and in gang participation in looting.

53. Interview, Mkhonza (HWSFP).

54. *The World*, 6 August 1976.

55. Interviews: Mofokeng, "Thabo," Simelane (b), Maseko. See also P. Frankel, "The Dynamics of a Political Renaissance: The Soweto Students Representative Council," *Journal of African Studies*, 7, 3, 1980, p. 174.

56. Cillie Report RP 55/1980, p. 138, par. 4.3.1.

57. Interviews: G. Khumalo, G. Dlamini, Xhaba, Tsotetsie, Mxadana, Duma; *The Star*, 17 June 1976; *The World*, 6 August 1976; Brooks and Brickhill, *Whirlwind*, p. 151 and p. 208. See also Mzamane, *Children of Soweto*, pp. 149–150.

58. Interview, Gibi; similar observations are made in interviews with C. Mbuli, G. Dlamini.

59. Cillie Report, RP 55/1980, p. 140, par. 4.3.8.

60. Brooks and Brickhill, *Whirlwind*, p. 208.

61. Interviews: Lebelo, Khoza, Tsotetsie, Morwa, S. Khumalo; Brooks and Brickhill, *Whirlwind*, p. 151. See also Mzamane, *Children of Soweto*, pp. 149–151.

62. Interviews: Gibi, Tsotetsie, Simelane (b), F. Mazibuko.

63. Interview, Zikalala.

64. Interviews: Masoka, Simelane (b), Mrs Dlamini (b).

65. For a detailed, blow-by-blow account of the SSRC's lifespan, see Kane-Berman, *Soweto*, chapters 9 and 10, pp. 109–152. For an assessment of the SSRC's effectiveness and popularity in Soweto see Frankel, "The Dynamics of a Political Renaissance." This section is not an exhaustive account of the SSRC; rather, I concentrate on the divisions within the youth constituency and on generational aspects of the council's activities.

66. Interview, Kheswa. Many informants observed a marked shift in the generational balance of power; see interviews: Moloantwa, Tsotetsie, Thabo, Duma, Mrs. Dlamini, Bothile (HWSFP), Morobe (HWSFP). The generational dynamics appear to have been similar in the African townships of Cape Town; for an interesting eye-witness account of the revolt in Guguletu, Nyanga, and Langa see C. Hermer, *The Diary of Maria Tholo*, Johannesburg, 1980, particularly pp. 21–29.

67. Interviews: Morobe (HWSFP), Duma.

68. Interviews: Seathlolo, Makhabela (HWSFP), Morobe (HWSFP), Gibi; *The World*, 3 and 17 August 1976; Kane-Berman, *Soweto*, p 132; Brooks and Brickhill, *Whirlwind*, p. 62; Hirson, *Year of Fire, Year of Ash*, p. 207.

69. Prior to June 1976, SASM had some links with the older generation through the Black People's Convention and the allied Black Parents' Association (BPA). Through the BPA, the SASM leadership had attempted to negotiate parental support for its educational demands. However, the BPA, rather than representing wider parent interests, consisted of a group of politically sympathetic parents.

70. For some examples of SSRC pamphlets, see Institute of Commonwealth Studies, London, Baruch Hirson Papers: Soweto Collection (ICS BHS), file B.

71. ICS BHS, file B, "Azikwhwelwa," SSRC pamphlet, September 1976.

72. *RDM*, 13 December 1976.

73. Interviews: Morobe (HWSFP), Bothile (HWSFP). See also ICS BHS file C, "The Story of the Soweto SRC," part 1, clipping from *The World*, ca. mid-1977.

74. See, for instance, reports on harassment of workers in *The World*, 4, 6, and 9 August 1976. Interviews: Xhaba, Mtshali.

75. Brooks & Brickhill, *Whirlwind*, p. 208.

76. Interviews: Morobe (HWSFP), Zodwa, C. Mbuli, Mkhonza; Glen Moss, "Crisis and Conflict: Soweto 1976-7," M.A. dissertation, University of the Witwatersrand, 1982, pp. 67–69; Kane-Berman, *Soweto*, pp. 113–114.

77. Interview, Mashiloane (HWSFP).

78. Kane-Berman, *Soweto*, p. 114. See Moss, "Crisis and Conflict," for a general analysis of the relationship between students and migrants during the Soweto uprising.

79. Kane-Berman, *Soweto*, pp. 127–128; ICS BHS, file C, "The Story of the Soweto SRC," part 2, clipping from *The World*, ca. mid-1977.

80. Interviews: Nzimande, G. Khumalo, Tsotetsie, Thabo.

81. Interview, Mofokeng.

82. Interview, Seathlolo.

83. Interviews: Seathlolo, Duma.

84. Interviews: Ndala, Nzimande, Maseko, Mhlambi, G. Khumalo, Zodwa, G. Dlamini, Mofokeng, Xhaba, Mokgotsi, Duma, Seathlolo. See also Kane-Berman, *Soweto*, p. 125 and p. 132.

85. Interview, Ndala.

86. Kane-Berman, *Soweto*, p. 125.

87. Interviews: Mowela, D. Nkosi, Thotela, Masoka, Mabhena, Mokgotsi, Mrs. Dlamini. See Kane-Berman, *Soweto*, p. 119 and p. 132; Hirson, *Year of Fire, Year of Ash*, p. 194.

EPILOGUE

The extraordinarily prevalent gang subculture was the most striking feature of the history of youth in Soweto from the 1940s to the early 1970s. At first glance, it might be tempting to conclude that the assertive youth politics of the mid-1970s were linked historically to the long tradition of aggressively antiestablishment youth gangs. This study explores the linkages between gang culture and youth politics in the three decades leading up to 1976 and finds that the youth uprising had its roots in the relatively insulated second-ary school environment, rather than on the streets. The gangs remained out-side the orbit of formal resistance politics up to and during 1976.

The polarity between the school and the gang should perhaps not be exaggerated. There was much shifting along this school–gang continuum over the decades. During the 1940s and 1950s, schooling beyond junior levels was a relatively marginal experience in the townships. High school students, though quite distinct, represented a tiny elite among the youth and offered no credible alternative role models to those of the gangs. With the massive expansion of primary schooling in the 1960s, school-ing up to Standard Five level became a far more common experience. During this decade the social gulf between older primary school stu-dents and gangs probably closed, although high school students remained a fairly remote elite. Throughout the time-span of this book, students and gang members had some social contact with each other at the neigh-borhood level. At times, especially in the 1970s, they shared feelings of rage about the political status quo.

It is important to emphasize, however, that the school and the gang spawned two very different traditions of political and social defiance. The high school provided a space for a more cerebral and disciplined form of politics to emerge. Student activists were idealistic and broad in vision; they saw themselves, by the mid-1970s, as the vanguard of a national black community. The gangs expressed themselves through subversive styles and violent territorial opposition to outsiders, including police and administrators. Their objective was to maintain de facto control of their streets; to keep intruders off their turf. They cordoned off and defended a space in which they were significant. Whereas the gang world was almost by definition internally divided and antagonistic, the school knitted together a student identity. The cohesive tendency of the school environment, coupled with the sudden expansion in high school numbers, explains the dramatic rise in importance of Soweto's student constituency during the first half of the 1970s. High schools competed for the allegiance of youths in precisely the same category as the gangs. More importantly, with the growth of black middle-class opportunities and aspirations, schooling began to offer an attractive, and visible counter-lifestyle. The school and gang cultures diverged and increasingly came into conflict.

Despite their spontaneous sympathy for the 1976 student uprising, gangs did not shed their gang identities or their criminal methods. Adult Sowetans, who had long been victimized by the likes of the Hazels and the Dirty Dozen, would not countenance a political alliance with the gangs. Student activists had to separate themselves clearly from the gang element if they were to establish credibility among older residents. In order to break out of its narrow generational mold and embrace adult workers and hostel residents, the Black Consciousness movement was forced to discard gangs as a political constituency. The Student Representative Council made the decision to submerge itself in the mainstream of the community and leave the gangs on the margins.

AFTER 1976 . . .

A number of studies have dealt with urban youth culture and politics in the post-uprising period.[1] It has been shown that student and youth politics became increasingly important during the late 1970s and 1980s; gradually politics forced gangsterism and other forms of youth subcultural expression onto the defensive. As youth activists demobilized during the negotiation and post-apartheid era, however, the townships experienced a resurgence of youth gangsterism. This concluding chapter draws on recent literature to follow the themes of the book into the 1980s and 1990s. It is a mere sketch of the key developments, an attempt to bring the story up to date.

After the turbulence of the 1976–1977 uprising, Soweto, like other townships around the country, returned to more predictable rhythms. The term *pantsula* (or *mapantsula* in the plural) came into vogue probably in the second half of the 1970s to describe the "clever" variant of the time. Much like the term *tsotsi* in the 1940s, Lunn suggests that it initially cut across criminal and noncriminal, gang and non-gang, but gradually developed a criminal connotation. *Mapantsula* style was antithetical to both the dandyish, middle-class "ivies" (who evolved into "cats" around the late 1970s) and to the political alternative that gathered momentum in the 1980s.[2] The lure of gang life and of the hedonistic, apolitical *mapantsula* style remained strong throughout the first half of the 1980s, but politics offered an increasingly powerful counterattraction to non-student youth.

By 1978 the Black Consciousness movement had been decimated by state repression. SASM and the SSRC had effectively disbanded in Soweto. Much of the student leadership was in jail or in exile. But, unlike the early 1960s, the apartheid state was unable to halt the momentum of internal political resistance. After a brief hiatus in 1978, opposition organizations began to rebuild themselves. Jeremy Seekings shows that the ANC, whose interest in internal resistance had been reawakened by the events of 1976–1977, identified youth and student politics as a priority. In 1979 it helped to set up the Congress of South African Students (COSAS), an organization that played a central role in resistance politics in the 1980s.[3]

COSAS drew primarily on a constituency of students and older ex-student veterans of the 1976 uprising. Initially it concentrated on educational issues. But COSAS did attempt to accommodate all youths who were looking for a political home. COSAS set up dozens of new branches throughout the country during the early 1980s, but it gradually came to the realization that it could not operate effectively as a catch-all organization for "youth" in general. Students had specific interests, and it became clear that non-students needed separate organizations. In 1982 and 1983, COSAS helped to establish a number of youth congresses, including the Soweto Youth Congress (SOYCO), to cater to a specifically non-student youth constituency. It was around this time, Seekings argues, that the term "youth" took on a powerful political connotation; it became a category to describe politicized young people who were not students. Students, whether at school or university, had their own political organizations. Although former student activists dominated the leadership core of the new youth congresses, they made significant progress in attracting the so-called "push-out" element: early school-leavers, the unemployed, and gang members.[4]

The United Democratic Front (UDF) was formed in mid-1983 to oppose both the government's tricameral parliamentary initiative and the township community council system. Both COSAS and the youth congresses were important affiliates of the front. The UDF was remarkably successful in discrediting the tricameral parliament and even more successful in rendering the community council system unworkable. The government sent in troops to restore and protect the community councils, which led to virtual war in numerous townships between 1984 and 1986. Two states of emergency were declared; the first in 1985 and the second, more severe and extensive, in 1986. Under the emergency measures, the security forces detained, or sent into flight, layers of political leadership down to the street level.

In a climate of confrontation, the non-student youth were increasingly drawn to the "struggle"; by 1985 almost every township had an active youth congress. Non-student youth lacked the political sophistication of the school students but with time on their hands and little to lose they became the most militant wing of the UDF; they were the most willing to risk their lives in confrontations with the security forces. From 1984 onward, youth congress activists, known as *comrades*, played a central, often unpopular, role in policing stayaways and consumer boycotts. The *comrades* were responsible for rendering numerous townships "ungovernable" between 1985 and 1987. Their willingness to confront the security forces and drive them from *comrade*-controlled areas was in many ways consistent with the territoriality of gang culture.

From 1984 onwards the Bantu Education system went into a crisis even more severe than that of 1976. The school system expanded throughout the early 1980s but learning conditions deteriorated. COSAS, partly in protest against appalling schooling and partly out of solidarity with broader national opposition to the apartheid government, initiated school boycotts, which soon swept the country. During the height of the school boycotts, 1984–1986, the distinction between student and non-student youth became less marked. The sense of pride in school identity disintegrated along with the credibility of the education system. COSAS, which offered a political identity linked to schooling, was banned in 1985. Away from the schoolyard for length periods, students tended to become integrated into the world of the street. Politicized students, without any organizational base, joined youth congresses.

While some youth congresses were tightly controlled and consulted thoroughly with other community representatives before taking action, *comrades* were not always responsive to centralized leadership, particularly if their own more politically astute leaders were in prison or on the run. Their activities were often spontaneous and violent and, in many cases, divided communities along generational lines. Their de facto power in the townships represented a direct challenge to traditions of hierarchy, and many older residents resented their arrogance and bullying. Under the two states of emergency, much of the student and youth congress leadership was detained and, Mark Swilling argues, the UDF found it increasingly difficult to impose organizational discipline on the *comrades*.[5]

The distinction between criminal and political activity also became hazy. Many unemployed youths who had become politically conscious were still involved in the criminal gang subculture, It was common for them to continue their criminal activity while identifying with the liberation struggle and acting politically. Some merely used the political climate opportunistically. During the mid-1980s these youths were often called *com-tsotsis*. The more politically disciplined and accountable youth congresses, eager to disassociate themselves from the criminal element, took it upon themselves to combat *com-tsotsis* and other young criminals. As with the SSRC in 1976–1977, the congresses' anti-crime campaigns were important in winning support from the older township residents and in cementing alliances with other community organizations.[6]

By the mid 1980s, the *comrade* bands were made up almost entirely of males. The street youth expressed their masculinity in militarized political activity. As the youth drifted beyond organizational control, physical prowess and street savvy began to replace articulateness and organizational skill as necessary leadership qualities. As the conflict became more violent, Seekings stresses, young women were increasingly marginalized and encouraged to play only a supportive domestic role in the struggle.[7]

The *comrades* formed a distinctive subculture with its own style and ritual. In many respects it involved a fusion of politicized student and gang cultures. The subculture included a spectrum of youths from highly disciplined politicos to *com-tsotsis*. But they all used a similar rhetoric, adhered to the same dress code (stereotypically, they wore cheap, unpretentious clothes with political T-shirts or sweaters), and clustered in predominantly male groups.[8] As the *comrades* gained power, the gangs and the *mapantsula* subculture went into retreat.

During the negotiation era between 1990 and 1993, the central political contest moved from the streets into conference rooms. In a number of townships on the Witwatersrand, *comrades* channeled their energy into defending their neighborhoods from migrant vigilantes. But the apartheid *casspirs* (armoured personnel trucks) had withdrawn and gradually they lost their sense of political purpose. Meanwhile, material conditions had not improved for young men; employment opportunities had, if anything, narrowed. Political activism lost its prestige and drawing power; gangs, less afraid of reprisals, regained confidence.

By the early 1990s, "jackroller" gangs were rampant in Soweto.[9] "Jackroll," in street argot, means to abduct and rape. Youth activists had limited gang rape in the 1980s, but their influence receded during the negotiation era. By the mid-1990s, unemployed male youths were increasingly attracted to the small-time, petty-criminal gangs, known as *abo-*

skroef ("screws"), or bigger-time criminal gangs, "schemes." The small-time, generally younger, "screws" aspire to become "schemes." The gangs sell their criminal services and pass on their stolen goods to the well-connected adult criminals known as *ama-bhoza* (the "bosses").[10] The youth gangs are not very different form the gangs of the 1950s or 1970s but the stakes have changed. Not only are guns more prevalent, but massive vehicle theft rackets and hard drugs have entered the equation. Crime is more streamlined under the management of sophisticated syndicates. Gangs have much more firepower and the opportunity to make much more money.

At the turn of the millennium, street and school cultures continue their tug-of-war for the souls of Soweto's male youth. The school option seems to be losing ground: job opportunities for school-leavers are scarce, and secondary schooling in Soweto is, by most accounts, in chaos. Purposeful, attractive student organization has disappeared. High school students in Soweto seem to have lost the sense of pride and distinctiveness that they possessed in the 1960s and 1970s; it is quite common for students to be involved in gangs, and girls are less well protected in the school environment than they used to be. Most of the useful schooling goes on outside of Soweto itself.[11] Those who do make it through school, who go to university or find good jobs, often leave Soweto, or at least the poorer neighborhoods, creating a scarcity of visible role models. The pull of gang life is more forceful than ever in the ghettos, offering young men a tangible route to material wealth, excitement, and local prestige.

The so-called "crisis of youth" cannot be regarded as a peripheral social issue. The South African population is getting proportionately younger and, if anything, the problems are deepening. The youth are at the heart of the most critical issues facing policy-makers: crime, education, and employment. What happens to South African youth will powerfully determine the country's future. In attempting to understand the attractions of gangsterism and criminality among South African urban youth, it is essential to probe beyond the obvious issues of urban poverty and unemployment. After all, gang life often proves more appealing than regular employment, and numerous relatively well-off youths are involved in gangs. This book has emphasized the importance of urban family structure, generational tensions, and the relationship between schooling and gang culture. It has also explored the style and value system of the gangs. Underpinning all of this is a stress on gender socialization, in particular, the historical construction of masculinity and the transition from adolescence to "manhood." This book does not pretend to offer any easy solutions to the crisis of youth, but it does reveal the complexity of the issue and it suggests, perhaps, some valuable lines of investigation.

NOTES

1. Helen Lunn, "Antecedents of the Music and Popular Culture of the African post-1976 Generation," M.A. thesis, University of the Witwatersrand, 1986, provides useful material on popular youth culture in Soweto. For insights into Soweto gang culture in the late 1980s and early 1990s, see Steve Mokwena, "The Era of the Jackrollers: Contextualising the Rise of Youth Gangs in Soweto," Seminar paper no. 7, Project for the Study of Violence, University of the Witwatersrand, 30 October 1991; and Sibusiso Mabena, *Violence in Diepkloof: Youth Gang Subcultures in Diepkloof, Soweto,* Johannesburg, 1996. On Cape Town youth gangs, see D. Pinnock, *The Brotherhoods: Street Gangs and State Controls in Cape Town,* Cape Town, 1987; and W. Scharf, "The Resurgence of Urban Street Gangs and Community Responses in Cape Town during the Late Eighties," in D. Hannson and D. Van Zyl Smit (eds.), *Towards Justice? Crime and State Control in South Africa,* Cape Town, 1990. See also Pinnock's *Gangs: Rituals and Rites of Passage,* Cape Town, 1997, in which he argues that rites of passage are an inevitable part of growing up and need not reinforce social marginalization. Rather, he argues, they can be molded ultimately to reintegrate youths into society, as was the case in precolonial Southern Africa. J. Seekings' *Heroes or Villains: Youth Politics in the 1980s,* Johannesburg, 1993, is a brief but astute overview of South African youth politics in the 1980s. For more localized studies of youth activism, see C. Carter, "'We Are the Progressives': Alexandra Youth Congress Activists and the Freedom Charter, 1983–1986," *Journal of Southern African Studies (JSAS),* 17, 2, June 1991; and M. Marks "Organisation, Identity and Violence amongst Activist Diepkloof Youth, 1984–1993," M.A. thesis, University of the Witwatersrand, 1993. A. Sitas, "The Making of the 'Comrades' Movement in Natal," *JSAS,* 18, 3, September 1992, and C. Campbell, "Learning to Kill? Masculinity, the Family and Violence in Natal," *JSAS,* 18, 3, September 1992, focus on the "comrade" culture of Natal. The psychological trauma of township youths at war is highlighted in G. Straker, *Faces in the Revolution: The Psychological Effects of Violence on Township Youth in South Africa,* Cape Town, 1992. Youth issues are also given prominence in several broad overviews of resistance politics in the 1990s. See in particular Tom Lodge, "Rebellion: The Turning of the Tide," in T. Lodge and B. Nasson (eds.), *All, Here, and Now: Black Politics in South Africa in the 1980s,* New York, 1991; and M. Swillling, "United Democratic Front and Township Revolt in South Africa," in W. Cobbett and R. Cohen (eds.), *Popular Struggles in South Africa,* London, 1988.

2. In retrospect, the "clever" style of the early 1970s is often described as *mapantsula,* but there is no evidence to suggest that the term was actually used until the later 1970s. See Lunn, "Antecedents," pp. 197–206, for a valuable description of *pantsula* style. Lunn's periodization, however, is vague.

3. Seekings, *Heroes or Villains?* pp. 29–30; p. 34. See also H. Barrell, "The Turn to the Masses: The African National Congress Strategic Review of 1978–9," *Journal of Southern African Studies,* 18, 1, March 1992.

4. Seekings, *Heroes or Villains?* pp. 29–34.

5. See Swilling, "United Democratic Front and Township Revolt."

6. See, for instance, Marks, "Organisation, Identity and Violence," pp. 155–157. In 1986, Diepkloof youth congresses came together to smash a particularly rapacious gang, the Kabasas, which operated in the Orlando East/Diepkloof area.

7. Seekings, *Heroes or Villains?* pp. 82–86.

8. Marks, "Organisation, Identity and Violence," sees the *comrade* subcultural identity as incorporating only the disciplined end of the spectrum. See, in particular, pp. 175–177. But this probably underestimates the degree of shading and ambiguity within the subculture.

9. See Mokwena, "The Era of the of the Jackrollers."

10. See Sibusiso Mabena, *Violence in Diepkloof.* This remarkable piece of research, based on participant observation, is the only contemporary anthropological work on Soweto gangs I have come across. Mabena was a postgraduate student at the University of the Witwatersrand, who died tragically in a motor accident in 1995. The study is therefore unfinished and unpolished, but the university decided to publish it posthumously because it offers unique insights into the world of Soweto gangs.

11. For recent surveys of secondary schooling in Soweto, see B. Maja, "The Future Trapped in the Past: A Case Study of a Soweto Secondary School," M.A. research report, University of the Witwatersrand, 1995; L. Chisholm and S. Valley, "The Culture of Learning and Teaching in Gauteng Schools: Report of the Committee on the Culture of Learning and Teaching," Education Policy Unit, University of the Witwatersrand (commissioned by the Department of Education, Gauteng), June 1996; Laduma Film Factory, "The Culture of Teaching and Learning: Drama Series Research Report" (commissioned by the South African Broadcasting Services), September 1997.

BIBLIOGRAPHY

SECONDARY LITERATURE: UNPUBLISHED

Bothma, C. V. "'n Volkekundige Ondersoek na die Aard en Ontstaans oorsake van Tsotsie-groepe en hulle Aktiwiteite soos Gevind in die Stedelike Gebied van Pretoria," M.A. thesis, departement van Bantoeltale en Volkekunde, University of Pretoria, July 1951.

Chisholm, L., and Valley, S. "The Culture of Learning and Teaching in Gauteng Schools: Report of the Committee on the Culture of Learning and Teaching," Education Policy Unit, University of the Witwatersrand (commissioned by the Department of Education, Gauteng), June 1996.

Eales, K. "Rehabilitating the Body Politic: Black Women, Sexuality and the Social Order in Johannesburg, 1924–1937," seminar paper presented at the African Studies Institute, University of the Witwatersrand, 2 April 1990.

Freed, L. F. "The Problem of Crime in the Union of South Africa: An Integralistic Approach," D. Phil. thesis, University of the Orange Free State, Bloemfontein, August 1958.

French, K. "James Mpanza and the Sofasonke Party in the Development of Local Politics in Soweto, Johannesburg," M.A. thesis, University of the Witwatersrand, 1983.

Giffard, C. "The Hour of Youth Has Struck: The ANC Youth League and the Struggle for a Mass Base," B.A. Honours dissertation, University of Cape Town, February 1984.

Glaser, C. "Students, Tsotsis and the Congress Youth League, 1944–1955," B.A. Honours dissertation, University of the Witwatersrand, October 1986.

———. "Anti-Social Bandits: Juvenile Delinquency and the Tsotsi Youth Gang Subculture on the Witwatersrand, 1935–1960," M.A. thesis, University of the Witwatersrand, 1990.

———. "Youth Culture and Politics in Soweto, 1958–1976," Ph.D. thesis, Cambridge University, England, 1994.

Hyslop, J. "Social Conflicts over African Education in South Africa from the 1940s to 1976," Ph.D. thesis, University of the Witwatersrand, 1990.

Khumalo, B. V. "Sources and Structure of Tsotsitaal," B.A. Honours dissertation, University of the Witwatersrand, April 1986.

Kieser, W. W. "Native Juvenile Delinquency," M. Ed. thesis, University of Potchefstroom, 1952.

Koch, E. "Doornfontein and Its African Working Class 1914–1935: A Study of Popular Culture in Johannesburg," M.A. thesis, University of the Witwatersrand, 1983.

Laduma Film Factory. "The Culture of Teaching and Learning: Drama Series Research Report" (commissioned by the South African Broadcasting Services), September 1997.

Lazar, J. "Conformity and Conflict: Afrikaner Nationalist Politics in South Africa 1948–1961," D. Phil. thesis, Oxford University, 1987.

Lebelo, M. S. "The Locations in the Sky Act and the Limitations of the Local State in the Era of High Apartheid: Ethnicity and Class in Early Soweto, 1960–1975," paper presented to the History Masters seminar, University of the Witwatersrand, 7 August 1990.

Lodge, T. "Insurrectionism in South Africa: The Pan Africanist Congress and the Poqo Movement 1959–1965," D. Phil. thesis, University of York, United Kingdom, April 1984.

Lunn, H. "Antecedents of the Music and Popular Culture of the African post–1976 Generation", M.A. thesis, University of the Witwatersrand, 1986.

Maja, B. "The Future Trapped in the Past: A Case Study of a Soweto Secondary School," M.A. research report, University of the Witwatersrand, 1995.

Manoim, E. "The Black Press in South Africa 1945–1953," M.A. thesis, University of the Witwatersrand, 1953.

Marks, M. "Organisation, Identity and Violence amongst Activist Diepkloof Youth, 1984–1993," M.A. thesis, University of the Witwatersrand, 1993.

Mokwena, S. "The Era of the Jackrollers: Contextualising the Rise of Youth Gangs in Soweto," Seminar Paper no. 7, Project for the Study of Violence, Department of Psychology, University of the Witwatersrand, 30 October 1991.

Moss, G. "Crisis and Conflict: Soweto 1976–7," M.A. thesis, University of the Witwatersrand, 1982.

Ntshangase, K. D. "Towards an Understanding of Urban Linguistic Varieties: The Case of Iscamtho in Soweto," paper presented to the Department of African Languages Seminar, University of the Witwatersrand, 6 May 1992.

Seekings, J. "Why Was Soweto Different? Urban Development, Township Politics and the Political Economy of Soweto, 1977–1984," paper presented to the African Studies Institute Seminar, University of the Witwatersrand, 2 May 1988.

———. "Quiescence and the Transition to Confrontation: South African Townships, 1978–1984," D. Phil. thesis, University of Oxford, 1990.

Soweto in Transition Project. "Soweto in Transition Project: Second Preliminary Report," Department of Sociology, University of the Witwatersrand, August 1997.

SECONDARY LITERATURE: PUBLISHED

Abrams, P. *Historical Sociology*, Shepton Mallet, England, 1982.

Adam, H. "The Rise of Black Consciousness in South Africa," *Race*, 15, 2, 1973.

Barrell, H. "The Turn to the Masses: The African National Congress Strategic Review of 1978–9," *Journal of Southern African Studies*, 8, 1, March 1992.

Beavon, K.S.O. "Black Townships in South Africa: Terra Incognita for Urban Geographers," *South African Geographical Journal*, 64, 1, April 1982.

Beinart, W. "The Origins of the Indlavini: Male Associations and Migrant Labour in the Transkei," *African Studies*, 50, 1991.

———. "Political and Collective Violence in Southern African Historiography," *Journal of Southern African Studies*, 18, 3, September 1992.

Boldror, S., and Humphrioo, R. *From Control to Confusion: The Changing Rule of Administration Boards in South Africa, 1971–1983*, Pietermaritzburg, 1985.

Black Community Programmes. *Black Review*, 1972 (ed. B. A. Khoapa), 1973 (ed. M. P. Gwala), 1974–1975 (ed. T. Mbanjwa).

Bonner, P. "The Russians on the Reef, 1947–1957: Urbanisation, Gang Warfare and Ethnic Mobilisation," in P. Bonner, P. Delius, and D. Posel (eds.), *Apartheid's Genesis, 1935–1962*, Johannesburg, 1987.

———. "Family, Crime and Political Consciousness on the East Rand 1939–1955," *Journal of Southern African Studies*, 14, 3, 1988.

———. "The Politics of the Black Squatter Movements on the Rand 1944–1952," *Radical History Review*, 46/47 (double edition), 1990.

———. "African Urbanisation on the Rand between the 1930s and the 1960s: Its Social Character and Political Consequences," *Journal of Southern African Studies*, 21, 1, March 1995.

Bozzoli, B. and Delius, P. "Radical History in South African Society," *Radical History Review*, 46/47 (double edition), 1990.

Brake, M. *The Sociology of Youth Culture and Youth Subcultures*, London, 1980.

Branch, T. *Parting the Waters: Martin Luther King and the Civil Rights Movement, 1954–1963*, London, 1988.

Brett, E. A., "African Attitudes," *South African Institute of Race Relations Fact Paper*, no. 14, Johannesburg, 1963.

Brooks, A. and Brickhill, J., *Whirlwind before the Storm*, London, 1980.

Bundy, C. "Street Sociology and Pavement Politics: Aspects of Youth and Student Resistance in Greater Cape Town, 1985," *Journal of Southern African Studies*, 13, 3, April 1987.

Campbell, C. "Learning to Kill? Masculinity, the Family and Violence in Natal," *Journal of Southern African Studies*, 18, 3, September 1992.

Carr, W. J. *Soweto: Its Creation, Life and Decline*, Johannesburg, 1990.

Carter, C. "'We Are the Progressives': Alexandra Youth Congress Activists and the Freedom Charter, 1983–1986," *Journal of Southern African Studies*, 17, 2, June 1991.

Clark, K. B. *Dark Ghetto: Dilemmas of Social Power*, London, 1965.

Clarke, J., Hall, S., Jefferson, T., and Roberts, B., "Subcultures, Cultures, and Class," in S. Hall and T. Jefferson (eds.), *Resistance through Rituals: Youth Subcultures in Post-War Britain*, London, 1976.

Clinard, M. B., and Abbott, D. J. *Crime in Developing Countries: A Comparative Perspective*, New York, 1973.

Cohen, A. K. *Delinquent Boys: The Culture of the Gang*, London, 1956.

Cohen, P. "Subcultural Conflict and Working Class Community," in S. Hall, D. Hobson, A. Lowe, and P. Willis, (eds.), *Culture, Media, Language*, London, 1980.

Coplan, D. *In Township Tonight! South Africa's Black City Music and Theatre*, London, 1985.

Davis, M. "Los Angeles: Civil Liberties between the Hammer and the Rock," *New Left Review*, 170, July/August 1988.

Delius, P. "Sebatakgomo: Migrant Organisation, the ANC and the Sekhukhuneland Revolt," *Journal of Southern African Studies,* 15, 4, 1989.

Dingake, M. *My Fight against Apartheid*, London, 1987.

Diseko, N. "The Origins and Development of the South African Students Movement (SASM)," *Journal of Southern African Studies*, 18, 1, March 1991.

Dlamini, M. *Robben Island: Hell Hole*, Nottingham, England, 1984.

Downes, D. *The Delinquent Solution: A Study in Subcultural Theory*, London, 1966.

———. *Crime and the City*, Basingstoke, England, 1989.

Easthope, A. *What a Man's Gotta Do: The Masculine Myth in Popular Culture*, London, 1986.

Edelstein, M. L. *What Do Young Africans Think?* Labour and Community Consultants, Johannesburg, 1974.

Ellis, H. and Newman, S. "The Greaser Is a 'Bad Ass'; the Gowster Is a 'Muthah': An Analysis of Two Urban Youth Roles," in T. Kochman (ed.), *Rappin' and Stylin' Out*, Urbana, Ill., 1972.

Everatt, D., and Orkin, M. *"Growing Up Tough": A National Survey of South African Youth*, Community Action for Social Enquiry (CASE) survey, commissioned by the Joint Enrichment Project, Johannesburg, 1993.

Everatt, D., and Sisulu, E. (eds). *Black Youth in Crisis: Facing the Future*, Johannesburg, 1992.

Fenwick, M. "'Tough Guy, eh?': The Gangster-Figure in Drum," *Journal of Southern African Studies*, 22, 4, December 1996.

Frankel, P. "The Dynamics of a Political Renaissance: The Soweto Students Representative Council," *Journal of African Studies,* 7, 3, 1980.

Gerhart, G. *Black Power in South Africa*, Berkeley, 1978.

Glaser, C. "Students, Tsotsis and the Congress Youth League: Youth Organisation on the Rand in the 1940s and 1950s," *Perspectives in Education*, 10, 2, 1988–1989.

———. "The Mark of Zorro: Sexuality and Gender Relations in the Tsotsi Youth Gang Subculture on the Witwatersrand," *African Studies*, 51, 1, 1992.

———. "When Are They Going to Fight? Tsotsis, Youth Politics and the PAC," in P. Bonner, P. Delius, and D. Posel (eds.), *Apartheid's Genesis 1935–1962*, Johannesburg, 1993.

———. "'We Must Infiltrate the Tsotsis': School Politics and Youth Gangs in Soweto, 1968–1976," *Journal of Southern African Studies*, 24, 2, June 1998.

———. "Swines, Hazels and the Dirty Dozen: Masculinity, Territoriality and the Youth Gangs of Soweto, 1960–1976," *Journal of Southern African Studies*, 24, 4, December 1998.

Goldman, P. *The Death and Life of Malcolm X*, Urbana, Ill. 1979.

Goodhew, D. "The People's Police-Force: Communal Policing Initiatives in the Western Areas of Johannesburg, circa 1930–1962," *Journal of Southern African Studies*, 19, 3, September 1993.

Guy, J. and Thabane, M. "The Ma-Rashea: A Participant's Perspective," in B. Bozzoli (ed.), *Class, Community and Conflict*, Johannesburg, 1987.

Hall, S. and Jefferson, T. (eds.) *Resistance through Rituals: Youth Subcultures in Post-War Britain*, London, 1976.

Hannerz, U. *Soulside: Inquiries into Ghetto Culture and Community*, New York, 1969.

Hebdige, D. *Subculture: The Meaning of Style*, London, 1984.

Hellmann, E. *Problems of Urban Bantu Youth*, Johannesburg, 1940.

Hermer, C. *The Diary of Maria Tholo*, Johannesburg, 1980.

Hirson, B. *Year of Fire, Year of Ash: The Soweto Revolt: Roots of a Revolution?* London, 1979.

Hobsbawm, E. J., *Bandits*, London, 1969.

Huddleston, T. *Nought for Your Comfort*, London, 1956.

Hudson, J. "The Hustling Ethic," in T. Kochman (ed.), *Rappin' and Stylin' Out*, Urbana, Ill., 1972.

Humphries, S. *Hooligans or Rebels? An Oral History of Working Class Childhood and Youth 1889–1939*, Oxford, 1981.

Hyslop, J. "School Student Movements and State Education Policy: 1972–1987," in W. Cobbett and R. Cohen (eds.), *Popular Struggles in South Africa*, London, 1988.

———. "State Education Policy and the Social Reproduction of the Urban African Working Class: The Case of the Southern Transvaal 1955–1976," *Journal of Southern African Studies*, 14, 3, April 1988.

———. "Schools, Unemployment and Youth: Origins and Significance of Student and Youth Movements, 1976–1987," *Perspectives in Education*, 10, 2, 1988–1989.

———. "'A Destruction Coming in': Bantu Education as Response to Social Crisis," in P. Bonner, P. Delius, and D. Posel (eds.), *Apartheid's Genesis 1935–1962*, Johannesburg, 1993.

Iliffe, J. *The African Poor: A History*, Cambridge, 1987.

James, W. *Our Precious Metal: African Labour in South Africa's Gold Industry, 1970–1990*, Cape Town, 1992.

Johnson, J., and Magubane, P. *Soweto Speaks*, Johannesburg, 1979.

Johnson, R. W. *How Long Will South Africa Survive?* London, 1977.

Johnson, S. "The Soldiers of Luthuli: Youth in the Politics of Resistance in South Africa," in S. Johnson (ed.), *South Africa: No Turning Back*, London, 1988.

Kane-Berman, J. *Soweto: Black Revolt, White Reaction*, Johannesburg, 1978.

Kochman, T. (ed.). *Rappin' and Stylin' Out*, Urbana, Ill. 1972.

Kuper, L. *An African Bourgeoisie: Race, Class and Politics in South Africa*, New Haven, Conn., 1965.

Kuzwayo, E. *Call Me Woman*, London, 1985.

La Fontaine, J. S. "Two Types of Youth Group in Kinshasa (Leopoldville)," in P. Mayer (ed.), *Socialization: The Approach from Social Anthropology*, London, 1970.

La Hausse, P. "The Message of the Warriors: The ICU, the Labouring Poor and the Making of a Popular Political Culture in Durban, 1925–1930," in P. Bonner, I. Hofmeyr, D. James, and T. Lodge (eds.), *Holding Their Ground: Class, Locality and Culture in 19th and 20th Century South Africa*, Johannesburg, 1989.

————. "'Mayihlome': Towards an Understanding of Amalaita Gangs in Durban, c 1900–1930," in S. Clingman (ed.), *Regions and Repertoires: Topics in South African Politics and Culture*, Johannesburg, 1991.

Lewis, O. *The Children of Sanchez*, London, 1964.

Lewis, R. B. "A 'City' within a City—The Creation of Soweto," *South African Geographical Journal*, 48, December 1966.

Lipton, M. *Capitalism and Apartheid: South Africa 1910–1984*, Aldershot, England, 1985.

Lodge, T. *Black Politics in South Africa since 1945*, Johannesburg, 1983.

————. "Rebellion: The Turning of the Tide," in T. Lodge and B. Nasson (eds.), *All, Here, and Now: Black Politics in South Africa in the 1980s*, New York, 1991.

Lodge, T., and Swilling, M. "The Year of the Amabuthu," *Africa Report*, 31, 2, 1986.

Mabena, S. *Violence in Diepkloof: Youth Gang Subcultures in Diepkloof, Soweto*, Johannesburg, 1996.

Mager, A., and Minkley, G. "Reaping the Whirlwind: The East London Riots of 1952," in P. Bonner, P. Delius, and D. Posel (eds.), *Apartheid's Genesis 1935–1962*, Johannesburg, 1993.

Manganyi, N. C., and du Toit, A. (eds.) *Political Violence and the Struggle in South Africa*, Basingstoke, England, 1990.

Mashile, G. G., and Pirie, G. H. "Aspects of Housing Allocation in Soweto," *South African Geographical Journal*, 59, 2, September 1977.

Mattera, D. *Memory Is the Weapon*, Johannesburg, 1987.

Mayer, I., and Mayer, P. "Socialization by Peers: The Youth Organization of the Red Xhosa," in P. Mayer (ed.), *Socialization: The Approach from Social Anthropology*, London, 1970.

Meier, A., and Rudwick, E. (eds.). *Black Protest in the Sixties*, Chicago, 1970.

Modisane, B. *Blame Me on History*, London, 1963.

Moller, H. "Youth as a Force in the Modern World," *Comparative Studies in History and Society*, 10, 1967–1968.

Moloi, G. *My Life*, vols. 1 and 2, Johannesburg, 1991.

Morris, P. *A History of Black Housing in South Africa*, Johannesburg, 1981.

Motley, W. *Knock on Any Door*, De Kalb, Illinois, 1989.

Msimang, C. T. "Impact of Zulu on Tsotsitaal," *South African Journal of African Languages*, 7, 3, July 1987.

Mzamane, M. *Children of Soweto*, Harlow, England, 1982.

————. "My Other Cousin Sitha," *Staffrider*, 7, 3 and 4, 1988.

Nattrass, J. *The South African Economy: Its Growth and Change*, Cape Town, 1981.

Niddrie, D. "New National Youth Congress Launched: Emergency Forces New Forms of Organisation," *Work in Progress*, 47, April 1987.

Nlutshungu, S. C. *Changing South Africa*, Manchester, England, 1982.

O'Donnell, M. *Age and Generation*, London, 1985.

Phillips, N. *The Tragedy of Apartheid*, New York, 1960.

Pinnock, D. *The Brotherhoods: Street Gangs and State Controls in Cape Town*, Cape Town, 1987.

————. *Gangs: Rituals and Rites of Passage*, Cape Town, 1997.

Pogrund, B. *How Can Man Die Better: Sobukwe and Apartheid*, Johannesburg, 1990.

Posel, D. *The Making of Apartheid, 1948–1961: Conflict and Compromise*, Oxford, 1991.

Rosenhaft, E. "Organising the Lumpenproletariat: Cliques and Communists in Berlin during the Weimar Republic," in J. Evans (ed.), *The German Working Class*, London, 1982.

Sammadar, R. "The Rebellious and Non-Conformist Youth of Bengal," in P. Sinha (ed.), *The Urban Experience: Calcutta*, Calcutta, 1987.

Sampson, A. *Drum: A Venture into the New Africa*, London, 1956.

Saul, J., and Gelb, S., *The Crisis in South Africa*, New York, 1981

Scharf, W. "The Resurgence of Urban Street Gangs and Community Responses in Cape Town during the Late Eighties," in D. Hansson, and D. Van Zyl Smit (eds.), *Towards Justice? Crime and State Control in South Africa*, Cape Town, 1990.

Seekings, J. *Heroes or Villains? Youth Politics in the 1980s*, Johannesburg, 1993.

Shepherd, R.H.W., and Paven, B. G. *African Contrasts: The Story of a South African People*, Cape Town, 1947.

Sikakane, J. *A Window on Soweto*, Johannesburg, 1977.

Simkins, C. *Four Essays on the Past, Present and Possible Future Distribution of the Black Population of South Africa*, Cape Town, 1983.

Sitas, A. "The Making of the 'Comrades' Movement in Natal," *Journal of Southern African Studies*, 18, 3, September 1992.

South African Institute of Race Relations. *A Survey of Race Relations in South Africa*, Johannesburg, annual publications, 1958–1977.

Spencer, P. *The Maasai of Matapato: A Study of Rituals of Rebellion*, Manchester, England, 1988.

Spergel, I .A. "Youth Gangs: Continuity and Change," *Crime and Justice*, 12, 1990.

Stadler, A. "Birds in the Cornfield: Squatter Movements in Johannesburg 1944–1947," in B. Bozzoli (ed.), *Labour, Townships and Protest*, Johannesburg, 1979.

Stein, P., and Jacobson, R. (eds.) *Sophiatown Speaks*, Johannesburg, 1986.

Straker, G. *Faces in the Revolution: The Psychological Effects of Violence on Township Youth in South Africa*, Cape Town, 1992.

Swilling, M. "United Democratic Front and Township Revolt in South Africa," in W. Cobbett and R. Cohen (eds.), *Popular Struggles in South Africa*, London, 1988.

Themba, C. *The World of Can Themba*, E. Patel (ed.), Johannesburg, 1985.

Thrasher, F. *The Gang: A Study of 1313 Gangs in Chicago*, J. F. Short (ed.), Chicago, 1963.

UNESCO. *Apartheid: Its Effects on Education, Science, Culture and Information*, New York, 1967.

Van Onselen, C. *Studies in the Social and Economic History of the Witwatersrand 1886–1914*, vols. 1 and 2, Johannesburg, 1982.

Van Tonder, D. "Gangs, Councillors and the South African State: The Newclare Squatters Movement in 1952," *South African Historical Journal*, 22, November 1990.

Vilakazi, A. *Zulu Transformations*, Pietermaritzburg, 1962.

Vundla, K. *P. Q.: The Story of Philip Vundla of South Africa*, Johannesburg, 1973.

Walshe, P. *The Rise of African Nationalism in South Africa*, Berkeley, 1970.
Wilson, M., and Mafeje, A. *Langa: A Study of Social Groups in an African Township*,
    Cape Town, 1963.
Wolfenstein, E. G. *The Victims of Democracy: Malcolm X and the Black Revolution*,
    Berkeley, 1981.

PRIMARY SOURCES

Government Commissions

Botha, M. C. *Verslag van die interdepartementele Komitee insake ledige en nie-werkende
    Bantu in Stedeleike Gebiede* (Report of the Interdepartmental Committee into
    Idle and Unemployed Bantu in the Urban Areas), Pretoria, 1962.
Centlivres, A. van der Sandt. *Report of the Riots Commission (Dube Hostel 14/15 Sep-
    tember 1957)*, Johannesburg, March/April, 1958.
Cillie, P. M. *Report of the Commission of Inquiry into the Riots at Soweto and Else-
    where from the 16th of June 1976 to the 28th of February 1977*, RP 55/1980,
    Pretoria, 1980.
de Villiers Louw, J. *Report of the Commission Appointed to Inquire into Acts of Vio-
    lence Committed by Natives at Krugersdorp, Newlands, Randfontein and
    Newclare*, UG 47/1950, Pretoria, 1950.
Fouche, M. L. *Report of the Commission of Inquiry into Housing Matters*, RP 74/1977,
    Pretoria, 1977.
Riekert, P. J. *Report of the Commission of Inquiry into Legislation Affecting the Utilisation
    of Manpower (Excluding the Legislation Administered by the Departments Of
    Labour And Mines)*, RP 32/1979, Pretoria, 1979.
Schlebusch, A. L. *Fourth Interim Report of the Committee of Inquiry into Certain
    Organisations*, RP 33/1974, Pretoria, 1974.
Viljoen, G. *Report of the Commission of Enquiry into the Penal System of the Republic
    of South Africa*, RP 78/1976, Pretoria, 1976.
Viljoen, S. P. *Report on the Inter-Departmental Committee on Native Juvenile Unem-
    ployment on the Witwatersrand and in Pretoria*, Pretoria, 1951.

Other Government Publications

Central Statistics Service. *Population Census*, 1960, 1970, and 1980.
Department of Bantu Education. *Bantu Education Journal*, 1960–1976.
Department of Welfare and Pensions. *Jeugmisdaad in die Republiek van Suid Afrika: 'n
    ontleding van beskikbare statistiek*, Publication no. 1 of 1972.

Archival Collections

Black Sash Collection, Historical Papers Library, University of the Witwatersrand,
    Johannesburg.
Carter and Karis Collection, microfilm copy, Historical Papers Library, University of
    the Witwatersrand, Johannesburg.

Ellen Hellmann Papers, Historical Papers Library, University of the Witwatersrand, Johannesburg (EHP).
Baruch Hirson Papers: Soweto Collection, Institute of Commonwealth Studies, London (ICS BHS).
Johannesburg Non-European Affairs Department Annual Reports, 1958–1972, Municipal Reference Library, Johannesburg (MRL JNEAD).
Joint Council Collection, Historical Papers Library, University of the Witwatersrand, Johannesburg (JC).
Jean McMurchie Collection, private papers, Johannesburg (JMC)
Political Parties Collection: Pan Africanist Congress, Institute of Commonwealth Studies, London (ICS PAC).
Albie Sachs Papers, Institute of Commonwealth Studies, London (ICS Sachs).
SASO/BCM Collection, University of South Africa Archive, Pretoria (UNISA SASO).
South African Institute of Race Relations Collection, Historical Papers Library, University of the Witwatersrand, Johannesburg (SAIRR).
Trade Union Council of South Africa Collection, Historical Papers Library, University of the Witwatersrand, Johannesburg (TUCSA).
Urban Bantu Councils Collection, University of South Africa Archive, Pretoria.
West Rand Administration Board Archive, Intermediary Archive Depot, Johannesburg (IAD WRAB). This collection is in the process of being moved to the Central Archive Depot, Pretoria.

Newspapers and Magazines

The Africanist.
Bantu World (BW), 1934–1955.
Drum, 1950–1959; scattered collection, 1960–1975.
Golden City Post (GCP), 1955–1965.
Post, 1966–1971.
South African Institute of Race Relations newspaper clippings collection, including *The Star* and the *Rand Daily Mail (RDM),* Historical Papers Library, University of the Witwatersrand, Johannesburg.
Umteteli wa Bantu.
Weekend World, 1958–1977.
The World, 1958–1977.
Zonk, scattered collection, 1958–1961.

Records of Trials

Saths Cooper and twelve others, 1975–1976, microfilm, Institute of Commonwealth Studies, London.
Criminal Cases of the Witwatersrand Legal Division (WLD), Central Archives Depot (CAD), Pretoria: WLD 437/60, WLD 504/60, WLD 570/61, WLD 186/63, WLD 248/69, WLD 474/72, WLD 174/73.
Philip Kgosana Trial, Albie Sachs Papers, Institute of Commonwealth Studies, London.

Oral Sources

The majority of these interviews were conducted either by myself or by a research assistant, Meverett Koetz, who is fluent in Zulu, Afrikaans, English, and the Soweto street argot. I compiled a list of questions to be covered but encouraged him to use his discretion and to digress where appropriate. We compiled no formal sample of interviewees, but he targeted people who had experiences and memories of specific Soweto gangs. Koetz's interviews were taped, translated, and transcribed. During six of the interviews he took notes without using a tape recorder. About half of my interviews were conducted without a tape recorder, either because I met my informant in a public space or because my informant felt uncomfortable with tape recording. In such cases I took thorough notes. The untaped interviews are indicated by the word "notes" in parentheses. All of the taped interviews will be deposited with the Oral History Project, African Studies Institute, University of the Witwatersrand. In addition, I was given access to videotaped interviews conducted by the History Workshop Soweto Film Project (HWSFP), University of the Witwatersrand, and several transcribed interviews conducted by colleagues. All of the interviews took place in the Johannesburg/Soweto area unless otherwise indicated. Informants often supplied only their surnames or nicknames, in some cases specifically to avoid easy identification.

Interviews with the Author, 1986–1992

Buthelezi, Q., 30 October 1991 (notes).
Carr, W.J.P., 15 April 1988 (a); 5 August 1992 (b) (notes).
Duma, L., 10 August 1992.
Kambule, T. W., 29 October 1991 (a); 4 December 1991 (b).
Kuzwayo, E., 23 May 1989 and 1 June 1989.
Lebelo, S., 27 September 1991.
Leeuw, L., 23 September 1988 (notes).
Magubane, P., 7 September 1988.
Manana, K., 21 September 1988.
Maponya, R., 28 October 1992 (notes).
Mattera, D., 5 June 1988 (a); 10 July 1988 (b).
Mazibuko, F., 5 December 1992.
Mbawu, "Babes," and Ngwenya, B., 20 April 1989 (notes); 27 April 1989 (notes).
McMurchie, J., 21 September 1992 (notes).
Mdlalose, "McCoy," 20 April 1989; 27 April 1989 (notes).
Miles, H., 4 April 1989 (a); 11 April 1989 (b); 16 November 1989 (c).
Mofokeng, S., 2 October 1991.
Moloi, Godfrey, 26 March 1988.
Motaung, I., 27 November 1991.
Motjuwadi, S., 29 September 1988.
Motlana, N., 2 October 1986.
Mphahlele, E., 29 September 1986.
Msimanga, J., 23 January 1992.
Mxadana, M., 31 January 1992 (notes).
Ndaba, Q., 15 September 1988 (notes).
Nhlapho, J., 9 May 1989; 12 May 1989 (notes).

Nkondo, C., 2 September 1992 (notes).
Nkosi, Norris, 25 September 1988.
Peggy Bel Air (E. Sinnle), 2 June 1989.
Pitje, G., 23 September 1986.
Seathlolo, K., 2 September 1992 (notes).
Shubane, K., 24 August 1992 (notes).
Siluma, M., 13 December 1991 (notes).
Thabethe, B., 18 January 1990 (notes).
Thwala, G., 21 September 1988 (notes).
Tloteng, S., 18 November 1991 (notes).
Zikalala, S., 2 October 1992.

Interviews with Meverett Koetz, 1992

"Bra Forker," Manfred, 17 June 1992.
Dlamini, G., December 1992.
Dlamini, Mrs., 5 September 1992.
Gibi, Mrs., August 1992 (a); December 1992 (b).
"Gladys" (Mzimhlophe resident), 15 June 1992.
Hlatswayo, C., 24 April 1992 (notes).
Hlatswayo, Mrs., and Moloi, Gertrude, August 1992.
"Johannes" (Phiri resident), 21 June 1992.
Kheswa, L., 21 June 1992.
Khoza, M., 12 April 1992 (notes).
Khumalo, G., December 1992.
Khumalo, Mrs. S., August 1992
Mabhena, P., 26 September 1992.
Makgene, T., August 1992.
Malaza, S., December 1992.
Mampiki, Mrs., 13 June 1992.
Maseko, L., 26 September 1992 (a); including "Thabo," December 1992 (b).
Masoka, S., December 1992.
Mawela, Mr., December 1992.
Mbuli, C., December 1992.
Mbuli, S., 11 April 1992 (notes).
Mhlambi, Mrs., December 1992.
Modise, M., 13 June 1992.
Mokgotsi, H., 5 September 1992.
Moloantwa, P., December 1992.
Moosie, Mrs., August 1992.
Morwa, G., August 1992.
Mtshali, Mrs., December 1992.
Ndala, "Oupa," 26 September 1992
Ndlovu, "Spokes," 22 June 1992.
Ngobese, A., 19 April 1992 (notes).
Nkosi, D., 5 September 1992.
Nkosi, L., August 1992.
Nkosi, T., 4 July 1992.

Ntsoaneng, Mr., 20 June 1992.
Nzimande, J., December 1992.
Radebe, J., 5 September 1992.
Sentsoe, Mrs., 4 July 1992.
Sibiya, Mrs., August 1992.
Sidu, Mr., December 1992.
Simelane, G., 18 April 1992 (a) (notes); December 1992 (b).
Sirurufera, M., 26 September 1992.
"Sister Grace" (Phiri resident), 17 June 1992.
Thape, Rev., 6 July 1992.
Thotela, "Zakes," 5 July 1992.
Tshabalala, Sam, 5 July 1992.
Tsotetsie, A., 26 September 1992.
Xhaba, M., December 1992.
Zodwa, Miss, December 1992.
Zwane, M., 23 April 1992 (notes).

Videotaped Interviews: History Workshop Soweto Film Project (HWSFP), 1991–1992

(Cassette numbers follow names.)
Bothile, N., HWSFP 21–23.
Khanyeza, J., HWSFP 10.
Khanyeza, W., HWSFP 10–11.
Leisa, E., HWSFP 4–5.
Makhabela, B., HWSFP 6C–9C.
Mashiloane, C., HWSFP 5B–7B.
Mazibuko, S., HWSFP 2–5.
Mkhonza, J., HWSFP 23–1B.
Moake, S., HWSFP 1–3.
Mohapi, T., HWSFP 11–12.
Morobe, M., HWSFP 10B–13B.
"Ndoza," HWSFP 16B.
Tshabalala, Stephen, HWSFP 6–8.

Transcribed Interviews in the Carter and Karis Collection

(All on microfilm, Historical Papers Library, University of the Witwatersrand.)
Kgosana, P., interviewed by Bob Hess, Addis Ababa, 15 August 1963.
Matthews, J., interviewed by Gwen Carter and Sheridan Jones, 9 March 1964.
Mbata, C., interviewed by Gwen Carter, 19 February 1964.
Nkomo, W., interviewed by Tom Karis, Pretoria, April 1964.
Ngubane, J., interviewed by Gwen Carter, Swaziland, 5 March 1964.
Nkoana, M., interviewed by Sheridan Jones, Cairo, 13 April 1964.

Other Transcribed Interviews

Mahwayi, J.; Mboweni, D.; Mbulani, H.; Ndlovu, Mr.; Ngenyama, J.: transcribed interviews with Chiawelo residents (1988–1991) in the possession of Philip Bonner.

Masondo, A., interviewed by Gail Gerhart, 5 July 1989.

Mattera, D., interviewed by Tom Lodge, 1979.

Molotsi, P., interviewed by Gail Gerhart, August 1969.

Mthembu, K., interviewed by Tom Karis and Gail Gerhart, New York, 24 February 1989.

Radebe, L., and Senakoane, S. (Madipere), interviewed by Jeremy Seekings, 7 May 1991.

Tlholoe, J., interviewed by Steve Lebelo, 13 August 1990.

INDEX

ABOUT THE AUTHOR

CLIVE GLASER lectures in history at the University of the Witwatersrand in Johannesburg. He specializes in South African urban history and has published several articles on urban youth culture and politics. He is a member of the Wits History Workshop.

ISBN 0-325-00219-3

90000>

EAN

9 780325 002194

HARDCOVER BAR CODE